Dowry

Bridging the Gap between Theory and Practice

Edited by

TAMSIN BRADLEY, EMMA TOMALIN and
MANGALA SUBRAMANIAM

Zed Books Ltd.
London & New York

Dowry: Bridging the Gap between Theory and Practice
was first published outside of South Asia in 2009
by
Zed Books Ltd, 7 Cynthia Street, London N1 9JF, UK
www.zedbooks.co.uk

Originally published in South Asia in 2009
by
Women Unlimited (an associate of Kali for Women)
K-36, Hauz Khas Enclave
New Delhi – 110016
www.womenunlimited.net

The rights of Tamsin Bradley, Emma Tomalin and Mangala Subramaniam to be
identified as the editors of this work have been asserted by them in accordance
with the Copyright, Designs and Patents Act, 1988

Distributed in the USA exclusively by Palgrave Macmillan, a division of St
Martin's Press, LLC, 175 Fifth Avenue, New York, NY 10010, USA

A catalogue record for this book is available from the British Library
Library of Congress Cataloging in Publication Data available

ISBN 978 1 84813 294 8 pb

Cover design: PealiDezine
pealiduttagupta@pealidezine.com

Typeset at Tulika, 35 A/1, Shahpur Jat, New Delhi – 110049
and printed at Raj Press, R-3 Inderpuri, New Delhi – 110012

Contents

iii

Contents

Acknowledgements

First and foremost we thank our families for their continued and sustained understanding and support. We also extend our gratitude to Ritu Menon and Ratna Sahai and the rest of the team at Women Unlimited for recognising the importance of this volume and for their commitment to the feminist visions it is based upon. We appreciate the support of Susannah Trefgarne in the publication of this volume through a Women Unlimited/Zed partnership. We are grateful to our anonymous reviewer who encouraged us to think carefully about how to approach the central theme—bridging theory and practice in research on dowry.

We must thank all those practitioners, activists and researchers whose commitment and energy to end dowry motivated us and our contributors who tirelessly revised their papers to ensure that their work spoke to each other and added to the global knowledge base on dowry.

This volume is dedicated to two wonderful and courageous scholars who remained committed until their deaths to seeing their academic work bring practical change to the lives of South Asian women. Julia Leslie was a founding member of the Dowry Project and without her efforts this volume would not have happened since all the contributors were brought together through the project's network. Her scholarly competence, love and enthusiasm for her subject, her inspiring presence and concern for her students were a great example to those around her. Jayoti Gupta's early death left many activists and scholars deeply saddened. Through writing and film, Jayoti had been working on dowry for some time. Relating the rising practice to her findings on agrarian change, women's land rights and law, she also followed the links with domestic violence and sex selective abortion. Her intellectual and research commitments were embedded in her concern for a political practice that would enable a mobilisation for social transformation. Both these scholars made important contributions to shaping the way researchers and activists think about and approach anti-dowry work and left a lasting influence on them. We hope that this volume stands as proof of their legacy.

Lastly, but most importantly, we thank and acknowledge all women whose lives are blighted by dowry. This book is intended to support their endeavours as agents shaping their destinies and fighting gender inequality and abuse.

TAMSIN BRADLEY
EMMA TOMALIN

Preface

This volume has its genesis in a network called the Dowry Project, which was established in 1995 at the International Conference on Dowry and Bride Burning at Harvard University, USA, with the aim of encouraging, sharing and disseminating research in the areas of dowry, bride burning and son preference in South Asia and the diaspora. It has now held six successful international conferences, which have attracted the participation of academics, practitioners and activists: Harvard University (1995, 1996 and 1998); the School of Oriental and African Studies, London (1997); and New Delhi (2001 and 2003). Three of the most prominent founding members were Himendra Thakur, Werner Menski and the late Julia Leslie.[1] Research undertaken in the early phase of the project had three main objectives. First, the production of reliable, in-depth studies of incidents recorded as 'dowry deaths' in order to be absolutely certain of the link between violence against women and dowry practices, to prove this link beyond doubt and to highlight that such deaths were not just accidental occurrences affecting relatively few Indian women. Second, that research should seek to uncover the motivations behind dowry related crimes and to prove that violence against women is not an inherent part of dowry (although high levels of domestic violence exist), but has been attributed to it by an increase in the level of greed from in-laws who see it as a means to improve their material well-being.

Third, to understand why anti-dowry campaigns have been largely unsuccessful. This research focused on the possibility that dowry persists because women themselves hold onto the practice, seeing it as a means to preserve their self-respect and negotiate their position as they make the transition into another family as married women.

The project's main goal of raising the visibility of issues relating to dowry through academic research, represents a very small part of the wider 'anti-dowry' movement. Moreover, it raises important questions about the relationship between academic theory, research and activism, with medical and legal practitioners and socio-political activists playing a vital role in the network in enhancing awareness of the type of research that is most needed. Thus, a network has emerged that offers academics, practitioners and activists the opportunity to disseminate their work and share experiences of dowry with the common objective of eradicating dowry injustice. The academics involved in the project are based mainly in India, the USA and Europe, and include medical and legal researchers, historians and social scientists. Research that members publish on dowry is disseminated across the network via group emails and a discussion forum.[2] The practitioners involved include health professionals, mainly female doctors, who have treated large numbers of women for injuries due to dowry harassment by husbands and in-laws. At the most recent conference a paper was presented by Dr Achla Daga on her experiences in a public hospital in Mumbai treating women who suffered from dowry-related injuries. Also contributing to discussions are non-governmental organisations, such as 'Point of View' in Mumbai (www.pointofview.org),[3] working on issues of gender injustice. The practising lawyers who are involved analyse the effectiveness of dowry legislation and catalogue dowry cases. All of them are concerned that research on dowry should translate into activism to end unjust cultural practices in the lives of South Asian women.[4]

Some of the contributors to this volume have attended one or other of the events hosted by the network whereas others are newer 'members', having more recently participated in a panel at the 2006 annual conference of the British Association of South Asian Studies at Birkbeck College, London. What unites all of them, however, is a commitment to bridge the gap between their academic research, practice and activism against dowry and to contribute to the eradication of violence against women that is occurring as a result of dowry practice. The main aim underpinning much of the research by current project members is to explore *practical measures* capable of responding to the deep-rooted and multiple impact dowry has on women's lives. The essays in this volume engage with the notion of 'feminist praxis' in considering that there should be a dialectical relationship between 'theory' and 'practice' (Stanley and Wise 1990). Such feminist activist scholarship (Naples 2006) is at the heart of the Dowry Project, which seeks to campaign for an end to dowry injustice through the generation of empirical and theoretical research that helps to extend and deepen our understanding of how and why dowry exists in both Hindu and non-Hindu communities. Members' research has looked at dowry through a range of interdisciplinary themes, some of which has been presented at the different conferences held by the network. Topics have included: 'the economics of marriage'; 'dowry, property and inheritance rights'; 'collective action to challenge the practice of dowry'; 'legal changes and domestic violence'; 'the women's movement and dowry'; 'caste and dowry'; 'dowry and Indian literature'; 'dowry and Hindu scriptures'; and 'dowry and son preference'. However, this volume reflects a move to broaden the focus in several key areas. Firstly, the emphasis to date has been largely legalistic with less attention paid to the role of other factors, such as the inherent gender discrimination within heterosexual marriage or the influence of patriarchal religious systems upon social attitudes towards gender that influence dowry practice. On the whole, the network did not examine dowry through a gendered methodology. In contrast, this volume places gender at the centre of its analysis. Secondly, the network has tended to draw attention to the most visually harrowing aspects of dowry harassment, such as bride burning, rather than a more complex analysis of the foundations of dowry (see also Narayan 1997; Rudd 2001).

The project's agenda is fluid and is not determined by a committee or director but by individual members whose work reflects their own experiences of dowry and relationships with South Asian women affected by it. Members benefit from being part of the overall network because it represents a forum for the exchange of ideas and enables encounters between people whose experiences differ yet can offer each other critical, supportive advice on their work. The transnational and interdisciplinary character of this volume is a positive step towards engagement between scholars from various regions of the world that has been facilitated by the relative ease of modern communication as a result of globalising trends. But it is also appropriate to acknowledge the challenges that we as editors have faced, mostly in bringing together the expert insights of authors trained in a variety of disciplines who also conform to different writing styles and the use of difference discipline-specific technical knowledge. Our efforts have been directed at staying focused on the central themes of the volume and ensuring that these contributions can be easily read and digested by readers coming from diverse backgrounds. But we have also endeavoured to retain the different styles, approaches and theoretical insights the contributors brought to the discussion.

The leading research on dowry that is presented here is a valuable tool for those seeking to pursue this topic in their work (including academics, policy makers and activists). The Dowry Project receives constant emails from researchers across the globe inquiring about the activities and publications of the network. It is clear that this volume is long awaited.

Notes

[1] Himendra Thakur is chair of the Board of Directors of the International Society Against Dowry and Bride Burning in India and an international activist working to eradicate dowry-related murders. Professor Werner Menski, based at the School of Oriental and African Studies, conducts research in South Asia on law, socio-legal and cultural studies, and religion

Preface

and law. The late Dr Julia Leslie was Reader in Classical Indology and
Sanskrit; her area of specialism was gender and Hindu scriptures. All three
founding members coordinated the network of scholars and organised the
six international conferences.

[2] http://www.londonmet.ac.uk/depts/dass/research/the-dowry-project/the-dowry-project_home.cfm

[3] Representatives from 'Point of View' attended the last Dowry Project
conference in New Delhi, 2003. Its members are largely from artistic and
media backgrounds and use their professional skills to raise awareness of
gender injustice, including dowry. Its photographic exhibition at the
conference was titled 'In black and white: What has independence meant
for women?'

[4] Further, information about the network, including future events, can be
obtained by emailing thedowryproject@hotmail.co.uk

References

Naples, N. 2006. 'Feminist Activism and Activist Scholarship in the 21st Century.'
FemTAP: A Journal of Feminist Theory and Practice. Summer. http://
femtap.com/sitebuildercontent/sitebuilderfiles/naples.pdf

Narayan, Uma. 1997. 'Cross-Cultural Connections, Border Crossings & Death by
Culture' in *Dislocating Cultures: Identities, Traditions and Third World Feminism.*
New York: Routledge. pp. 81–117.

Rudd, J. 2001. 'Dowry-Murder: An Example of Violence Against Women.' *Women's
Studies International Forum* 24. pp. 513–22.

Stanley, Liz and Sue Wise. 1990. 'Method, Methodology, and Epistemology in
Feminist Research Processes' in *Feminist Praxis: Research Theory and
Epistemology in Feminist Sociology.* ed. Liz Stanley. New York: Routledge.
pp. 4–19.

Foreword

I am deeply grateful for the invitation to write a foreword for this book. A landmark in dowry studies, it is focused on a gender-centred methodology and represents a clarion call for transformative action. I have learnt an immense amount from reading its detailed case studies that reveal the complexity and diversity of dowry practices in South Asia. The rich empirical data assembled here is analysed within a theoretical framework that provides readers with helpful explanations for understanding the concepts, attitudes and social practices associated with dowry. There is also a strong emphasis on the need for social action and change at the level of local, national and international communities.

Without wishing to anticipate the substantial arguments and descriptions of the following papers, I want to say a few words about the book and its contributors, and also about one of the prominent founder members of the Dowry Project, the late Dr Julia Leslie, from the School of Oriental and African Studies, University of London.

An international group of women scholars collaborated over several years to create this book. The results of their research show what dowry means in practice in different social, cultural, religious and legal contexts, how it is understood and practised differently among different ethnic and religious communities, and how it affects particular groups of women in particular places. However, they also show how dowry practices are being transformed by the processes of globalisation and transnational transactions.

The preface to the volume outlines the origin, rationale and motivation of the research presented in this book, and the introduction analyses the concepts and theories surrounding dowry practices and studies, pointing out that debates about dowry have been developed since the 1960s, especially since the rise of the Indian women's movement. The discussions show how the current research is rooted in the international Dowry Project founded in 1995 with the purpose, in the words of one of the editors, 'to research in the areas of dowry, bride burning and son preference in South Asia and the diaspora'. The Project developed through a series of international conferences held at Harvard University, USA, the School of Oriental and African Studies, London, and New Delhi, India. While the Dowry Project was first described in an earlier publication (*South Asians and the Dowry Problem,* 1998) in more general terms, the present work breaks new ground in making gender analysis the main focus of all the cases presented here, providing proof, if any proof is needed, that gender is central for understanding dowry in many different contexts, including its abuses. The book also demonstrates the changing patterns of dowry through detailed case studies ranging from Bangladesh to North and South India. Finally, the volume also reveals a concern with different forms of activism that increasingly call into question the practice of dowry, challenging its very idea, its gender inequality and abuse, and also the continuity for son preference, often associated with it. The contributors offer activists a methodology that enables them to gain a clearer insight into the complex realities of dowry, so that they can plan their interventions more effectively.

Research into traditional and changing dowry practices is immensely challenging; it is an exciting and socially sensitive, profoundly relevant undertaking that requires much sensitivity and critical self-reflexivity on the part of researchers, well demonstrated in this book. Its carefully researched studies open up new perspectives that reveal dowry as a multi-stranded web of many dimensions, only to be dealt with collaboratively by drawing on many different disciplines, theories and actions. The burning issues of dowry practice are of great transnational importance; they are not only of relevance in relation to the acute suffering in countless women's lives but also have to take their place within the ongoing international discussions of women's human rights, especially in association with the work of the United Nations, and in current work pertaining to the interaction between gender, religion and development.

All these concerns were close to Julia Leslie's heart. As one of the founding members of the international Dowry Project she provided much inspiration for her colleagues and collaborators. I want to end by paying tribute to this brilliant woman scholar whose life was tragically cut short through cancer.

I knew Julia for many years as an esteemed colleague and scholar who undertook an impressive range of research and publications for which she gained an international reputation. Even during her final illness, just a few months before her death, she was determined to complete a long entry on 'Gender and Hinduism' for the revised, internationally renowned *Encyclopaedia of Religion* (Macmillan), the premier reference work in the field of Religious Studies, published in its second edition in 2005. This excellent article, together with another on sati, one of her specialist interests, were her last pieces of scholarly writing, as she herself proudly told me about two weeks before she died. These are fine pieces by which she will be long remembered.

The large number of tributes sent by scholars from England, Germany, India and the USA to Julia Leslie's funeral service were an extraordinary testimony to the international impact she had made and recognition gained through her scholarly work and warm friendship with so many different people. This was the result of her passionate engagement with Indian religions, gender studies and Hindu communities in Britain as well as her strong support for her many students and colleagues. Given this international impact and reputation, and taking into account what she achieved through her own research and teaching at the School of Oriental and African Studies, particularly in setting up the Centre for Gender

Foreword

and Religions Research, in attracting grants, postgraduate students and visiting scholars from around the world to regular research seminars and conferences, it is most appropriate that Julia Leslie should be one of the two scholars to whom this volume is dedicated. She would have felt honoured and delighted as well as proud of it. This book sets a new standard and horizon for dowry research as a project of international collaboration. Its informative chapters are full of new insights, helpful analyses and impressive bibliographical resources for anyone seeking information, explanations and understanding of a widespread social practice which has disempowered women for so long. It is a practice which urgently demands more effective strategies and commitment on the part of women and men to achieve necessary social changes for greater gender justice and equality in the world. Because of its immense social, economic and political importance, dowry research needs to attract much more international attention and discussion than hitherto. The excellent contributions to this volume provide a significant step towards reaching this goal.

URSULA KING, FRSA
Professor Emerita of Theology and Religious Studies and
Senior Research Fellow, Institute for Advanced Studies,
University of Bristol Professorial Research Associate,
Centre for Gender and Religions Research, School of
Oriental and African Studies, University of London

Introduction

EMMA TOMALIN

It is difficult to provide a precise definition of dowry since it has undergone distinct transformations over time, and it can encapsulate a range of different practices of marital gift-giving. Both dowry and bride price in South Asia have been identified as oppressive practices (Unnithan-Kumar 2005: 27), but it is dowry that has attracted most attention for its association with different strands of violence against women. As described below, dowry itself is not a violent practice and in its most basic form has been interpreted as a form of pre-mortem inheritance for women who otherwise lack inheritance rights equal to those of men. However, evidence has amassed of abuses against women that can be associated with the system. Dowry is not uniquely South Asian and the exchange of goods or money at the time of marriage is a custom that has been found across the globe since antiquity. However, in South Asia by the 1980s it had become the focus of an 'anti dowry' or 'dowry boycott' campaign, a sustained and vocal campaign fronted by the women's movement (Palriwala in this volume).

Dowry-related harassment, sometimes resulting in so-called 'dowry death' or 'bride burning' (Leslie 1998; Butalia 2002; Stone and James 1995; Sirohi 2003), became an increasing burden facing women from all castes and classes in modern India as well as the diaspora. What was once a practice largely confined to upper caste

Hindus in the north of India, spread to other castes, religions and regions. The reasons for this are complex and are, at least partially, dependent upon a combination of Sanskritisation (upper caste emulation), neo-liberalisation and rise of cash incomes (Banerjee and Jain 2001; Banerjee 2002). Moreover, there is some perception[1] that the size of dowries has grown in recent decades putting increased pressure on families to prefer sons to daughters, thereby exacerbating an existing tendency towards son preference.[2] The impact of this upon the 'reversed sex-ratio' in India is well documented with the numbers of 'missing' females due to sex selective abortion and female infanticide on the increase in many regions (Basu 1999a; Banerjee 2002; Dreze and Sen 2002; Jayaraj and Subramanian 2004; Sen 1992, 1993; Sunder Rajan 2003).

While dowry practices can be linked to different forms of violence against females, others argue that the practice itself is inherently sexist since it can be seen as a measure of women's lack of status and empowerment as they are effectively traded on the marriage market. The spread and inflation of dowry further entrenches the notion that marriage is compulsory for women, and it also inhibits opportunities for women and girls on many levels. For instance, critics frequently point towards the development costs of dowry for women, focusing upon its expense and its links to poverty. Women often do not retain any sort of ownership of their dowry and money spent on it can mean that fewer resources are available for girls before their marriage. That dowry reflects and reinforces existing gender hierarchies in India is emphasised throughout this volume. It is argued that although there has been a tendency in anti-dowry initiatives to focus upon the violent aspects of dowry-giving (as they are the most politically visible), as well as legal solutions to the problem, we cannot begin to understand the hold and consequences of dowry nor hope to deal with them effectively, without understanding and tackling structural gender inequalities in society more broadly.

The exact nature of the dowry problem and how to approach it is by no means straightforward. Thinking about different sorts of dowry practices (from the seemingly benign to the pernicious) urges us to reconsider whether it is the dowry system itself or, more specifically, its abuse (linked to dowry escalation and harassment) that should be rallied against. This issue has been a matter for debate, with key activists in the field actually shifting their position over time. Most notably, Madhu Kishwar—editor of the feminist magazine *Manushi*—had been one of the key proponents of the 1980 'dowry boycott' (Kishwar and Five Others 2005 [1980]: 265; Palriwala in this volume) but by 1988 had rethought her position. Frustrated at the lack of success and support for the 'dowry boycott' she came to the conclusion that, without widespread change for women in Indian society, including a strengthening of women's inheritance rights, a boycott could in fact be counterproductive (Kishwar 2005 [1988]). For Kishwar, the potential of dowry to provide women with some form of inheritance that could improve their position within their marital homes meant that for 'women to refuse dowry and go empty-handed to their marital homes is to suggest that they make even greater martyrs of themselves than society makes of them' (2005 [1988]: 269; 1989). While Kishwar has been criticised for effectively sidelining considerations of gender she promotes her view as more realistic of the way that women view dowry (Basu 2005: xix).

Others, including Palriwala (1989) and Lakshmi (1989), have strongly rejected this and consider that dowry itself is inherently problematic for women because it is primarily transacted between men (with women having no involvement in marriage negotiations which ultimately affect them) and because it is premised upon the inferiority of the bride's future contribution to her husband and his family who must thereby be financially compensated for 'taking her on'. Palriwala and Lakshmi do concur with Kishwar that strengthening inheritance rights is crucial, but disagree that this should be approached apart from the anti-dowry campaign. As Sirohi summarised: 'the two problems had to be tackled simultaneously. Dowry ... is a reality which often envelops other forms of oppression. Dowry and other practices degrade women, and one is not exclusive of the other' (2003: 53).

In this introduction I will first discuss some definitions of 'dowry' for readers who are unfamiliar with this practice and its history in South Asia. Then I will move on to look at the ways in which dowry has become transformed over recent decades. Although any form of dowry does involve a transaction that places value on women, and as such its gendered consequences need to be investigated, there is a widespread consensus that it is the modern form of dowry in South Asia (what Srinivas calls the 'new dowry') that is particularly problematic, as well as the fact that it perseveres in its most pernicious form, despite the strong presence of the campaigns of the women's movement in India (Srinivas 1984; Menski 1998: 17). How have scholars explained and theorised this 'new dowry': who and what underpins the cycle of culpability and how can it be broken?[3]

What is dowry? different interdisciplinary theories and perspectives

Srinivasan and Lee (2004: 1108) suggest that dowry in India grew from a number of different ritual exchanges:

> The dowry system—payments from the bride's family to the groom or groom's family at the time of marriage—has a long history in India and other Asian societies ... The modern Indian dowry system has its roots in the traditional upper-caste practices of *kanyadhan* (literal meaning: gift of the virgin bride), *varadakshina* (voluntary gifts given by the bride's father to the groom), and *stridhan* (voluntary gifts given by relatives and friends to the bride ...). Traditionally, although these gifts could be significant, they were often small tokens of good wishes. More recently, however, the dowry has come to involve a substantial transfer of wealth from the bride's family to the groom's, and has become a major factor in marriage negotiations.

Scholars have also portrayed dowry as a form of pre-mortem inheritance for women (Tambiah 1973; Caplan 1984; Palriwala; and Basu in this volume). The link between dowry as an upper caste custom and dowry as a form of inheritance is also relevant, since upper caste women were less likely to participate in employment away from the home (see Dalmia and Lawrence in this volume). Thus, dowry can be seen as:

> a way of compensating the groom and his family for the economic support they would provide to the new wife, because women had little or no role in the market economy and would be dependent upon their husbands and in-laws ... This interpretation is consistent with the fact that the dowry was historically practised largely in the upper castes, among whom women's economic roles were particularly restricted. In the lower castes, where women were more likely to be economic contributors to their families, the custom of the bride price was more common (Srinivasan and Lee 2004: 1108–09).

However, it is the consequences of the spread and inflation of dowry during the latter half of the 20th century and its inclusion on the agenda of the women's movement that transformed it into an issue that has attracted the interest of scholars from across disciplines. Anthropologists discuss dowry in terms of the literature on gift, reciprocity and exchange, marriage and kinship rites (Unnithan-Kumar 2005; Evans Pritchard 1951; Levi-Strauss 1949), whereas sociologists consider it in terms of theories about social problems (Sitaraman 1999), the family (Banerjee 1999; Prasad 1994) and the response of society (community, media, institutions, activists) (Palriwala 1989; and in this volume). Economists, such as Dalmia and Lawrence (in this volume), focus their attention on data about the amounts exchanged and the bargaining that takes place (Anderson 2003; Bloch, Desai and Rao 2004; Bloch and Rao 2002; Rao 1993) and legal scholars (see Basu in this volume) are interested in legislative attempts to curb dowry (Sandanshiv and Mathew 1995; Basu 2005; Butalia 2002; Sitaraman 1999; Menski 1998). Human geographers reflect upon the demographics of the practice (e.g. Bhat and Halli 1999) and historians attempt to locate dowry within texts and practices from the past (Oldenburg 2002; Nabar 1995). We also find contributions from psychologists (Rastogi and Therly 2006) and within medical journals (Jutla and Heimbach 2004; Kumar and

Tripathi 2004) as researchers aim to document and theorise the profound mental and physical impact of dowry violence upon the lives of many women.[4]

Despite this great effort from within academic disciplines to reflect upon dowry and its consequences, defining dowry in South Asia can still be challenging and problematic, particularly since it has undergone distinct transformations over time. Modern dowry can be seen as gifts of cash and/or kind from the family of the bride to that of the groom as a condition of marriage (Rudd 2001; Srinivasan and Lee 2004; Sirohi 2003; Tambiah 1973). However, considering the fact that today requests for dowry often continue after a marriage, Rastogi and Therly define dowry as 'the wealth a bride brings to her husband *at the time of and after* the wedding'[5] (2006: 67, emphasis mine). Dowry payments can range from large and ostentatious gifts that can seriously stress the financial security of the bride's family, to smaller offerings that are more nominal in character. Some families make open demands whereas others see dowry as an unspoken condition. Nonetheless, what is of concern is evidence of the ways in which dowry is dangerous for women since it leaves them vulnerable to violence and underpins damaging gender hierarchies. Dowry was outlawed in 1961 in the Dowry Prohibition Act, but this has been ineffectual in bringing the practice to an end. Instead, social norms prevail and, as Rastogi and Therly note, it continues to be true that 'dowry is exchanged in the majority of Indian weddings' (2006: 66).

Dowry should not, however, be essentialised as one type of practice with a predictable set of effects and Menski differentiates between three related understandings of dowry. First, 'what a woman brings or takes into her new home ... this is property that, in normal circumstances, belongs to the woman, should be owned by her absolutely, and should help her to build up her status as a married woman in the new home' (1998: 16). Second, 'what a woman's natal family spends on her wedding ... again, inflation and inflated expectations might cause problems, but the social customs are, at least in their origin, positive elements of social exchange and of bonding between the two families' (1998:

16–17). Third is Srinivas' 'new dowry', which involves 'property or cash demanded or in various forms expected by the new groom's family' (1998: 16). The most pernicious aspect of this 'new dowry' is the possibility that the groom's family will continue to ask for more 'dowry' after the wedding, a demand that can normally not easily be met. The significance of this financial outlay needs to be emphasised, because the bride's family tends to save for her dowry from birth and usually does not have a second pot of savings available to meet additional dowry demands. It is at this point, Menski argues, that women are placed most at risk from violence and/or other abuses: caught between their in-laws' demands and their parents' inability or unwillingness to meet them.

As this volume illustrates, the idea of dowry as voluntary, pre-mortem inheritance for women[6] and as a custom confined to upper castes has undergone substantial shifts. Dowry has *spread* to different regions, religious groups and castes, and it has *inflated*. From the mid-20th century the literature begins to discuss the ways in which the traditional understanding of *stridhan* (i.e. gifts given to a woman at the time of marriage, corresponding more or less to Menski's first understanding of dowry) is superseded by modern marriage payments (Caplan 1984; Gough 1956). In particular, there is a shift from goods taken into a marriage that remain the property of the woman to gifts presented to the bridegroom and his family by the woman's parents. Accompanying this shift is a trend towards competition for grooms, whereby the woman who can come up with the largest dowry can secure the best match. Moreover, dowry practices have spread to other castes, religions and regions of South Asia (Dalmia and Lawrence in this volume), including groups that previously practised bride price[7] (Jehan; and Rozario in this volume).

This volume provides an overview of these debates and discussions as they have developed since the 1960s, with the emergence of the Indian women's movement in particular. However, this more familiar material is located within the context of new research that asks important questions which aim to contribute towards a greater understanding of the shifting dynamics of the dowry terrain, as well as the contribution of academic research and theory to practice. In what ways and why has dowry spread? What is the role of gender in underpinning dowry abuse and how might academic research feed into practical strategies to deal with this? What sorts of data are useful for understanding the changes in dowry practice to help avoid over-simplistic and inaccurate conceptions of dowry? How is the practice being resisted both within nations, particularly in South Asia, as well as globally? What roles do religion, culture, economics, class or caste play in shaping dowry practices as well as perpetuating the abuse of dowry customs that result in death or injury to women across South Asia? The dynamics of these changes and the complexities they involve are analysed and explored.

Avoiding an emphasis upon 'dowry violence'

In addition to the debate about what should form the primary focus of dowry activism, this volume explores the ways in which dowry is 'framed' from different points of view (Subramaniam, Remedios and Mitra). This framing is discussed in terms of differences between approaches at local, national and international levels as well as shifts in its framing over time (Basu). Subramaniam, Remedios and Mitra draw attention to the focus at a global level (e.g. UN documents and events), which subsumes dowry within the larger category of violence against women. Basu, by contrast, outlines the decline in feminist activism against dowry, specifically since the 1980s, as women's 'organisations now address more broad-based problems located in economic entitlements of marriage and the dailiness of violence rather than looking to the largely ineffective Dowry Prohibition Act (1984) and to piecemeal demonstrations around alleged "dowry deaths" and their legislative trajectories'.

In particular, a number of scholars (in both this volume and in the broader literature) have assessed the implications of the framing of dowry as an issue primarily concerned with violence typically leading to the death of women (see Narayan 1997). For instance, the National Crime Records Bureau of the Government of India collects statistics on dowry deaths and in 2004 it recorded 7026 such deaths.[8] However, these statistics are notoriously slippery since we can assume that not all the actual cases of dowry deaths are recorded—some women's groups argue that the number is in fact many times higher. Moreover, acts of violence sustained by women as a result of dowry, but not resulting in death, are not systematically collated. As Narayan notes, the collection of statistics on dowry deaths is the only area in which domestic violence of any sort is recorded statistically by the Indian government (1997: 97). Thus, the way in which 'dowry murder' has come to be framed in India as a specific public issue has an impact upon the type of data that are collected, which in turn then has the effect of reinforcing the perception of 'dowry murder' as virtually the only form of domestic violence that women in India suffer. Dowry violence appears to be a rather small part of the broader rubric of domestic violence (it is the part that is most politically visible).

The emphasis upon dowry violence can draw attention away from other proximate causes of violence as well as the ways in which these are more substantively linked to gender. Dowry can, and does, marginalise and oppress women in many ways, and violence is only one of its outcomes. Although dowry-related violence may diminish, the practice itself is still problematic for women unless its gendered dimensions are addressed more broadly. Alternatively, while many activists and scholars continue to call for the eradication of dowry altogether, others argue that if we actually speak to women themselves they may not want to give it up. Academic research can contribute here in highlighting the value of making women's opinions about dowry visible, in addition to the more familiar portrayal of them as victims of dowry violence. Moreover, as Palriwala and Basu discuss in their papers, the framing of dowry as a violent practice led the women's movement to call for a total dowry boycott as the solution to the problem and this had an influence upon state interventions with the passing of the Dowry Prohibition Act in 1961. However, as the contributors to this volume argue, curing the problems associated with dowry is not just a matter of passing legislation but requires deeper social change around gender.

Avoiding an emphasis upon legislation

Despite the Dowry Prohibition Act and subsequent amendments, legislation has proved unable to end this practice. Some point out that the legislation has been poorly implemented or that the legislation itself is limited (Menski 1998; Basu 2005), while others argue that this is not an issue that can be dealt with through legal pressure alone. Instead, deeper and more sustainable social change is necessary that elevates the status of women throughout society as a whole in order to transform a mindset that views women as economic commodities to be traded on the marriage market. Scholars and activists are divided about whether this means that dowry should or will be banned, or that this implies the need to focus on ending the *abuse* of the practice that often results in dowry harassment and bride burning.

Bridging the gap between theory and practice

This volume aims to make a contribution to ongoing discussions on dowry in a number of ways. First, contributors argue for the application of a gender analysis to the study of dowry as well as to the consideration of solutions to the problem. Second, rather than focusing upon the violent aspects of dowry, they regard dowry in its different manifestations as related to structural gender inequalities in society. While the fact that many women do not want to give up dowry may be interpreted as a 'patriarchal bargain' that they enter into because they believe it serves their interests (Kandiyoti 1988: 282–3), their views are often constrained by their position in the gender hierarchy. Appropriate strategies that deal with gender relations more broadly in society are necessary if women are to be able to adopt values and undertake courses of action that do not place them at a disadvantage.[9] Thus, while some advocates argue (Basu 2005: liii, fn 20) for dowry to be retained because it is part of Indian culture, others favour it because women do obtain some short-term benefit although under ideal conditions of gender equality they may well choose to reject it (or dowry would then only exist as a modest symbolic gesture).

Finally, as the title of the volume reveals, our aim is to highlight the role that academic research can play in furthering our understanding of the dowry problematic and in identifying solutions to deal with it.

From practice to praxis

This interdisciplinary and integrative, or intersectional, approach looks at different factors and issues that shape dowry practices. While the 'dowry issue' is multifaceted, the contributors are all of the view that it operates through gendered constructions of femininity and masculinity. Practice that is not informed by gender analysis is unlikely to bring about any change. The term 'praxis' is used to refer to theoretically informed practice. Gender analysis, which enables identification of power relations and challenges hierarchies based on perceived differences between the sexes (Scott 1986), is central to the theoretical framework underpinning this book. Gender, however, is not a homogenous category: it is internally differentiated and elaborated by different factors, including, class, race/ethnicity, age, religion and education, and scholars have proposed an 'integrative' or 'intersectional' framework that emphasises the social processes through which interactions between factors such as class relations, racialisation and engendering take place (Acker 2000; 2006; Hill-Collins 1990; Andersen 1993; Glenn 2000). However, while gender is manifested in different ways, depending, for instance, on one's location, sociological analyses emphasise that gender, like race and class, is a social experience of both men *and* women: dowry has become embedded as an aspect of gender identity for both men and women (see Jehan in this volume).

Apart from Jehan's paper, the others in this volume concentrate upon women's gendered experience of dowry. We present research that understands dowry and anti-dowry activism as beginning with each woman's own relationship to and with dowry and includes an appreciation of how it forms part of her identity, often simultaneously contested and accepted. Identities are created out of group histories and structural positions that are influenced by caste, class, wealth and land ownership. Dowry endorses these positions by acting as a mechanism through which these identifying markers are publicly displayed (see Palriwala). Increasingly, as Palriwala, and Dalmia and Lawrence show, dowry is used by a family to renegotiate their social positioning by marrying their daughter upwards into a family of higher social position. Thus, dowry must be understood both physically and symbolically. Basu's (1999b) ethnographic research highlights that women acknowledge the 'physical' injustice dowry brings to their lives, as a proxy for the absence of inheritance, a lack of financial independence and vulnerability to violence. However, dowry is also part of a woman's identity, symbolising her soon-to-be marital status and the position of a married woman is important as it brings respectability. We are concerned to look at how activism can intersect with these different and contradictory aspects of dowry.

This volume is also attuned to the 'politics of location' that should begin with women's lived experiences of oppression (Rich 2003). Individual experiences are politicised by the recognition that other women share similar experiences, from which alliances and networks emerge. The aim, therefore, is to make the links between gendered experiences of dowry and activism clearer in order to bring into focus the options available to women who want to politicise their experiences and become active in anti-dowry campaigning. Despite this emphasis on lived experiences of dowry as the foundation for activism and the caution applied in how women outside these experiences may talk and write about dowry, our contributors do not feel it is necessary to have experiential knowledge to make a meaningful contribution to dowry campaigns. In other words, the volume does not outline what Lewis and Mills (2003) describe as a 'hierarchy of oppression' in which the more intense your suffering the greater your 'right to speak about dowry'.

Nonetheless, we recognise the need to be sensitive to post-colonial calls for self-reflection to ensure that ethnocentrism does not determine how South Asian women are represented. This can, however, prove difficult to enact. Narayan's much referenced 1997 essay, 'Cross-Cultural Connections, Border-Crossings, and "Death by Culture",' draws our attention to the ways in which the physical, social and cultural distance between Indian women and scholars within India and across national borders, can distort both the description of, and the meaning assigned to, dowry practices (see Basu, and Subramaniam et al. in this volume). Narayan highlights the ways in which the framing of dowry in terms of its violent aspects, in particular by western feminists who are intrigued and outraged by descriptions of 'bride burning' and 'dowry murder', also encourages us to see it as a 'cultural product'. She argues that the framing of this in terms of the

> 'alien' features of 'burning' and 'dowry' help to further code the phenomena as 'Indian' and 'Other' and intersect to expunge any trace of the phenomenon's connection to the more 'familiar' domestic category of 'domestic violence' ... Indian women's murder-by-fire seems mysterious, possibly ritualistic, and one of those factors that is assumed to have something to do with 'Indian culture' (1997: 101–02).

Basu similarly writes that in western feminist contexts 'dowry gets read as a peculiar Indian problem of "culture"' and that 'few parallels are drawn with problems related to marriage as an institution or women's access to financial resources, or violence against women in ways that affect women in the US or Europe' (Basu 2005: iv). Basu considers that this idea of 'dowry as culture' did not ask for dowry and the gender inequality it causes to be abolished, just for women to be treated better:

> ... the series of conferences dealing on dowry sponsored by Harvard (e.g. Menski 1998: 18–20) carefully bemoan excesses in dowry and dowry-related deaths, while explicitly confirming the validity of dowry and the

patrilocal joint family as important 'Indian' institutions, a position reminiscent of 'culture' based apologia from legislators (2005: liv).

While feminism is a politically driven vision that seeks gender equality, it has been criticised for reflecting a western bias and projecting a patronising and unhelpful view that 'other women' in the 'third world' lead inferior lives (Mohanty 1988). For some researchers (e.g. Basu, Palriwala) feminist convictions underpin their desire to combine research with activism and they argue that feminism remains an important part of the anti-dowry movement. Oldenburg, for example, is clear in her reasons for using the word feminist:

> Feminism has a long history and is no longer monolithic; multiple feminisms abound, and feminism is capable of the same kinds of distinctions one would expect in any analysis of the word patriarchy. I define the word feminist in its simplest political sense, a person (and not necessarily a woman) whose analytical perspective is informed by an understanding of the relationship between power and gender in any historical, social, or cultural context. To me, the argument against using the word feminist is weakened by the fact that terms and theories of equally western provenance—Marxist, socialist, Freudian, or post-structuralist—do not arouse similar indignation and are in fact (over) used as standard frameworks for analyses of Indian society by Indian scholars (1994: 103).

Despite the cautious use of the term, this volume considers that gender analysis is itself a 'feminist' activity, which if carried out with sensitivity and awareness is capable of 'crossing borders'. However, in asking, 'how well does the political identity "feminist" travel?' we are aware that 'in response to their different histories and local economies, women activists and their allies in different parts of the world have developed diverse definitions of feminism' but also that other 'women activists refuse to identify under the political identity, "feminist"' (Naples 2006: 6–7). While there is diversity in orientation to the term feminist (from embracing it to dismissing it) we support the view that there continues to be a role for feminist scholars and activists since:

As feminist scholars and activists point out, there are 'gender dimensions' to all struggles for social justice, and 'feminists better be in these struggles and bring out those dimensions because certainly nobody else will.' Feminist scholars consistently demonstrate how gendered and race-based inequalities undergird capitalist expansion and argue that even broader left movements have yet to incorporate the ways that gender and race inequalities constitute the foundation for many of these economic and political projects (Naples 2006: 7).

This issue of crossing borders is also central to our theme of linking theory and practice through 'feminist praxis'. The post-colonial critique of western (second wave) feminism has led to the emergence of styles of feminist theorising and activism that reflect the diverse positions of subordination that women experience across the globe.

This volume's originality and major contribution is its central theme, which seeks to consider how the gap between theory and practice may be bridged. Attempts have been made throughout to show how theoretical and empirical research may inform and shape approaches to activism to eradicate dowry and/or its abuse. In the process, some researchers analyse why so many of the current initiatives fail to have significant impact. Basu and Palriwala highlight that legislation has been mistakenly prioritised as the primary route to eradicating dowry. As they point out, dowry must be challenged through a theoretical framework capable of unravelling its complex hold over women's lives. Theory is understood here as a set of ideas that explains the existence of dowry and which then enables the critical evaluation of its continued presence. Academic research, therefore, has a role to play here in the generation of theories about the limitations of anti-dowry or dowry reform initiatives, as well as in producing empirical case studies and collecting data.

Although the pursuit of practical outcomes from academic research may seem idealised, this volume is founded on a conviction that the two can fruitfully intersect. For this research to have significance beyond the text, it must be deliberately focused to achieve this in diverse ways. First, the gap between theoretical ideas about dowry produced by academics and the women whose lives are affected by it is bridged through face-to-face contact with those women who live with its fall out. Failure to bridge this gap leads activists and policy-makers to limited conclusions about the strategies to adopt to end dowry abuse. At its worst, research directing activism, development projects and government policy towards specific women-focused anti-dowry initiatives can actually make things worse (Srinivasan and Bedi 2007). Second, the gap in abstract theorising about dowry that is not easily translated into activism is overcome by contributors who have expounded clear arguments, relevant for activism. Despite its diversity of perspectives, the volume has an integrity born of each scholar positioning her work according to her disciplinary base and/or experience of working with women on dowry, to feed the wider debates of the network. Therefore, throughout the volume scholars reflect on how their work intersects with that of other contributors, while cross-referencing between them helps highlight areas of agreement. The contributors also indicate gaps in our knowledge and areas where further research is necessary, in particular on diaspora experiences and masculinities.

The term 'activism' in this volume describes the kind of political, social action we hope to inform; the methodologies used help activism to emerge by forcing a critique of work on dowry to reveal assumptions and misrepresentations, and by pinpointing strategies that might or might not work. In particular, the term 'praxis' specifically locates the intersection of theory and practice. (Stanley and Wise 1990; Harding 1991). On the one hand, the work presented here aims to contribute towards 'praxis' in generating research that can have a useful impact on ending dowry injustice; on the other it is also considered in itself as an example of 'feminist praxis'. This praxis may be divided into three types, along a continuum, reflecting the various forms of action that the authors discuss or seek to connect with:

- First, a methodological critique of past and current research and activism in the area of dowry (Rozario; Bradley; Dalmia and Lawrence; Palriwala; Basu);

16

- Second, reviewing the progress of current anti-dowry initiatives and how they frame the dowry problem, by looking at how dowry has changed and adapted around such campaigns and legislation (Rozario; Palriwala; Basu; Subramaniam);
- Third, by producing research that updates our collective understanding of how dowry impacts on the lives of men and women—in particular, the material pull that globalisation has had on the changing face of dowry gift-giving (Rozario; Jehan; Dalmia and Lawrence).

This emphasis upon praxis cautions against reifying theory, calling instead for grounding research in experience and basing it in possible social change action. As Harding explains:

> ... feminist politics is not just a tolerable companion of feminist research but a necessary condition for generating less partial and perverse descriptions and explanations. In a socially stratified society the objectivity of the results of research is increased by political activism by and on behalf of oppressed, exploited and dominant groups (1991: 127).

Thus, the term 'praxis' is used to encompass a methodological concern to bring forward women's lived experiences with specific attention to the impact dowry has on them, as well as identifying and analysing specific forms of anti-dowry activism with the hope that research may fruitfully pick out and/or influence successful initiatives. The formulation of the Dowry Project is itself an attempt to bring about a convergence of methodological considerations and political action, in that it acknowledges the mutual interdependence of theory and practice which combine in the process of listening to and recording women's own experiences of dowry. These women are also active agents who frequently pursue strategies to end dowry and its related gender inequalities. The three concerns of feminist praxis exist as a continuum, and contributors have placed their work along it choosing to focus their attention on one or two aspects. It is important that taken collectively research feeds into all points on this continuum because in its entirety it can make for a solid foundation for anti-dowry campaigning. Thus, praxis encompasses individual challenges, (such as research, writing and action) as well as collective action to question and resist dowry.

Overview of contributions

Most contributors to this volume are situated in academic institutions in the UK and the USA, and it therefore reflects a particular locational politics of knowledge. Although the Dowry Project itself is 'based' in the UK, it is a network rather than an organisation and, as such, is open to inputs and participation from scholars working across all areas affected by dowry, in South Asia as well as beyond. The contributions here do not tell the whole story, but reflect a selection of papers that offer important insights into certain key themes, which we believe have been undertheorised. Dowry is explored here through an interdisciplinary lens that emphasises the intersectionality of different axes of inequality, such as gender, socio-economic status, class, caste, religion and location. Anchoring their analyses across disciplines acknowledges the different facets of the dowry system and deters a universalising of experiences.

The first four papers discuss the rapidly shifting dowry terrain. In what ways and why has it spread? What is the role of gender in underpinning dowry abuse and how might academic research feed into practical strategies to deal with this? What sorts of data are useful for understanding changes in dowry practice to help avoid over-simplistic and inaccurate conceptions of it?

Santi Rozario analyses the reasons why dowry in Bangladesh tends to be treated as an intractable problem and suggests some strategies that might have the possibility of real impact. Dowry is a relatively new phenomenon among non-Hindu families in Bangladesh, and Rozario discusses the reasons for the shift from 'bride wealth' to 'dowry'. Although dowry is officially illegal in Bangladesh, as in India, it continues to spread and is a major cause of high levels of indebtedness and impoverishment. There is a long history of attempts to discourage it, but virtually all marriages in Bangladesh involve large dowry payments and the availability of microcredit has led to a further substantial inflation.

In particular, Rozario considers that the dowry problem can only be solved in Bangladesh if there are associated attempts to deal with the broader issue of patriarchy. This, she suggests, could include challenging village stereotypes of women through the use of media, education and role models, and working with religious authorities such as local imams, and encouraging them to raise awareness about the situation of women.

An awareness that gender transformation is complex and multifaceted, yet central to dealing with dowry, is also a central theme of Kate Jehan's paper. She examines male dowry narratives across three generations in the southern Indian state of Tamil Nadu. She argues that while dowry tends to be seen as a women's problem, and they are its most prominent victims, we cannot hope to have an impact on curbing oppressive dowry practices without an understanding of men's experiences. She links her discussion to a broader shift within gender and development discourse that calls for the inclusion of men's voices and attitudes, since an exploration of both women and men's subjectivities 'provides data on how and why people uphold, resist and contest dominant values or unequal social relations' (Vera-Sanso 2001: 180). Jehan aims to contribute to the key concern of this volume: how might theory be linked to practice? As she asks, how might a positive impact be made on an area replete with so many 'gender pathologies'? The recent growth of dowry in South India demands an exploration of men's dowry behaviours and beliefs in tandem with the changing context in which they occur. She not only asks how men's perspectives intersect with religion, caste or class, but also how they have been shaped in the modern era by economic reforms and globalisation.

Tamsin Bradley extends this consideration of gender, through looking at the role that religion and culture play in supporting gender hierarchies that feed into dowry abuses. She discusses the work of the late Julia Leslie, founder member of the Dowry Project and a scholar of religion, who was particularly attuned to the ways in which religious teachings, practices and myths impact upon women's roles and status in society. While dowry itself is not a practice that is sanctioned by religious texts, Hinduism does nonetheless influence social attitudes towards women that arguably allow particular practices such as dowry, and more importantly its violent manifestations, to persist. Bradley investigates this claim by looking closely at Leslie's work and the potential of religious myths and practices to empower women, and how this could be used to transform abusive dowry practices. Bradley emphasises the importance of responsive approaches, which support women's own experiences of dowry and build solutions out of direct dialogues with those affected.

Shifting economic conditions in India, particularly since liberalisation in the early 1990s, are crucial to understanding the spread and inflation of dowry. Sonia Dalmia and Pareena Lawrence specifically focus on this terrain and discuss economic data on the regional distribution of dowry and bride price across India. Although the north-south dichotomy in marriage transactions has been widely discussed in the literature, this essay has significant practical importance since a majority of the studies are based on ethnographies that are now over 35 years old. In particular, it draws attention to the fact that in the past several decades, marital transfers in India have experienced significant changes, including the adoption and inflation of dowry across regions and communities. As a result, more recent survey data from representative samples are essential for an accurate picture of the shifts in regional socio-cultural variations in marriage payments in India. Dalmia and Lawrence use retrospective data on marriage transactions and on the personal and family traits of marriage partners collected from the states of Uttar Pradesh (North India) and Karnataka (South India) in order to examine the patterns and variations in dowry transactions based on the cultural, social, demographic and economic organisation of each region.

Whereas the first three papers look at the underlying factors supporting dowry practices, specifically the ways in which patriarchal gender hierarchies are maintained and may be dismantled, Dalmia and Lawrence emphasise the importance of collecting and analysing data on dowry practices and distribution as a crucial factor in bridging the gap between theory and practice. The final three papers bring us more squarely into the realm of practical initiatives and activism, and critically analyse specific anti-dowry campaigns and types of activism that are and could be further used by NGOs, social movements and governments. They indicate women's agency, individual and collective, and enable us to reconsider their portrayal only as victims. Women's activism clearly points to the fact that seeking change from within the community is possible. It may be slow, but it can facilitate building a foundation for a larger movement of change in social relations based on the intersections between gender, caste, and religion. Such change through a collective process is relevant under circumstances in which seeking individual change is a difficult and complex process.

As these final three papers illustrate, autonomous groups and organisations within the women's movement at the grass roots, national and transnational levels have vigorously pursued protests and campaigns against dowry. Rajni Palriwala examines in detail the All India Democratic Women's Association (AIDWA) survey of dowry practices in India, conducted in 2002 (AIDWA 2003). She focuses on the processes behind the AIDWA survey, considering it a form of activism, and presents its findings as one aspect of the movement against dowry. The key point here is the significant shift in focus from recording dowry-related violence to an examination of the causal factors behind it. She addresses the question of why AIDWA decided to conduct the survey, through a brief consideration of the nature and outcomes of the earlier mobilisation of the 1980s and the critiques that were raised of it, as well as issues of perspective and strategy from within the Indian women's movement. In presenting some of the findings of the survey for selected states and through key examples, she maps the

21

changes in the practice of dowry and its implications. The stimulus for the survey was to strategise on furthering the struggle against dowry, and she concludes with these discussions, illustrating the multiple experiences men and women have of dowry, indicating the need for an equally complex set of responses to it.

Srimati Basu continues this discussion centring on the question: how have discourses around dowry violence changed in the Indian women's movement over the decades? She argues that although the legislative history of dowry reflects the strong influence of the women's movement, in terms of delineating the word 'dowry' in legal parlance, the Dowry Prohibition Act (1984) that emerged at the end of political negotiations was a weak legal tool, at odds with both feminist definitions and cultural practices of dowry. On the one hand, legal remedies did not take into account feminist critiques, such as the gendered differences in power in parties to the marriage, and the problems of looking to dowry as women's optimal, if indirect, access to property resources. On the other, it failed to distinguish coercion from custom, and gift from demand, and to clearly demarcate who should be held criminally liable in marriage exchanges. In the ensuing decades, while the women's movement has targeted loopholes in the prosecution and proliferation of dowry, and the linkage of dowry to other forms of violence (infanticide, sex-selection, domestic violence), cultural practices have adapted to these loopholes, transforming the scope and form of dowry. Basu analyses recent feminist discourses of anti-dowry mobilisation and other marriage- and violence-related campaigns, alongside fieldwork data on dowry that emerged in the course of studying the workings of family law, to foreground the evolution of dowry demands, and the ways in which women's organisations manage these emergent forms. Her analysis reveals that simultaneous attention to fundamental issues of marriage, access to resources and entitlement to uses of property help illuminate the ever-changing forms of dowry practices.

Mangala Subramaniam, Karen Remedios and Debarashmi Mitra shift our attention away from a focus on the Indian women's movement and place dowry in the context of the international women's movement, represented by various forms of transnational networks. They highlight the ways in which the international women's movement has been significant in naming and bringing the issues of violence against women into the public arena. This effort has included connecting violence in the private and public spheres with issues of power. Women's groups and networks have been persistent in seeking mandates and conventions from the United Nations in an attempt to put pressure on nation states to commit to implementing anti-violence measures. The authors examine transnational activism against dowry violence, with specific attention to the Convention of Elimination of all Forms of Discrimination Against Women (CEDAW). In particular, they are critical that experiences of violence, such as 'dowry deaths', are mentioned without reference to women's subordination as related to dowry and marriage; nor is any information included about women being harassed and abused for dowry without being murdered. They suggest that the reasons for this can be seen as deliberate or strategic, and therefore dowry is framed as an issue of violence rather than as gendered cultural practice, in order to circumvent the cultural relativism debate and simultaneously demonstrate sensitivity to a cultural practice.

A final concluding paper is aimed specifically at consolidating some key themes of the volume, as well as thinking about future directions of the Dowry Project. We present suggestions made about the sorts of activism and action that are necessary to end dowry injustice and to highlight the particular role that academic research can play. In order to bring our discussion beyond the legal dimensions of dowry and to be able to target appropriate interventions, it is necessary to ask 'who and what underpins the cycle of culpability and how can it be broken?'

Notes

[1] Dalmia and Lawrence in this volume, however, discuss data that suggest that this is only the case if we compare 'real values' of dowry (i.e. the values of

dowry at a particular point in time without any adjustment for inflation). If we compare the 'nominal values' of dowry (i.e. the values of dowry with adjustment for inflation) then such increases are negligible.

[2] Traditions of son preference exist in South Asia apart from dowry pressure. For instance, many women feel that they have failed in their wifely duty if they produce daughters rather than sons. The reasons for this are that a higher social, economic and religious value is placed upon males compared to women in South Asian societies (see Robinson 1999). For instance, in Hinduism only men can carry out the last rites for their parents, women are typically considered to be a lower rebirth than men and the texts (e.g. the Laws of Manu) contain references to the fact that the birth of girls is to be lamented.

[3] This will be returned to in the conclusion to this volume.

[4] I would like to acknowledge Kate Jehan for initially drawing my attention to this wide range of interdisciplinary sources on dowry.

[5] The reasons for this escalation are discussed by a number of contributors to this book (see Rozario; and Dalmia and Lawrence).

[6] Discursively people still refer to it as such (Basu 1999b).

[7] Although as Unnithan-Kumar argues, despite that fact that 'gender theorists have ... championed the cause of bride price as it supposedly acknowledges the work "value" of women ... bride price payments do not improve upon the structural gender inequalities found in dowry-paying communities' (2005: 27).

[8] http://ncrb.nic.in/crime2004/cii-2004/CHAP5.pdf

[9] See the concluding essay in this volume.

References

Acker, Joan. 2000. 'Rewriting Class, Race, and Gender: Problems in Feminist Rethinking' in *Revisioning Gender*. eds. Myra Marx, Judith Lorber and Beth Hess. Walnut Creek, CA: AltaMira Press. pp. 44–69.

———. 2006. *Class Questions: Feminist Answers*. Walnut Creek, CA: AltaMira Press.

AIDWA. 2003: *Expanding dimensions of dowry*. Delhi: AIDWA.

Andersen, Margaret L. 1993. *Thinking about Women: Sociological Perspectives on Sex and Gender*. New York: Macmillan.

Anderson, S. 2003. 'Why Dowry Payments Declined with Modernisation in Europe but are Rising in India'. *Journal of Political Economy*. 111(2). pp. 269–310.

Banerjee, K. 1999. 'Gender Stratification and the Contemporary Marriage Market in India'. *Journal of Family Issues*. 20(5). pp. 648–76.

Banerjee, N. 2002. 'Between the Devil and the Deep Blue Sea: Shrinking Options for Women in Contemporary India' in *The Violence of Development: The*

Politics of Identity, Gender and Social Inequalities in India. ed. K. Kapadia. London: Zed Books. pp. 43–68

Banerjee N. and D. Jain. 2001. 'Indian Sex Ratios through Time and Space: Development from Women's Perspective' in *Enduring Conundrum: India's Sex Ratios*. eds. V. Mazumdar and N. Krishnaji. New Delhi: Centre for Women's Development Studies. pp. 73–119

Basu, A.M. 1999a. 'Fertility Decline and Increasing Gender Imbalance in India, Including a Possible South Indian Turnaround'. *Development and Change*. 30(2). pp. 237–63.

Basu, S. 1999b. *She Comes to Take Her Rights: Indian Women, Property and Propriety*. Albany: SUNY P.

Basu, S. ed. 2005. *Dowry and Inheritance*. New Delhi: Women Unlimited.

Bhat, M. and Halli, S. 1999. 'Demography and Brideprice and Dowry: Causes and Consequences of the Indian Marriage Squeeze'. *Population Studies*. 53(2). pp. 129–48.

Bloch, F., S. Desai and V. Rao. 2004: 'Wedding Celebrations as Conspicuous Consumption: Signaling Social Status in Rural India'. *Journal of Human Resources* 39(3). pp. 675–95.

Bloch, F. and Rao, V. 2002. 'Terror as a Bargaining Instrument: A Case Study of Dowry Violence in Rural India'. *American Economic Review*. 92(4). pp. 1029–43.

Butalia, S. 2002. *The gift of a daughter: Encounters with victims of dowry*. New Delhi: Penguin Books India.

Caplan, L. 1984. 'Bridegroom Price in Urban India: Class, Caste and "Dowry Evil" Among Christians in Madras'. *Man*. New Series. 19(2). pp. 216–33.

Dreze, J. and A. Sen. 2002. *India: Development and Participation*. Oxford: OUP.

Evans Pritchard, E.E. 1951. *Social Anthropology*. London: Cohen and West.

Glenn, Evelyn Nakano. 2000. 'The Social Construction and Institutionalization of Gender and Race: An Integrative Framework' in *Revisioning Gender* eds. Myra Marx, Judith Lorber and Beth Hess. Walnut Creek, CA: AltaMira Press. pp. 3–43.

Gough, K. 1956. 'Brahman Kinship in a Tamil Village'. *American Anthropologist*. New Series. 38(5). pp. 826–53.

Harding, Sandra. 1991. *Whose Science? Whose Knowledge? Thinking from Women's Lives*. Ithaca, NY: Cornell University Press.

Hill-Collins, Patricia. 1990. *Black Feminist Theory: Knowledge, Consciousness and the Politics of Empowerment*. Cambridge, MA: Unwin Hyman.

Jayaraj, D and S. Subramanian. 2004. 'Women's Wellbeing and the Sex Ratio at Birth: Some Suggestive Evidence from India'. *The Journal of Development Studies.*40(5). pp. 91–119.

Jutla, R. and D. Heimbach. 2004. 'Love burns: An essay about bride burning in India'. *The Journal of burn care and rehabilitation*. 25(2). pp. 165–70.

Kandiyoti, D. 1988. 'Bargaining with Patriarchy'. *Gender and Society.* 2(3). pp. 274–90.

Kishwar, M. and Five Others. 2005 [1980]. 'Beginning with our own lives: a call for dowry boycott' in *Dowry and Inheritance.* ed. Srimati Basu. New Delhi: Women Unlimited. pp. 265–67.

Kishwar, M. 1989. 'Dowry and Inheritance Rights'. *Economic and Political Weekly.* 24(11). 18 March. pp. 587–88.

———. 2005 [1988]. 'Rethinking the Dowry Boycott' in *Dowry and Inheritance.* ed. Srimati Basu. New Delhi: Women Unlimited. pp. 268–78.

Kumar, V. and C.B. Tripathi. 2004. 'Burnt wives—a study of suicides'. *Burns.* 29(1). pp. 31–5.

Lakshmi, C.S. 1989. 'On Kidneys and Dowry'. *Economic and Political Weekly.* 24(4). 28 January. pp. 189–91.

Leslie, J. 1998. 'Dowry, dowry deaths and violence against women: a journey of discovery' in *South Asians and the Dowry Problem.* ed. W. Menski. London: Trentham Books. pp. 21–35.

Levi-Strauss, C. 1949. *The Elementary Structures of Kinship.* London: Eyre and Spottiswoode.

Lewis, R. and S. Mills. 2003. 'Introduction' in *Feminist Postcolonial Theory A Reader.* eds. R. Lewis and S. Mills. New York: Routledge.

Menski, W. 1998. 'New Concerns about Abuses of the South Asian Dowry System in *South Asians and the Dowry Problem.* ed. W. Menski. London: Trentham Books. pp. 1–20.

Mohanty, C. 1988. 'Under Western Eyes' in *Third World Women and the Politics of Feminism.* eds. C. Mohanty and A. Russo. Bloomington: Indiana University Press.

Nabar, V. 1995. *Caste as Woman.* New Delhi: Penguin Books International.

Naples, N. 2006. 'Feminist Activism and Activist Scholarship in the 21st Century'. *FemTAP: A Journal of Feminist Theory and Practice.* Summer. http://femtap.com/sitebuildercontent/sitebuilderfiles/naples.pdf

Narayan, Uma. 1997. 'Cross-Cultural Connections, Border Crossings & Death by Culture' in *Dislocating Cultures: Identities, Traditions and Third World Feminism.* New York: Routledge. pp. 81–117.

Oldenburg, Veena T. 1994. 'The Roop Kanwar Case: Feminist Responses' in *Sati The Blessing and The Curse.* ed. J.S. Hawley. New York and Oxford: Oxford University Press.

———. 2002. *Dowry Murder: The Imperial Origins of a Cultural Crime.* New York and Oxford: Oxford University Press.

Palriwala, R. 1989. 'Reaffirming the Anti-Dowry Struggle'. *Economic and Political Weekly.* 24(7). 29 April. pp. 942–44.

Prasad, B.D. 1994. 'Dowry-related violence: A content analysis of news in selected newspapers'. *Journal of Comparative Family Studies.* 25(1). pp. 71–89.

Rastogi, M. and P. Therly. 2006. 'Dowry and its Link to Violence Against Women in India'. *Trauma, Violence & Abuse.* 7(1). pp. 66–77.

Rao, V. 1993. 'The Rising Price of Husbands: A Hedonic Analysis of Dowry Increases in Rural India'. *The Journal of Political Economy.* 101(4). pp. 666–77.

Rich, A. 2003. 'Towards a Politics of Location' in *Feminist Postcolonial Theory A Reader.* eds. R. Lewis and S. Mills. New York: Routledge.

Robinson, C.A. 1999: 'Tradition and Liberation: The Hindu Tradition in the Indian Women's Movement'. Richmond, Surrey: Curzon.

Rudd, J. 2001. 'Dowry-Murder: An Example of Violence Against Women'. *Women's Studies International Forum* 24. pp. 513–22.

Sandanshiv, D.N. and J. Mathew. 1995. 'Legal reform in dowry laws' in *Kali's Yug: Empowerment, Law and Dowry Death.* ed. Rani Jethmalani. New Delhi: Har-Anand. pp. 79–93.

Scott, Joan. 1986. 'Gender: A Useful Category of Historical Analysis' *American Historical Review.* 91(5). December. pp. 1053–75.

Sen, Amartya K. 1992. 'Missing Women'. *British Medical Journal.* 304(682/). March. pp. 587–88.

———. 1993. 'The Economics of Life and Death.' *Scientific American.* 268. May. pp. 40–47.

Sirohi, S. 2003. *Stories of Dowry Victims.* New Delhi: HarperCollins.

Sitaraman, B. 1999. 'Law as Ideology: Women, Courts and "Dowry Deaths" in India'. *International Journal of the Sociology of Law.* 27(3). pp. 287–316

Srinivas, M.N. 1984. *Some reflections on dowry.* Delhi: Oxford University Press.

Srinivasan, S. and A. Bedi. 2007. 'Domestic Violence and Dowry: Evidence from a South Indian Village'. *World Development.* 35(5). pp. 857–80.

Srinivasan, Padma and Gary R. Lee. 2004. 'The Dowry System in Northern India: Women's Attitudes and Social Change'. *Journal of Marriage and Family.* 66. pp. 1108–17.

Stone, L. and C. James. 1995. 'Dowry, Bride-Burning, and Female Power in India'. *Women's Studies International Forum.* 18(2). pp. 125–34.

Sunder Rajan, R. 2003. *The Scandal of the State: Women, Law, and Citizenship in Postcolonial India.* Durham: Duke University Press.

Stanley, Liz and Sue Wise. 1990. 'Method, Methodology, and Epistemology in Feminist Research Processes' in *Feminist Praxis: Research Theory and Epistemology in Feminist Sociology.* ed. Liz Stanley. New York: Routledge. pp. 4–19.

Tambiah, S.J. 1973. 'Dowry and bridewealth and the property rights of women' in *Bridewealth and Dowry.* eds. Jack Goody and Stanley J. Tambiah. London: Cambridge University Press. pp. 59–169.

Unnithan-Kumar, M. 2005. 'Girasia Brideprice and the Politics of Marriage Payments' in *Dowry and Inheritance*. ed. Srimati Basu. New Delhi: Women Unlimited. pp. 27–41.

Vera-Sanso, P. 2001. 'Masculinity, Male Domestic Authority and Female Labour Participation in South India' in *Men at Work: Labour, Masculinities, Development*. ed. C. Jackson. London: F. Cass.

Dowry in Rural Bangladesh
An intractable problem?

SANTI ROZARIO

Introduction

Over the last two to three decades, there has been a complex range of developments in rural Bangladesh. These have included the increased monetarisation of the village economy, the gradual disintegration of extended family networks, the progressive breakdown of patron-client relationships, improved roads and transport infrastructure, the rise of garment industries, increased levels of rural-urban migration and landlessness, an expansion of education and health facilities, and the growing presence of non-government organisations and microfinance institutions. All these have had consequences for rural women (Kabeer 1985; Lindenbaum 1981; Wood 1994).

NGOs, microfinance institutions and garment industries have become the major agents of change in the lives of rural Bangladeshi women in recent years. Usually referred to as signs of improvement of women's status and of their 'empowerment',[1] these changes include their increased participation in paid employment, their greater presence in public spaces, higher levels of female school attendance, greater access to finance through microcredit schemes, access to better health provisions and so on. It is true that compared to 15 or 20 years ago, a greater number of women are engaged in paid employment with NGOs and microfinance institutions as

29

health and family planning visitors, family welfare visitors, teachers, bankers, or workers on income-generating projects. In the urban areas, garment factories have provided one of the major sources of employment to relatively poor rural female migrants, as well as to poor urban women. Some middle class women have also taken up jobs in these factories, while a significant proportion of them are in paid employment in the various government sectors, NGOs, and the private sector. In addition, the growth of microcredit institutions aimed primarily at women, initiated by Grameen Bank, has, on the surface at least, led to much higher levels of independent access to finance for rural women, even those from relatively poor backgrounds.

However, the puzzle remains: if these positive changes have resulted in women's 'empowerment', why has there not been the kind of improvements in women's position that might be expected, such as the reduction or abolition of dowry payments, or a reduction in domestic violence? Indeed, if anything, these tend to be going in the opposite direction (Rozario 2007; Huda 2006; Naved et al. 2007; Suran et al. 2004).

Methodology

This paper is based on my field research in rural Bangladesh since the early 1980s in a village in the region of Dhaka containing a mixed population of Muslims, Christians and Hindus. As the focus was on gender relations in a rural region, dowry[2] was quite understandably one of the main issues that stood out and formed a large section of my subsequent books (Rozario 1992, 2001a). Between 1991 and 2007, I made 18 field research trips to Noakhali, Bogra, Rajshahi and Dhaka districts working with rural Bangladeshi women of all three religious communities in relation to their reproductive health concerns, the status of the local birth attendants, the role of NGOs and microfinance institutions in alleviating poverty, women's empowerment and solidarity, as well as the question of dowry itself. Dowry was constantly present as a major issue in women's lives and during this period, I observed its spread and inflation among all rural and urban classes.

Since 2000, I have interviewed rural women in other parts of Bangladesh including most of the north of the country (Dinajpur, Rangpur and Bogra districts), and gained a broad picture of the changing gender relations in Bangladesh.[3] In 2005, a series of focus group discussions with poor rural women in northern Bangladesh highlighted that their biggest problem was almost unanimously 'dowry' (CARE reports 2004, 2005). Dowry is a relatively new phenomenon among non-Hindu (Muslim and Christian) families in Bangladesh. This essay discusses its root causes, examines the impact of recent developments in relation to women, including NGO activities, garment factories and the spread of microfinance around rural Bangladesh and analyses how within the modern capitalist socio-economic context, dowry has become one of the most critical sources of capital for men and their families. This explains the resistance or reluctance to do away with dowry on the part of village, urban, poor and middle class families.

Why dowry?

To understand how dowry (*dabi* or *joutuk*) came about among non-Hindu families in Bangladesh, and how the earlier practice of bride wealth, or marriage payments (*pon*),[4] from grooms' families to brides' families, has shifted to the opposite direction, we need to grasp the social processes which sustain Bengali gender ideologies. These in turn are enmeshed in everyday social practice. Thus the questions of marriage, dowry and the dependency of women on men are interrelated.

The ideology that supports patriarchy in Bangladesh centres on concepts such as *izzat* (honour, focusing in particular on the control of women's sexuality), *lajja-sharam* (shame), and *parda* (purdah, restrictions on women's mobility). These concepts pervade society as a whole and indeed support its class structure, since the practicalities of survival mean that the poor are less able to meet the demands of honour, shame and purdah than the better off. In the present context those who stand to gain from the hierarchical

31

class structure of Bangladeshi society, women as well as men, feel threatened by any attack on these principles.

In particular, patriarchy would not survive without the cooperation of women, especially women from the 'middle' and 'upper' classes, both in the villages and in urban contexts.[5] These women cooperate in part at least because they stand to gain from the hierarchical class structure. It is through their 'purity' and 'honour' *(izzat)* that their men can retain their own honour and position within the class hierarchy. And of course the honour of their men has a flow-on effect on themselves (see Rozario 2001a).

Of course, these women are also subject to the Bangladeshi patriarchal norms in their day-to-day living. Poor and illiterate women are not necessarily more adversely affected by patriarchy than the middle and upper middle classes, although it is true that their poverty often makes their situation much more unbearable in material terms. In some ways, the physical constraints of patriarchy *(parda* etc.) are more directly experienced by middle class women who do not necessarily find it easy to fight it (Jackson 1998). In a society such as Bangladesh, which lacks any effective State-provided social security system, most women are ultimately dependent on the men of their family for support, and they cannot afford to alienate them. Marriage is regarded as essential for all women, and this in turn is linked to patrilocal residence, patrilineal inheritance, and the lack of any socially approved place for a woman outside her husband's home.

At the same time, the relatively high status of middle and upper class women in the system is tied up with their accepting the assumptions on which it is built. It is not surprising that most of them go along with what Kandiyoti has called the 'patriarchal bargain' by which they receive security and protection in exchange for accepting their own subordination (Kandiyoti 1988: 282–3).

Thus it is the middle and upper classes, women as well as men, who continue to keep the gender ideology of Bangladeshi society in force, not least by their attitudes and behaviour to those who step out of line. This includes lower-class women who are forced for survival to take on jobs that are seen as compromising

32

their purity and *izzat* (e.g. in garment factories), as well as women of all classes who choose not to marry. Perhaps above all, women as well as men fuel the demand for the ever-increasing dowry payments that quite literally devalue women in relation to men. Until these middle-class gender values and behaviours change, it is unlikely that there will be a real change to Bangladeshi patriarchy as a whole. But first, I discuss the growth of dowry in Bangladesh.

The rise of dowry

Dowry has had a long tradition in Hindu marriage in South Asia, albeit in different forms in lower and upper castes and in various regions. Different forms of dowry practised among Hindu castes have been extensively discussed, especially in the Indian context (Tambiah & Goody 1973, 1989; Boserup 1970; Epstein 1973; Srinivas 1984; Fruzzetti 1982; Randeria and Visaria 1984).

Dowry among non-Hindus in Bangladesh is a much more recent phenomenon. During my doctoral fieldwork in Dhaka district in the mid 1980s, dowry was only gradually becoming the norm among the non-Hindus (Muslims and Christians) in the village. Muslim and Christian women stated that of the two generations of women in most households, the older generation were married with the payment of *pon* to the bride's parents, not dowry (*dabi* or *joutuk*) to the bridegroom's which shows how recent this practice is. The timing of this shift from *pon* to *dabi* is not clear and it may vary from region to region. Amin and Cain's (1997) findings from two villages in Rajshahi district reveal that dowry replaced bride price from 1964 quite abruptly and since then it has become the norm, whereas in the Dhaka region of my research villagers generally talked about the shift having taken place since the early 1970s.

In the mid 1980s, I identified four interrelated reasons for the emergence of dowry and they are still of help today in understanding the perpetuation and inflation of dowry in Bangladesh:

33

- demographic imbalance: surplus of women and shortage of men;
- socio-economic transformation: dowry as the product of modernity;
- ideological justification: valorisation of men *vs.* devalorisation of women;
- disjunction between culture and economy.

The demographic imbalance: surplus of women and shortage of men

To explain the shift from a *pon* to a *dabi* system, villagers usually pointed to the shortage of men and surplus of women. Other researchers in Bangladesh and India have also had similar responses (Lindenbaum 1981). Indeed in my field visits to northern Bangladesh in 2004 and 2005, women and men gave me exactly the same response. Yet, it is well known that, demographically, the sex ratio for all age groups in Bangladesh shows considerably more males than females.[6]

There are, however, social reasons for the rural perception of a female surplus. Although 18 has been set as the minimum legal age of marriage for women, in practice women are still married from the age of around 14, sometimes even earlier. On the other hand, before marriage can be considered, a man today has to be at least 20 and preferably to have established himself by acquiring economic autonomy or a monthly income. Thus, while a woman becomes marriageable from the age of 14, a man is usually not established satisfactorily and become a desirable groom till about 25, or even older. Thus, at any given time, the number of women available in the marriage market is always greater than the number of available men and although the absolute number of women is smaller than that of men, the socially imposed difference in the age of marriage creates a real imbalance in the number of available men and women (Rozario 1992, 2001a). It is this imbalance between marriageable girls and men that helps in legitimation and perpetuation of dowry and gives rise to competition among potential brides' families for suitable grooms, further inflating the amount of dowry demanded and paid by brides' families.

The socio-economic transformation:
dowry as the product of modernity

The emergence of dowry is directly linked to the socio-economic changes in Bangladesh over the last few decades. While agriculture was the main source of livelihood for most people, men were tied to the land and marriage was seen as one way of gaining extra labour. However, the number of men dissociating themselves from agricultural work has been increasing. The importance of land has not decreased, but educated men have become interested in different kinds of work. They go to the city for higher education and employment and become accustomed to an urban culture. This male urban migration became necessary following the decrease in the size of landholdings and the increase in landlessness as well as the new aspirations of upper middle and middle class men. Such male urban migration is linked to the transition of Bangladesh from its pre-capitalist agricultural relations to its incorporation into the capitalist world economy. Working on the land lost its former high status, while prestige became increasingly attached to income from urban centres.

This pattern of urban migration and the associated penetration of capitalist methods of production into the countryside affected the value system, including the status of women. Associated with these changes is a shift in the prestige system 'from one based on land and aristocratic values to one based on the accumulation of money,' with the possibility of translating occupation and commercial success into a new status hierarchy (Lindenbaum 1981: 396).

As many men began to take advantage of these changes, acquiring education, wealth and new status, women began to pay a price for their success. With the decline in family-based farming, the traditional productive role of women suffered more than men's, largely because societal pressure on sexual segregation prevented them from seeking opportunities parallel to men's (Kabeer 2001). Thus until recent times education and urban employment were largely restricted to men.

This led the parents of grooms to see it as appropriate to make a *dabi* or 'demand' for cash or other items from parents of brides as a return for their investment on their sons. While in most cases the bride's parents respond to a demand for *dabi* made by the groom's parents, in some cases the bride's parents volunteer a dowry so that their daughter can marry a son-in-law with a good education and urban occupation.

Such practices have been referred to in the Indian context as the 'status game of hypergamy'[7] for brides (Caldwell et al. 1983). This certainly applies to the development of the practice of dowry among non-Hindus in Bangladesh as well. The shift from bride wealth to dowry occurred first in urban centres among wealthy families and gradually spread among the rural upper and middle classes (Lindenbaum 1981). The nouveau riche of Bangladesh spent their wealth on conspicuous consumption rather than investing in productive activities. As black-marketeers, contractors, bureaucrats, army officers, politicians and the like, they acquired considerable wealth in a very short period of time (Ahmed and Naher 1986, 1987). Lacking the status of the landed aristocratic class, they engaged in status hypergamy through marriage. They spent enormous amounts at the weddings of both sons and daughters, and paid large dowries at their daughters' marriages to display their wealth and to secure a groom with a good education and occupation. Although the urban middle and lower middle class could not afford to be as spendthrift, they began to emulate the nouveau riche.

In the villages of my doctoral research, several returnees from the Middle East had initially engaged in a similar practice of hypergamy by giving large dowries for daughters and displaying their wealth through elaborate weddings for sons and daughters. These conspicuous displays of wealth gradually influenced other grooms' families to ask for *dabi* for their educated sons and placed families of brides under pressure to meet such demands In some cases they voluntarily offered dowry to prevent the families of prospective grooms from being tempted away by the offer of a large dowry elsewhere.

In recent interviews (CARE Report 2005) with village women in north-western Bangladesh they gave examples of how the families of mature girls compete for suitable grooms. One woman said, 'Dowry has become like a competition. If one family wants to give less dowry, another will offer more to marry their daughter.' Another woman said, 'Fathers of daughters have to sell their land and the bull they plough with to pay dowry.' Different villages had similar responses: 'When a groom's family see a girl and like her, they start negotiating about dowry. Often poor families cannot meet the demand for a high dowry and they offer a somewhat lower amount. But the groom's family does not budge. At this time, some neighbouring family, who might be somewhat better off and have a marriageable daughter, offer a few thousand takas extra (perhaps five or ten thousand)[8] and "buy the groom" for their daughter.'

The ideological justification: valorisation of men vs. devalorisation of women

Village men formerly married between the ages of 18 to 22, but with increased urbanisation and education, they began to postpone marriage until a much later age and now do not marry until 25 to 30. Yet while men identify with the modern practice of economic autonomy before marriage, they still define women's status in traditional terms. They still value female sexual purity, and consequently do not marry women of their own age, whom they consider likely to be sexually suspect. Men in their late 20s and 30s now prefer to marry women between the ages of 15 and 19. For every man who marries a much younger woman, there is a corresponding unmarried woman of his own age. While a man can remain unmarried until he is 30 or even 40, a woman who is not married by the time she is 20 is labelled as unmarriageable. This attitude often prevents women from having aspirations to higher education or outside employment.

As the number of never-married women began to increase, parents became anxious about the marriage prospects of their daughters, prompting them to make dowry payments. This is often the case even where the parents of the prospective groom either have no expectation of dowry or do not demand one. Through dowry, men are looking for compensation for taking the risk of marrying women whose purity is becoming increasingly difficult to control. As Caldwell et al. (1983: 359) argue, 'dowry provides a powerful mechanism in South Asia, unlike the rest of the Third World, for mitigating the impact of the marriage squeeze,' i.e. the imbalance of marriageable men and women.

The ideological basis of dowry is maintained through the notions of purity and honour. The responsibility of guarding the purity of mature women is seen as such a burden that even when unmarried women are economically viable the parents are anxious to marry them off (Rozario 2001b; Dennecker 2002). The economic contribution of mature unmarried women is not a desirable alternative to their marriage. Caldwell et al. (1983) report that in South India the size of dowry increases from menarche onward and older women's families pay higher dowry. They point out that even among the lower castes young girls are withdrawn from outside paid work for fear of damaging their marriage prospects. In my field visit to north-west Bangladesh I found that this analysis still applies there. Parents of *kachi meye* (young, unspoiled, and pure girls) can get away with paying a smaller dowry. Thus, I would argue that the ideological justification for dowry centres around the concern about women's virginity and purity.[9] However, while there is a cultural preference for men to marry 'pure' women, other assets (fair complexion, wealth, education) of women play almost equally important roles in determining their desirability as brides. Nevertheless, whether or not all men succeed in marrying a so-called 'pure' woman, the ideology of 'purity' has the effect of enforcing female subordination and maintaining *dabi*. The notion of purity has the effect of distinguishing between 'good' (therefore marriageable) and 'bad' (therefore unmarriageable) women, and thereby justifying and inflating the amount of dowry as brides' families compete with each other to secure 'good' grooms for their daughters (Rozario 2002b).

Thus the shift from a *pon* system to a *dabi* system is linked

38

to a combination of factors: the socially created surplus of never-married mature women; socio-economic changes over the last few decades, resulting in valorisation of men and consequent devalorisation of women; and the significance of the ideology of purity in defining desirable brides.

The disjunction between culture and economy

In discussing the problems facing Bangladeshi women, it is common to see Bangladeshi 'culture' as the problem. 'Culture' is an increasingly problematic concept in anthropology, and it is not possible to analyse here how 'culture' in general might be defined. However, it is important to understand that what is popularly seen as 'culture' or 'cultural' values does not function in isolation from socio-economic and political structures. In other words culture and social structure are part of the same process of social life, although there is not necessarily a neat 'fit' between them in all aspects of social life.

There is indeed a significant disjunction between the demands of the economy (or the wider social structure) and the system of values in Bangladeshi society. Over the last two decades, women have been joining the outside paid workforce in large numbers. It is clear that many families can no longer afford to confine all their women to their households. To a certain extent, Bangladeshi society now tolerates women's presence in the men's world, i.e. the public sphere, although the increased incidents of sexual harassment and other forms of violence on women in public spaces can be seen as a form of backlash.[10] Yet women's status is still defined in terms of traditional ideologies of purity and honour, and their families now have to pay large dowries to ensure a 'good' marriage for them.

The shift from bride wealth to dowry and its escalation in recent years is a consequence of this disparity between the cultural values and the changing economic practices in Bangladesh. Drastic changes in its economy have not been reflected in the ideology of gender.[11] Hence, parents are desperate to marry off their daughters despite the fact that women are presently less of an economic

SANTI ROZARIO

burden than they were in the past. This explains why men want it both ways (i.e. women who are young/pure/fair/useless as well as educated/rich/income-producing). Bangladeshis want the fruits of modernity (radios, televisions, motorcycles, cars, apartments equipped with the latest gadgets) but are not willing to pay the price (increasing incorporation of women in the workforce) since this is seen as threatening their purity.

It is important to understand that it is in the interest of the dominant classes to try to maintain the traditional values, which continue to subordinate women and now are also responsible for the shift to and escalation of dowry. This is because the gender hierarchy is an essential component of the Bangladeshi social hierarchy in general. Hence purity, which devalorises women and thus justifies the new dowry system, serves an important function for the social order. Moreover, like purity, the system of dowry facilitates the maintenance and reproduction of status and social hierarchies. Tambiah's analysis of Indian dowry payments also helps us in understanding the system as they 'allow the creation of alliances and ties between elite groups of approximately similar status (or between groups whose exchange of prestige for wealth close status gaps)' (Tambiah 1989: 22).

The contemporary situation and inflation of dowry

Changes over the last few decades in the agricultural economy and in the urban sector through capitalism, the activities of hundreds of NGOs, and microfinance institutions in rural areas brought both positive and negative changes in women's lives. The decline of family-based farming left women more vulnerable and dependent on men. Rural poverty and increasing polarisation between the landed and landless began to 'undermine the material basis of kinship solidarity and cooperation—the "moral economy" of the peasantry' (Kabeer 1988: 105) and made unmarried, widowed and female-headed households much more vulnerable. At the same time, NGOs such as BRAC (Bangladesh Rural Advancement Committee), Proshika, Nijera Kori and others engaged in many income-generating projects as well as consciousness-raising programmes for women. Most of the income-generating projects for women, many financed with microcredit, are undertaken within the confines of the household. More often than not, microcredit is used by men in rural families and invested in activities outside the household and do not involve women. This is done to maintain the general norm of *parda* or sexual segregation and thereby the honour and reputation of individual families. Despite these constraints many women have accessed job opportunities provided by the village-based development programmes linked to government and NGOs.

In more recent years, very poor women, who traditionally often worked in wealthy households, have begun to take up outdoor jobs provided by the local government or bilateral agencies in road construction, or various other farming activities. Some of these are related to the special projects involving the 'poorest of the poor'. Since these jobs are perceived both as menial and as very public, most families would prefer their women not engaging in them for fear of their losing their honour. Thus no women from reasonably well-off families would ever be allowed to take up these jobs, which also come with low pay for very difficult physical labour.

Another significant development since the 1980s has been the rise of garment factories in the main urban centres of Bangladesh. Much has been written about how this new development has generated outside paid employment for large number of poor and not so poor women (Paul-Majumdar & Sen 2000; Dennecker 2002; Kabeer 1994, 2001; Siddiqui 1991). Like women's access to microcredit, this employment too has made a significant difference to many poor women's lives, such as their increased status in relation to husbands and other family members. Many of them who used to work as domestics with middle class families found this work more appealing both in terms of money earned and the number of hours of work. However, this work is on the whole very lowly paid, with very long hours and such rigid discipline that married women with small children often find it difficult to cope. Nevertheless, it provides relative freedom compared to working as domestics and being on call 24 hours a day, seven days a week. Female garment workers, like their poor sisters in outdoor paid employment, such as in construction industries in the urban areas or road building and farm work in rural areas, were seen to have departed from the norms of *parda* and faced public condemnation, particularly if they were young and unmarried. But these women themselves did not see their taking up paid employment as breaking of *parda*, and, instead, they redefined and renegotiated it (Siddiqui 1991; Kabeer 2001).

Though these new forms of employment have led to some subtle shifts in the arena of decision-making whereby women's needs and wants are given more importance, on the whole, there has not been a significant change in the intra-household power relationships—women very rarely can decide to take up outside paid employment without the permission of their husbands, and often they have little or no control over their own earnings.

Microcredit and inflation of dowry

The most significant single development in the 1990s for women in rural areas has undoubtedly been the growth of microcredit schemes aimed at them which has made considerable difference to their lives. Many women, who derived great benefits from their access to loans from Grameen Bank or other microcredit institutions, referred to Grameen Bank as their mother and father. Many reported how microcredit made it possible for them to send their children to school, to build a house, to instal a tubewell, and also helped them to marry their daughters by being able to pay dowry. Some women also reported that their ability to borrow money from an NGO or Grameen Bank increased their value in the eyes of their husbands or in-laws.

At the same time, however, there have also been heartbreaking stories from women being subjected to regular violence from their husbands when asking them for money for the weekly payments on microcredit borrowings. Typically, in these cases, the husband may have spent the borrowed money in gambling, drinking or womanising.

Although advocates for microcredit place great emphasis on lending to women, it is common knowledge among borrowers and bank workers alike that, whilst loans are taken by women, they are mostly used by their menfolk, husbands, brothers, sons, fathers or fathers-in-law (Goetz and Gupta 1996; Rahman 1999a; 1999b).[12] In recent years this has been explicitly acknowledged through the practice of requiring the signature of the husband or son who will use the loan before it is approved (Rozario 2002a). Women borrowers often take no part in deciding how the money is to be spent.

The creation of 'solidarity' or 'empowerment' among women in Bangladeshi villages has often been claimed as one of the major aims of microcredit programmes. In fact, while this has positive benefits for many women, including improvement of their economic status and their status within their families, it does not necessarily build female solidarity, and in fact can have a destructive effect upon it (Rozario 2002a).[13] The emphasis on repayment discipline means increased peer group pressure rather than mutual support for each other. In my own field research in a number of Bangladeshi communities where Grameen Bank-style microcredit had been introduced, loan repayments were regular causes of fights and conflicts among women, which worked against any form of solidarity they might have developed otherwise from their group meetings.

In the words of one Grameen Bank officer, the main strategy adopted by bank workers in collecting weekly repayments is to 'Keep the group under pressure. To threaten them that no new loan will be given to anyone in the group unless 100 per cent loan was collected' (*Groupkey chaper mukhey rakha hoy. Rin na deyar humki deya hoy*). For microcredit institutions, while group collateral is a way of giving loans in the absence of any other collateral, a high price is being paid by women for this collateral. Members resent defaulters, both because the entire group may be unable to obtain future loans, and also because it has to stay together at the meeting until the missing payment has somehow been produced. It is particularly women from poor families who lose out here. They are less likely to be admitted to microcredit schemes in the first place, and are usually at the receiving end of squabbles and fights over repayments within the group and between them and their husbands. In one case the corrugated roof of a poor woman's house was taken away by her fellow group members when she failed to come up with the repayment on the due date. This has an adverse impact on women's solidarity at village levels.

In the absence of solidarity among women and thereby absence of collective female empowerment (Rozario 1997, 2002a, 2002b) it is not surprising that microcredit does not necessarily lead to the removal of oppressive aspects of gender norms, including dowry, domestic violence and early marriage. While women's *collective* interest may be to reduce dowry payments and avoid early marriage, in practice they subordinate their interests to those of the extended family into which they are married, and these are tied up in various ways with the maintenance of dowry payments, gender norms and early marriage.

Indeed Grameen Bank-style microcredit schemes themselves operate in ways that reinforce this subordination of women's interests to the wider family context. All NGOs and microfinance institutions continue to define women by their relationship to other men: to their fathers, brothers, husbands and sons and thereby contribute to perpetuating women's dependency on men. As White (1992) has argued in another context, women use their resources not so much to be independent of their husbands or husbands' families but rather to improve the relationship of dependence they have with them.

Thus it would seem Grameen Bank and NGOs activities have failed to change anything within the existing gender relations in Bangladesh. The payment of dowry is a key example here, since in theory Grameen Bank and most other NGOs are opposed to it. In fact, one of the Sixteen Decisions ritually affirmed by Grameen Bank meetings reads in part 'We shall not take any dowry in our sons' weddings, neither shall we give any dowry in our daughters' weddings. We shall keep the centre free from the curse of dowry.' On the loan papers, loans are never described as being paid for use as dowry, but for income-generating projects or other officially acceptable purposes. In practice, though, among the most common uses of microcredit are to pay for women's dowry, to save for little girls' future dowry payment, to make jewellery to be part of a daughter's dowry package and to meet wedding expenses. The village-level bank officials are often aware of this strategy and turn a blind eye to it.

Women complain about having to pay dowry, but say that they do not have a choice, because without a dowry they cannot attract grooms for their daughters. A typical rural dowry might amount to Tk. 30,000 (about £240) plus a TV and jewellery. In negotiating dowry amounts, if the bride's family members plead with the groom's family that they cannot afford to pay the amount demanded, the groom's family will readily say, 'What about a loan from Grameen Bank or BRAC?'[14] Often village leaders get drawn into such negotiations and as the following example shows, they back up the demands that the bride's father comes up with an appropriate dowry. The following is an example (from my field notes in 2005) illustrating these points:

> Kalu Ahmed is a poor labourer without any land, and can only get work for part of the year. He has three daughters and married the first two with great difficulty. He married the third at age 15 with the promise of Tk. 30,000 dowry but has been unable to pay it. The girl was abused mentally and physically by her husband and mother-in-law, and they repeatedly sent her back to her father's house for dowry. Eventually she became pregnant, but they treated her with more violence and forced her to have an abortion. Her parents fought with the husband's parents and a village *shalish* (court consisting of prominent village leaders) was arranged with the Union Chairman and many prominent village men. They told Kalu Ahmed to pay some of the dowry as a condition for the girl to go back to her husband, although they know well that he will be unable to do so and she will be forced to remain with her parents.

In this example, we see that the village leaders insisted on dowry being paid, even though they were fully aware that the family did not have the resources. Another example from the same field research:

Ruksana comes from a poor family. She is the second of four sisters; there is also one brother. Her elder sister was married 10 years ago. The third sister worked in someone's house for eight years, after which they paid for her marriage. Ruksana, who is good-looking but not fair in complexion, began a romantic liaison with her cousin Ataul (mother's brother's son). Her mother let them mix freely as she thought it might lead to marriage, but people started to talk and said he might not marry her later, and they should arrange the marriage. However, Ataul's parents disapproved of the marriage (apparently mainly on the grounds of the family's poverty), began to look for another wife for Ataul, and stopped him going to Ruksana's house.

Ruksana managed to speak to Ataul by phone and told him that her mother was very ill. Ataul came to her house, and village leaders then negotiated a marriage between them with a *mohr* (payment from Ataul's family to Ruksana's) of Tk. 80,000. However, when Ruksana went to Ataul's house after marriage, her mother-in-law mistreated her and demanded a cycle, some jewellery and Tk. 30,000 from her. Ruksana's mother took a Tk. 7000 loan from Grameen Bank, bought a cycle and made some earrings in the hope that the mother-in-law (her own brother's wife) would treat Ruksana better but the mother-in-law pressured her for more money. Ruksana did not want to tell her parents since they were already struggling to keep up payments on the first loan and could not afford enough food. Her mother-in-law tricked her into signing divorce papers (she told her that the papers were to obtain another loan, from BRAC), forced her to return to her parents' house, and arranged a new marriage for Ataul. Ruksana has sold the earrings so she has the money to try to bring a legal case against Ataul's family for violence and dowry offences (Rozario 2005).

In Ruksana's case, the village leaders recognised her father's inability to pay and attempted to negotiate a practicable settlement. However, her in-laws refused to recognise the settlement, although they were close relatives of Ruksana's own mother, and the village leaders did nothing to intervene. Meanwhile, her parents were forced to take out a loan they could not afford, making their already very bad economic situation even worse. In yet another case, when a poor father pleaded with one of the village leaders to intervene in his negotiation with a potential groom's family as he was unable to pay any dowry for his daughter, the leader responded, 'Are you a beggar that you can't pay anything for your daughter?' To me, this was a way of the village leader to get the poor man to draw a boundary between himself and a beggar, instilling a sense of superiority in relation to the latter, and thereby forcing the poor village father to borrow or do whatever in order to pay for his daughter's dowry.

There are many more examples like these, and they illustrate the centrality within Bangladeshi society of the question of dowry, which is at the root of a whole series of other problems for women including early marriage, violence, and the impoverishment of families through continual payment of dowries. It is not surprising that dowry was named as one of the biggest problems by almost all of the 47 focus group discussions held with village women with whom CARE Bangladesh had been working in north-western Bangladesh (Rozario 2005).

Dowry is such a common practice with all classes and religious communities in Bangladesh at present that, as noted above, Grameen Bank and NGO workers will often knowingly give out loans for this purpose. Indeed, members of their staff, although officially preaching against the practice of dowry, are known to demand and accept dowry at their own family marriages. The failure of Grameen Bank-style microcredit to make any difference in this field is more than evident. In fact microcredit is not simply perpetuating the practice of dowry, it is helping to inflate the amount of dowry demanded and paid by contemporary rural families.[15]

Here the comment of an NGO official of the Bangladesh Unemployed Rehabilitation Organisation (BURO), Tangail, whom I interviewed is significant. He said with regard to dowry, '*Shamajik pratha, ta toe mantey hobey*' (It's a social norm, it has to be followed).

From my research with Grameen Bank, BRAC and other NGOs that have followed the Grameen Bank model in their microcredit schemes, it is evident that rather than facilitating in the reduction or abolition of dowry, unwittingly they have contributed to its inflation. As already mentioned, one of the common uses of microfinance is for dowry (Hussain 1998; Rozario 2002a, 2002c). This has become so prevalent that village people not only look to microfinance for a one-off dowry payment, but as an ongoing source of finance. Thus the grooms' families often send their newly married women to their parents to ask their mothers to take further loans from one of the many microfinance NGOs to pay them additional dowry. This practice has become common all over Bangladesh, and is not necessarily only linked to microcredit. However, the knowledge that parents of brides can borrow money through a microfinance NGO provides an additional temptation to families of grooms.

Dowry as the source of capital for grooms and their families

In 1980 dowry was made illegal in Bangladesh, yet far from it disappearing, the practice has persisted and the amounts involved keep escalating. The Dowry Act appears to have had no impact here. As we have seen, dowry came about with the new socio-economic development in the country. Subsequently, it began to escalate, as if to keep pace with further changes in the economy, with the greater penetration of foreign capital in the country and the exposure of people to the latest consumer items in the global market. In the rural areas, since the early 1980s, Grameen Bank-style microcredit has unwittingly been contributing to the inflation of dowry amounts (Rozario 2002a). Dowry has now become very much the norm for both urban and rural families, and the question of a marriage without it is almost unthinkable. An important aspect of this development is the role which dowry is now increasingly taking as a source of capital for the bridegroom. Indeed for many grooms' families, access to modern goods, modern salaried jobs for the grooms, a new business venture, or expansion of an existing business is only possible through a large *dabi* from the brides' families.

Dowry as a form of inheritance for women?

Almost every day the newspapers publish reports of dowry-related violence, murders, divorce and so forth. For example Bangladesh

48

National Women Lawyers' Association (BNWLA 2005), cited in Huda (2006) reported '371 cases of dowry-related violence in 2004, taking a variety of forms'. At the same time, there is a kind of apathy about its presence. During my 2004–5 CARE research a few professional men suggested that dowry could not be easily abolished as it was actually a form of inheritance for women. It is true that in the Hindu Indian context, Tambiah and Goody (1973: 1) saw dowry 'as a type of pre-mortem inheritance to the bride'. However, as has been argued even in the case of India, dowry as a form of inheritance or property of women does not make sense (Ram 1991) as dowry is not so much a 'gift' from parents to daughters, but demands made by grooms' families, and is clearly a product of modernity in Bangladesh. It is well known that dowry is normally used by grooms and their families, and is not under the control of brides whose parents pay this, usually upon demands made by grooms' families in the first place. Thus to suggest that dowry in Bangladesh is a form of inheritance makes no sense whatsoever.

And, as shown above, dowry is good for women because when it is paid brides are treated well and are not subjected to violence by their husbands and in-laws. However, some recent research revealed interesting results. Naved and Persson (2007: 1) found that 'women married without dowry demand were less frequently abused compared to women who fulfilled dowry demands ... The likelihood of experiencing severe physical violence was less when dowry was not demanded in marriage ...' They concluded that it is the patriarchal attitudes of particular families that are a better predictor of violence against women compared to payment of dowry. Suran et al. (2004: 12) also found that women who did not pay dowry at all are one of the groups with the lowest risk of violence. Thus there can be no direct association between dowry and well being of women.

Thus the issue of dowry in Bangladesh is a complex one and I sum up the main points raised above:

- The practice of dowry remains universal because marriage

(and dependence on a husband) is thought essential for women;
- The necessity for all women to be married, with the perceived 'risks' posed by an unmarried woman to her family honour, means that families feel pressured to marry off their daughters as soon as possible;
- This depresses the marriage age for women, and creates a perceived surplus of women in relation to men, who are not under the same pressure to marry and generally marry later in life;
- This in turn leads to further inflation of dowries and to the further devaluing of women in relation to men;
- The failure of the Bangladesh government in providing security for girls at home and in public places adds to the pressure for the early marriage of girls;
- The poverty level of some families also lead to early marriage of girls, who are seen as financial burdens on their fathers.

These factors form a vicious circle that contributes to both the perpetuation and inflation of dowry demands and payments in today's Bangladesh.

Conclusion

As outlined above, government policies and programmes in relation to health, law, education and development, NGO activities in these same fields, women's access to microcredit and income-generating activities, and to large scale employment opportunities through garment factories have led to major changes in the position of women in Bangladeshi society. These social and economic transformations have brought many problems with them. However, it cannot be denied that, despite these problems and limitations, significant positive changes have taken place in the lives of millions of individual women who have been exposed to these opportunities and changes. Many of them have had the scope to exercise agency within their own family or community contexts, albeit within patriarchal and wider structural constraints. It is these structures that continue to stand as barriers in the path of a genuine empowerment of women that might finally help eradicate the evils of dowry, early marriage, and violence against women, among others.

Nevertheless, as pointed out in my CARE 2004 report, various women's organisations, especially the legal ones (Mohila Parishad, Naripokko, Ain-O-Shalish Kendra, Bangladesh National Women Lawyers' Association) and NGOs working with women, such as Nijera Kori, BRAC and many others have played and continue to play significant roles in addressing these problems.

It is clear, however, that dowry cannot be dealt with in isolation from many other problems of women, all of which are associated with their devalued status in society, with Bangladeshi patriarchy in its modern form. To tackle the problem of dowry, we need to a large extent to be able to challenge both the local class and patriarchal hierarchies. These hierarchies plague women in every culture, and are not peculiar to Bangladesh except that the specific forms that patriarchy has taken in this country have contributed to those difficult and widespread problems.[16]

However, we need to acknowledge the role of women, especially middle class women, in perpetuating the gender status quo. Middle class women stand to gain from both the gender and social status hierarchy, since social status is built, among other things, on the gender values of honour, shame, purity and purdah. That also means that if we seek to change the status quo, we need to work with middle class women and convince them that what they may gain in status terms from the present situation is less valuable than what might become available to them and to their daughters, and to Bangladeshi women as a whole, if genuine change were to come about in Bangladeshi's gender values. These gender values are proving difficult to shift even in the face of major structural changes in which women are playing a critical role. It is these same values which continue to enforce universal marriage at an early age for women, thereby also placing pressure on parents of girls to pay dowries to attract husbands for them.

Given the structural interest of middle class women in

maintaining the system as it is, they are not going to be easily mobilised to bring about a change in this status quo. Perhaps we are more likely to see change come about from below, since it is the women in lower income groups who have a more direct interest in bringing about change, despite the obstacles that are placed in their way.

These relatively less well-off women are now generally aware as a result of development activities that dowry is illegal, and that they are legally entitled to many rights which they are in practice denied by their men and families. Our challenge is to find ways to mobilise these women and give them support to challenge the hard rock of patriarchy which is at the root of their suffering. There are a number of ways in which support can be given. Four ways that seem to be particularly important in the Bangladeshi context (see Rozario 2004) are:

- collaboration between institutions working for women's right to campaign on dowry, inheritance rights and domestic violence;
- development of a large-scale rural legal aid service following the model already developed by ASK (Ain-O-Shalish Kendra) and BRAC;
- working with religious authorities such as local imams, to encourage them to raise awareness about the situation of women; and
- use of media, education and role models to contest village stereotypes of women.

Given a continual and systematic approach along the above lines, there may be some cause for optimism, despite the intractable barriers which poor rural women still face. Perhaps the time is ripe at last for these women, with appropriate support, to start denting and making holes in the patriarchal shield. In time, perhaps, Bangladeshi society as a whole will see the uselessness and irrelevance of these defences of the patriarchal order, and be willing to abandon them and move on to a new and better social order.

Notes

[1] The term 'empowerment' is used commonly in the development context, especially in relation to women. However, as I have argued elsewhere (Rozario 1997), this is a problematic concept, particularly as it often implies a focus on the 'empowerment' of individuals rather than changes to the gender hierarchy and other features of the social structure as a whole.

[2] Dowry, referred to in Bangla as *joutuk* or *dabi,* is a demand commonly made by grooms' families to brides' families for payments in money and/or goods as a condition for accepting the latters' daughters as brides.

[3] Since 2000 I have also been involved in a number of consultancies with DFID (Department for International Development, UK) and with CARE Bangladesh. The two DFID consultancies were for four weeks in 2000 and five weeks in 2001. I spent one month with CARE in 2004 and seven weeks in 2005.

[4] In Bangla *pon* implies marriage-money, given either to the bridegroom or to the bride. Sometimes a differentiation is made between these two types: *kannyapon* for bride price and *barpon* for groom price. In my book (1992, 2001a) *pon* refers to *kannyapon* or bride price, which is how it was used by the village women themselves. This was apparently used for the wedding expenses in the bride's house. Thus, during the time of the *pon* system, the bride's family spent very little at weddings, reflecting the relatively higher status of women compared to the present situation. *Pon* should not be confused with the practice of *mohr* or dower, which is a compulsory requirement for a Muslim marriage contract. *Mohr* is given by the groom to the bride, part of it before the marriage is consummated and the other part in the event of a divorce. The actual amount of *mohr* varies depending on the couple's class position. However, in practice women often do not demand *mohr* to be paid before the consummation of marriage as the bride and her family expect her husband to treat her well. See Lindenbaum 1981; Rozario 1992, 2001a; Amin & Cain 1997; also Huda (2006) who argues for dowry having replaced dower for Muslim Bangladeshi women.

[5] The term 'middle and upper classes' (or just 'middle class') is used as shorthand for households whose material status is relatively secure, who are able to meet survival needs without difficulty, and who are in a position to invest in secondary and perhaps tertiary education for their sons and daughters, etc. The class structure of Bangladeshi society is complex and cannot be dealt with in detail here. There are significant differences between the rural class structure in the north-west and the southern and eastern regions such as Dhaka, Comilla etc. (Wood 1994). However, in both areas the wealthier families define themselves and justify their position in terms of honour, purity and the observance of *parda*. The same is true in the cities,

with the partial and limited exception of a small westernised and more internationally oriented component of the urban elite.

6 The following are 2002 estimates: at birth: 1.06 male(s)/female; under 15 years: 1.05 male(s)/female; 15–64 years: 1.05 male(s)/female; 65 years and over: 1.18 male(s)/female; total population: 1.05 male(s)/female. From www.discoverybangladesh.com/meetbangladesh/statistic.html (accessed 18 May 2008).

7 Hypergamy is marriage to a person of superior caste or class. In the South Asian context, it always refers to a woman marrying a man of higher caste or class.

8 5000 takas correspond to about £40 and is a considerable sum for a poor village family.

9 See Rozario (1992, 2001a) for a distinction between virginity and purity. Briefly, the term 'virginity' is obvious. However, 'purity' encompasses virginity as well as other feminine and modest behavioural aspects of women. Inappropriate behaviour on the part of a woman can lead to her being labelled as potentially impure and thereby perhaps not a virgin.

10 On one of my research visits in 2005 some boys in a Bangladeshi village commented: 'Women themselves caused their own devalorisation—they are now everywhere, on the streets, at the cinemas, everywhere'.

11 This does not mean that there have not been any changes at all within the value system. The re-definition of *parda* to justify their entry into the paid workforce by garment workers and women in rural areas is a good example of how there have been some shifts in this sphere (Siddiqui 1991; Kabeer 1994, 2001). Yet, there is a quality of resilience about the ideologies of purity and honour that is clearly perpetuating the overall subordinate status of women in Bangladesh, including the practice of dowry.

12 There has been extensive criticism of microcredit schemes in relation to poverty alleviation (Montgomery, Bhattacharya and Hulme 1996; Montgomery 1996; Sobhan 1997; Wood & Sharif 1997); of microcredit replacing other development activities in the area of health and education (Rogaly 1996); of microcredit institutions' overemphasis on their financial sustainability and 'scaling up' at the expense of the interests of the rural poor (Rogaly 1996; Rahman 1999a, 1999b; Ebdon 1995). A review of this literature is beyond the scope of this paper. However, for criticisms more directly concerned with women's situation, refer to Ebdon 1995; Rogaly 1996; Goetz & Gupta 1996; Kabeer 1994; Montgomery 1996; Rahman 1999a, 1999b.

13 I emphasise that I am speaking specifically of Grameen Bank-style microcredit, which is the dominant model in Bangladesh at present. There are other models, some of which I have explored in Rozario (2001b), which do not necessarily have such destructive effects on women's solidarity. See

also Naila Kabeer's discussion of the Swedish International Development Cooperation Agency (SIDA) microcredit scheme in Kabeer 1998.

[14] A typical example from my fieldwork is that of Jasmin, whose husband has left her. She has two daughters and one adult unmarried son who runs a shop selling tea and snacks. Since her son has a regular income, she has been able to join the Grameen Bank group and borrow. She is trying to arrange the marriage of her elder daughter. She expects to get a lump sum distribution from the Bank within a few weeks, of around Tk. 12,000 which will go towards the dowry. Her next loan from the Bank will be to make jewellery for her daughter's dowry (field notes, March 2000).

[15] For example, one of my informants, with four marriageable daughters and a member of the NGO, Nijera Kori, which does not have microcredit provision, was told by a fellow village woman, a BRAC member, that her only hope was to join BRAC and take credit from them so she could pay dowry for her daughters. This was in a Muslim village in northern Bangladesh. Both women understood that without dowry the young daughters were not going to be accepted by potential grooms' families. When quizzed why they continue to pay dowry after reciting at their weekly meetings that they will not demand or give any dowry, one woman said, 'Well, dowry is of course always there, there is no marriage without dowry. Some people give goods instead of money; some people give dowry even when there is no demand for it. Times are no good, parents are anxious about their daughters; they marry them off early.' Her remarks suggest that dowry inflation may in fact be a cause of early marriage.

[16] The question of the overall gender ideology of Bengali patriarchy, with its systematic devaluation of women and its denial of their right to an independent existence without male guardianship is well known. It is worth noting that while similar ideas are found in other Islamic countries, this is not a specifically Islamic ideology. Within Bangladesh, these attitudes are shared by the majority population of Muslim Bengalis (around 88 per cent of the population), by Hindu Bengalis (about nine per cent), as well as by the much smaller populations of Christian and Buddhist Bengalis.

References

Ahmed, R. & M.S. Naher. 1986. 'Changing Marriage Transactions and the Rise of the Demand System in Bangladesh'. *The Journal of Social Studies*. 33. pp. 71–107.
——. 1987. *Brides and the Demand System in Bangladesh*. Dhaka University: Centre for Social Studies.
Amin, Sajeda and Mead Cain. 1997. 'The Rise of Dowry in Bangladesh' in *The Continuing Demographic Transition*. eds. G. Jones, R.M. Douglas, J.C. Caldwell and R.M. D'Souza. Oxford: Clarendon Press. pp. 290–306.

Boserup, E. 1970. *Women's Role in Economic Development*. London: George Allen & Unwin.

Caldwell, J.C., P. Reddy, and P. Caldwell. 1983. 'The Causes of Marriage Change in South India'. *Population Studies* 37. pp. 343–61.

Dennecker, P. 2002. *Between Conformity and Resistance: Women Garment Workers in Bangladesh*. Dhaka: Dhaka University Press Ltd.

Ebdon, R. 1995. 'NGO Expansion and the Fight to Reach the Poor: Gender Implications of NGO Scaling-up in Bangladesh. *IDS Bulletin* 26(3). pp. 49–55.

Epstein, T.S. 1973. *South India: Yesterday, Today and Tomorrow: Mysore Villages Revisited*. London: Macmillan.

Fruzzetti, L.M. 1982. *The Gift of a Virgin: Women, Marriage and Ritual in a Bengali Society*. New Jersey: Rutgers University Press.

Goetz, A.M. & R.S. Gupta. 1996. 'Who Takes the Credit? Gender, Power and Control Over Loan Use in Rural Credit Programmes in Bangladesh'. *World Development* 24(1). pp. 45–63.

Huda, Shahnaz. 2006. 'Dowry in Bangladesh: Compromising Women's Rights'. *South Asia Research*. vol. 26. no. 3. pp. 249–68.

Hussain, A.M.M. ed. 1998 *Poverty Alleviation and Empowerment: The Second Assessment Study of BRAC's Rural Development Programme*. Dhaka: BRAC Centre.

Jackson, Cecile. 1998. 'Rescuing Gender from the Poverty Trap' in *Feminist Visions of Development: Gender Analysis and Policy*. eds. Cecile Jackson & Ruth Pearson. London: Routledge.

Kabeer, Naila. 1985. 'Do Women Gain from High Fertility?' in *Women, Work, and Ideology in the Third World*. ed. Haleh Afshar. London: Tavistock Publications Ltd. pp. 83–106.

———. 1988. 'Subordination and Struggle: Women in Bangladesh'. *New Left Review* 168. pp. 95–121.

———. 1994. *Reversed Realities: Gender Hierarchies in Development Thought*. New Delhi: Kali for Women.

———. 1998. '"Money Can't Buy Me Love"? Re-evaluation of Gender, Credit and Empowerment in Rural Bangladesh'. IDS Discussion Paper. 363.

———. 2001. *The Power to Choose: Bangladeshi Women and Labour Market Decisions in London and Dhaka*. London and New York: Verso.

Kandiyoti, D. 1988. 'Bargaining with Patriarchy'. *Gender and Society*. vol. 2. no. 3. pp. 274–90.

Lindenbaum, Shirley. 1981. 'Implications for Women of Changing Marriage Transactions in Bangladesh'. *Studies in Family Planning* 12(11). pp. 394–401.

Montgomery, R. 1996. 'Disciplining or Protecting the Poor? Avoiding the Social Costs of Peer Pressure in Microcredit Schemes'. *Journal of International Development* 8(2). pp. 189–305.

Montgomery, R., D. Bhattacharya & D. Hulme. 1996. 'Credit for the Poor in Bangladesh: The BRAC Rural Development Programme and the Government Thana Resource Development and Employment Programme' in *Finance Against Poverty.* vol. 2. eds. David Hulme and Paul Mosley. London and New York: Routledge. pp. 94–176.

Naved, R.T. & L.A. Persson. 2007. 'Dowry and Spousal Physical Violence against Women in Bangladesh: Is Payment and/or Patriarchy the Main Issue?' ICDDR,B, Dhaka and Department of Women's and Children's Health. IMCH. Uppsalla University, Sweden. http://www.icddrb.org/pub/publication.jsp?classificationID=1&pubID=7960

Paul-Majumdar, P. & B. Sen. eds. 2000. *Growth of Garment Industry in Bangladesh: Economic and Social Dimensions.* Dhaka: Bangladesh Institute of Development Studies.

Rahman, A. 1999a. 'Microcredit Initiatives for Equitable and Sustainable Development: Who Pays?' *World Development* 27(1). pp. 67–82.

——. 1999b. *Women and Microcredit in Rural Bangladesh: An Anthropological Study of Grameen Bank Lending.* Oxford: Westview Press.

Ram, K. 1991. 'Capitalism and Marriage Payments' in *Mukkuvar Women: Gender, Hegemony and Capitalist Accumulation.* Sydney: Allen & Unwin.

Randeria, S. and L. Visaria. 1984. 'Sociology of Bride-Price and Dowry'. *Economic and Political Weekly.* XIX. 15. pp. 648–52.

Rogaly, Ben. 1996.'Micro-finance Evangelism, "Destitute Women", and the Hard Selling of a New Anti-Poverty Formula'. *Development in Practice* 6(2). pp. 100–12.

Rozario, Santi. 1992. *Purity and Communal Boundaries: Women and Social Change in a Bangladeshi Village.* Sydney: Allen and Unwin; London: Zed Books.

——. 1997. 'Development and Rural Women in South Asia: the Limits of Empowerment and Conscientization.' *Bulletin of Concerned Asian Scholars.* vol. 29. no. 4. pp. 45–53.

——. 2001a. *Purity and Communal Boundaries: Women and Social Change in a Bangladeshi Village.* Dhaka: University Press Limited. 2nd ed. with new introduction.

——. 2001b. 'Women and Poverty: Is Grameen Bank the Answer?' *Journal Interdisciplinary Gender Studies.* vol. 6. no. 2. pp. 60–82.

——. 2002a.'Grameen Bank-Style Microcredit: Impact on Dowry and Women's Solidarity.' *Development Bulletin.* 57. Feb. pp. 67–70.

——. 2002b. 'Poor and "Dark", What is My Future?': Identity Construction and Adolescent Women in Bangladesh' in *Coming of Age in South and Southeast Asia: Youth, Courtship and Sexuality.* eds. Lenore Manderson and Pranee Liamputtong Rice. Richmond, UK: Curzon Press. pp. 42–57.

——. 2002c. 'Gender Dimensions of Rural Change' in *Hands Not Land: How Livelihoods are Changing in Rural Bangladesh.* eds. Kazi Ali Toufique and Cate

Turton. Dhaka: Bangladesh Institute of Development Studies. pp. 121–130.

——. 2004. *Building Solidarity Against Patriarchy in Bangladesh.* CARE Bangladesh.

——. 2005. *Solidarity Against Patriarchy: The Village Perspective.* CARE Bangladesh.

——. 2007. 'The dark side of microcredit.' http://www.opendemocracy.net/article/5050/16_days/dowry_microcredit

Siddiqi, D.M. 1991. 'Discipline and Protect: Women Factory Workers in Bangladesh'. *Grass Roots.* vol. 12. pp. 42–50.

Sobhan, R. 1997. 'The Political Economy of Micro Credit' in *Who Needs Credit? Poverty and Finance in Bangladesh.* eds. G.D. Wood & I.A. Sharif. Dhaka: Dhaka University Press Ltd. pp. 131–41.

Srinivas, M.N. 1984. *Some Reflections on Dowry.* New Delhi: Oxford University Press.

Suran, L., S. Amin, L. Huq & K. Chowdury. 2004. 'Does Dowry Improve Life for Brides? A Theory of Dowry in Rural Bangladesh'. *Population Council.* no. 195.

Tambiah, S.J. and J. Goody. 1973. *Bridewealth and Dowry.* Cambridge: Cambridge University Press.

Tambiah, S.J. 1989. 'Bridewealth and Dowry Revisited: The Position of Women in SubSaharan Africa and North India'. *Current Anthropology.* 30.4. pp. 413–45.

White, S. 1992. *Arguing with the Crocodile: Gender and Class in Bangladesh.* Dhaka: Dhaka University Press Ltd.

Wood, G. 1994. *Bangladesh, Whose Ideas, Whose Interests?* Dhaka: Dhaka University Press Ltd.

Wood, G.D. & I.A. Sharif. eds. 1997. *Who Needs Credit? Poverty and Finance in Bangladesh.* Dhaka: Dhaka University Press Ltd.

Heroes or Hondas?

Analysing men's dowry narratives in a time of rapid social change

KATE JEHAN

Is it a choice between heroism or haggling for Hondas? There must be another way.

—Surya, auto-driver, 23

Introduction

In India, the practice of dowry has long been of central concern for those committed to gender justice. Legislation enacted in 1961 was followed by decades of activism in view of the continued intractability of the issue. More recently, alongside the protests, there have been keen efforts to theorise dowry in a push to understand how and why the practice persists. These efforts have been accompanied by the pressing sense of, 'But what can we *do* about it?' A dowry boycott was advocated (Kishwar 1980); then repealed to the dismay of many (Palriwala 2006 [1989]). Feminists and others committed to tackling the issue have been unable to reach consensus on how to approach 'the dowry problem'. This paper aims to contribute to the key concern of this volume: how might theory be linked to practice? How might a positive impact be made on an area replete with so many 'gender pathologies'? Dowry continues to represent the social and economic dependence of women, their increased vulnerability to gender-based violence, a debt-trap for low and middle income families, and a possible (though by no means isolated) catalyst for son-preference practices.

Dowry is often conceived of as solely a 'women's problem' within the popular discourse and, without doubt, women bear a disproportionate share of the suffering engendered by dowry. Yet to exclude men from the debate entirely seems erroneous. Firstly, men are dowry givers as well as takers. Secondly, achieving justice for both genders requires a critical engagement with both women's and men's roles. A pragmatic approach to dowry that incorporates men's experiences is recommended. The data on which this paper draws is part of a larger study of women and men, but as men are typically given less space in the dowry literature, the focus here is on men's perspectives.

The case for including men

Since the 1990s, a number of arguments have called for the inclusion of men within the gender and development discourse. Unease that such a move might dilute feminist concerns has been offset by an acknowledgement that uncritically 'stereotyping men as the oppressors and women as the oppressed' (Cleaver 2002: 7) is unhelpful in understanding social problems. Vera-Sanso argues that an inclusion of men does not mean 'moving from a pro-female bias to a pro-male bias' (2001: 182). Rather, an exploration of both women and men's subjectivities 'provides data on how and why people uphold, resist and contest dominant values or unequal social relations' (2001: 180). A pragmatic lens that sees competing narratives as useful insights into how others perceive themselves, their roles and the world as they see it is necessary.

> If we take our role as researchers not so much as collectors of facts ... but witnesses to *discursive stratagems* [that] shape definitions of persons, needs, rights and responsibilities, we can sidestep the dilemma of whose account, men's or women's, we are to believe.
>
> (Vera-Sanso 2001: 195; emphasis mine)

According to Pineda (2001) this would change the emphasis from women's 'victim-hood' and 'subordinate place in gender relations and power' to one that:

finds potentials, social support conditions and individual characteristics that enable many men to *challenge* hegemonic forms of masculinities.

(Pineda 2001: 73; emphasis mine)

This approach is critical and signposts the way in which a holistic gender approach may be put to practical use. By identifying conditions under which new masculinities might emerge, we may 'derive lessons for possible future action' (ibid.). A detailed analysis of the men's narratives is not possible here, but a range of themes will be discussed as exemplar and conclude with the modest lessons that may be learned to enable a constructive progression from theory into practice. The ultimate goal is to encourage the formulation of an appropriate dowry response with holistic gendered policy.

Research aims and background to the study

The core aim of this study is to analyse men's subjectivities in relation to dowry—their beliefs about dowry and their experiences of it throughout their lives. Particular attention is paid to men's stated beliefs in comparison with their stated practice as there is frequent dissonance between the two. Sunder Rajan notes that dowry remains 'embedded in a complex and complicated matrix of cause and effects' (2003: 204). This study is sceptical of reductionist approaches that aim to pinpoint causative relations for a phenomenon that is simultaneously socio-political, socio-cultural and socio-economic. Instead it employs a grounded approach by which recurring themes as stated by the men themselves become the focus for attention. This enables an analysis of factors that either influence attitudes or practice, or what men *claim* to be influential, and both are of interest. The key is an understanding of the manner in which a dominant culture perpetuates itself. This may help us map the factors that facilitate change.

Sixty-nine semi-structured interviews were conducted in 2007 in the southern Indian state of Tamil Nadu.[1] The study took a broad-brush approach to enable as inclusive a sample as possible in a highly stratified society. Within Tamil Nadu and in South India more widely, the threat of a perceived move away from relatively egalitarian gender relations has been a cause of concern for some decades (see Srinivas 2006 [1984]).[2] The comparatively gender equitable relations here have been challenged by a declining sex ratio and a rise in dowry in recent years (Basu 1999). Though dowry across India has undergone a succession of transformations over centuries, it is agreed the most significant of these have occurred mainly within the last 10, 15 or 20 years (AIDWA 2003). Though there is much community differentiation, the overall trend has been a move away from voluntary gift-giving at marriage towards that which more closely resembles a commercial exchange. This is discussed in some detail in this volume by Dalmia and Lawrence. Marriage is increasingly contingent on the value of the dowry given, leading to an inflation of dowries, and the exchange is primarily transacted between men (Geetha 2007).

The recent growth of dowry in South India therefore demands an exploration of men's dowry behaviours and beliefs in tandem with the changing context in which they occur. What are men's own perspectives and how do these intersect with religion, caste or class? Pearson notes that, in general, the implications of globalisation for men have gone under-researched (2001: 219). The supposition of a positive correlation between modernising (and now globalising) forces and the growth in dowry is not new, yet grounded empirical studies are few.[3] Srinivasan (2005) argues that establishing a linear relationship between economic reforms and rising dowry practice is not practicable (due to conflicting data on the impact of reforms and unreliable data on an illegal practice). Nevertheless, the impact of structural adjustments on dowry can be understood as 'less direct and more indirect through their impact on the material bases of people's lives' (Srinivasan 2005: 605).[4] It is these relationships that the following explores.

Socio-economic context to changes to dowry in Tamil Nadu

Whilst no word for 'globalisation' exists in Tamil, the notion of *nagareegam* (modernisation) and increased interconnectivity with the outside world was readily recognised by both rural and urban men in this study. India moved to liberalise in 1991, initiating a broad-ranging process of social change. Tamil Nadu's commitment to liberalisation in the early 1990s has had far-reaching effects in subsequent years and it now stands among the most highly industrialised in India.[5] State policy may hope to render it a 'global centre for business process outsourcing (BPO)' and to 'bridge the digital divide' (Government of Tamil Nadu 2003: 7), but what has been the outcome for other sectors? The government concedes that agricultural output has been 'in rapid decline' (2003: 5), in spite of nearly half the state continuing to rely on it as its primary source of income (2003: 19).[6] With structural changes, the government acknowledges that industrial and service sectors will have to play a greater role but, in an ironic twist, confesses that greater automation and use of IT means that opportunities for semi-skilled and unskilled workers in this sector will 'decline over the next decade' (2003: 132).

Under such conditions, 'un- or under-employment is high', with the Work Participation Rate (WPR) in 'severe decline' across all sectors in recent years (2003: 19). The number of marginal workers has almost tripled in a decade (2008).[7] It is unsurprising to learn that poverty in rural areas is 'widespread', that 16.5 per cent of the urban population lives in slums, and almost a third of the population (both rural and urban) remains under the poverty line (2003: 5). It is under these circumstances that the following narratives must be understood.

Men's observations on changes to dowry practice

The men interviewed in the sample reported significant transformation of *varadakshanai* or *seeru* (dowry)[8] over recent years. For Hindu men of Backward Caste (BC), Most Backward Caste

63

(MBC) and Scheduled Caste (SC) communities, and for men from Muslim and Christian groups, there is a clear transition in which the youngest group of respondents recognise a prevalence of dowry as the norm, whereas this was not necessarily the case for the middle age group, and certainly not the case for the older age group when either of those groups were of marriageable age.[9] Indeed, the majority of older and middle aged men in both urban and rural settings described a clear transition from practices prevalent in their youth. These changes relate chiefly to the spread, inflation and mutation of dowry into a mandatory practice. The shift was perceptible amongst all classes though clearly the value of dowries rose with class. Such shifts have been amply discussed elsewhere (see Rozario; and Dalmia and Lawrence in this volume). It is important to note, however, that historically, the practice of dowry has been much less prevalent in South India than in the North. Whilst both North and South favour caste endogamy (same caste marriage), the traditional South Indian preference for consanguineous ('same blood') marriage occurs within the family. It also often occurs (though not necessarily) within the same village (village endogamy) (Reddy 1993). This is in stark contrast to the North Indian preference for hypergamous marriage and village exogamy (in which a woman's husband is selected from a higher status group and from a different geographic locale). In South India, this close-knit pool of marriage partners may be supposed to have precluded the need to attract a higher status, outsider groom with a dowry (Basu 1999).[10] In Tamil Nadu, however, so-called 'cousin', 'uncle-niece' and other close-kin marriages have always been less popular among Tamil Brahmins than they have among other castes,[11] and the Brahmin men in this study report that dowry has been practised for several generations in their communities.

Outside of these so-called 'forward' castes for whom dowry has a longer history, dowry in its present form in Tamil Nadu follows an overall South Indian pattern, in which a substantial change from earlier precedents for the vast majority of communities is reported. The data show that modern dowry 'cuts across

geographical barriers, caste divisions and rural-urban differences'
(Karanth 1997: 102). However, a popular misconception is that
this means there has been a dramatic reversal in custom 'from
bride price to dowry' for lower status communities.[12] Kodoth
(2006) notes that this ignores the heterogeneity of older forms of
gift exchange and that a more accurate conception is of a *two-way*
exchange of goods, where the emphasis placed on the bride's family
as gift-giver grew over time. (See also Dalmia and Lawrence in this
volume). Certainly, among the older respondents it was widely
confirmed that lower status men paid a *parisam* (fixed sum at the
time of marriage), but there were varied accounts of exactly which
goods were given by which house and to whom. Nevertheless, in
contradistinction to the so-called 'forward' (OC) castes in whose
communities dowry has been longer established, the fact that
dowry in its present form is considered a new phenomenon was
emphasised by all older and middle-aged respondents of the
Backward, Most Backward, and Scheduled Caste communities.
Some men of the Scheduled Tribe (ST) communities maintained
that bride price practice was maintained, whilst others reported a
similar move toward dowry-like conventions.

Patriarchy, masculinities and modernisation: unpacking male dowry behaviours and beliefs

These critical changes to dowry were reported by Tamil men
themselves. We now turn to an analysis of men's own beliefs about
dowry and their attitudes to it in relation to the changing contexts
in which they occur within the current socio-economic
environment. It enables a contrastive inquiry into men's dowry
beliefs as compared with their stated practice. From this, an
understanding of how dowry culture may be perpetuated, co-
opted, or resisted by men might be reached which may enable an
exploration of how dominant models supporting dowry may be
challenged.

Kandiyoti (1988) argues that the widespread presence of
dowry in a society is characteristic of what is called 'classic

patriarchy'. An approval of dowry promotes (or allows) adherence to a patriarchal world view and assumes that a growing hold of dowry culture is a countervailing trend to women's empowerment. By contrast, efforts to tackle the problem will enable a progression toward gender equity.[13] The interviews carried out with Tamil men in both urban and rural areas revealed many narratives, yet not all of the voices rang in unison, or were uniformly 'patriarchal'. On the contrary, a number of competing voices emerged that could be conceived of as occupying a number of different positions on a continuum.

The following framework has been constructed in order to make those voices more clearly understood. It draws on Elson and Pearson's conception of a possible 'intensification', 'recomposition' or 'decomposition' of women's subordination under conditions of industrialisation and a changing global order (1980: 27). Their tripartite analysis is harnessed here as it reflects most accurately the processes unfolding in the narratives. It is clear that the majority of men interviewed are experiencing an *intensification* of dowry practice that had not in fact been customary in previous generations. This intensification in *practice* or *behaviour* is not, however, necessarily matched by an intensification of *support* but on the contrary, might be met by a range of perspectives: from willingness to indifference, reluctance to resistance. It is evident that dowry is rising, but it is men's personal beliefs and attitudes with which we are now concerned here. A man's dowry practice might be intensified due to social pressures and expectations, but his personal level of support might be situated anywhere along the continuum: an *intensification*, a *recomposition*, or a *decomposition* of support for dowry.

Intensification of support for dowry

Men who claimed to have intensified their support for dowry, or who attributed a growing support for it to other men, grounded it within the current socio-economic context. Overwhelmingly, they pointed the finger at one key 'cause'—*nagareegam* (modernisation) which was considered a catch-all reason to explain it. *Nagareegam* was couched in terms of inevitability in the current context and a fate that could not be avoided. One phrase that was frequently repeated was *kalam mari poradu* (times have changed). It is interesting that although many men framed their rise in support for dowry to this, there were conflicting opinions on the precise relationship between *nagareegam* and dowry. Some men argued that modernisation could be held responsible for this because there was 'lots of money' (*romba panam*) around, due to rising incomes. But an almost equal number of men (and sometimes, strangely, the same men) argued that modernisation meant that people had *less* money (*panam kami*) due to higher living costs and/or greater workplace insecurity. This too, it was claimed, was likely to see an intensified support for dowry.

There seemed to be a paradox. There also seemed to be no clear class differentiation between the kinds of men likely to adhere to one view or the other. According to many men from lower status communities, for example, education and jobs were seen to positively correlate with dowry. The men of these groups singled out those who had benefited from reservation and secured higher degrees, government jobs or migrated abroad as those most likely to ask for a large dowry. As one man said: 'Once the boy is abroad, the family of the boy don't even need to open their mouths. The money and gifts will come pouring in.' Other working class men disagreed, however. Although they concurred that men of higher status could expect large dowries, they also said that jobless or 'layabout types' amongst them would also take dowry. It was pointed out frequently that, 'Nowadays, even agricultural labourers can expect a good bike and 10 sovereigns of gold.'

Similarly, disagreement existed amongst men from higher status communities. Some of them identified dowry as most rife amongst lower status communities. But others of the same social standing were keen to point the finger at their own class or caste members as the worst offenders (the Nattakottai Chettiars and Nadars were frequently implicated, for example). Among such groups government jobs no longer held much allure, and men with jobs in the private sector, with multinational companies and preferably as software engineers or MBA graduates within these, were seen as most likely to intensify their support for dowry. Such discordant responses were initially confusing. Modernising or globalising processes were being universally 'blamed' for dowry, but if this were so, how could two such opposing narratives be proposed: the one that sees *successful* men more likely to take a dowry; the other that sees *unsuccessful* men more likely to take a dowry?

It became clear that the two narratives are not mutually exclusive, as may first appear. Indeed, many men found themselves supporting one notion, then switching to the other. Both discourses exist side by side due to the *uneven nature of globalising processes.* Economic restructuring renders a rise in some men's incomes, in others a fall. The man who finds himself one of globalisation's 'winners' commands a fat dowry; the man who finds himself one of globalisation's 'losers' asks for one anyway.[14] Whilst one scenario spurs on status displays and consumer culture, the other inspires feelings of inadequacy and failure. In dowry, such men have found the solution to both needs. As noted by V. Geetha, men have an uncanny ability to 'interpret historical changes and developments on their own terms, and to their advantage' (2006: 22).

Whilst globalisation was offered as one explanation, the notion of the 'provider' was also deemed important, though experiences of this were again far from uniform. Amongst many of the working class 'intensifiers', the notion that the men had been increasingly unable to fulfil their role as a provider was a recurring one. Livelihoods were reported obsolete or in decline due to automation, inappropriate farming technology, competition from foreign exports—a wide number of causes. In all such cases, the argument maintained was: 'Suppose people are not able to support themselves. They can use the dowry to come up in life.' Tamil masculinity depends on the ability to provide, for that is what constitutes a *nalla mappillei* (a good groom). But for others, dowry was by contrast a means of *avenging* the loss of men's provider roles. One fisherman said: 'Only somebody who's jobless will ask for dowry, then he'll pawn it and spend it on drink. Somebody who works hard wouldn't ask.'

At the same time, men who have no trouble fulfilling their provider roles (the software engineers, the MBA graduates) see themselves rewarded for doing so (the higher the status, the higher the dowry). What seems strange is that educated brides with good jobs are also expected to give dowry. This renders the rationale that many men use for dowry appear illogical (e.g. that dowry is compensation for the men's education; that the bride should not come empty-handed to her new home). Far from empty-handed, many such women bring large salaries. Whereas men are rewarded for their achievements, however, women meet with no such privileges. When I asked: 'Why does dowry persist in marriages where the wife is also educated and earning?', most men looked troubled that they were unable to answer the question. Two factors are at play, however. Firstly, gender relations worldwide tend to see women's labour as devalued, and India is no exception. Secondly, it is widely known that even in the more equitable marriage market of South India, it is not considered 'appropriate' for a woman to marry a man with fewer qualifications than herself or in a lower position than herself. Regardless of the woman's own income or standing, the man remains in the position of the 'dominant' provider. In so doing, his family may feel justified in asking for dowry. Should a woman marry a man with *fewer* qualifications or earnings than herself, this asymmetry does not seem to result in any tangible difference. (Certainly in one urban slum, interviews with women as part of the larger study described their husbands' earnings as 'insignificant' compared to their own, yet they were still expected to give dowry). Even where a man fails in this role, the durability of the myth of 'man as provider' continues to the extent that the sense of entitlement to be *regarded* as such (and to demand a dowry to boost this role, if it has not been fulfilled) remains.

Finally, when asked whether a proper implementation of equal inheritance rights might encourage the men to give up dowry, they answered negatively. Men were unlikely to give up their 'privilege' of dowry, regardless of whether women were given separate inheritances. The widespread feeling is that present-day dowry can no longer be considered a pre-mortem inheritance, as men do not view it as such. Instead, dowry is viewed as capital for the husband, or his family, which may or may not bring direct benefit to the wife. Dowry was hardly viewed as a woman's inheritance but as capital on which the whole family (or husband) would draw. When dowry is spoken of as a woman's 'protection', it is largely meant as her protection from emotional, mental or physical onslaught—rarely economic.

Recomposition of support for dowry

A number of issues raised by the men signalled a deviation of beliefs from the straightforward notions of the 'intensifiers'. Indeed, a large number of men seemed engaged in an internal dialogue or struggle, in which competing mini-narratives took place that modified, questioned and contested hegemonic beliefs. One prevalent notion was that the concept of dowry was permissible as long as no demand took place. As one young man from a slum area said: 'When it comes to money at the wedding, if the bride's family wants to give something, then that's the best thing. You shouldn't desire too much.' Others with a similar perspective considered that to demand was somehow a 'poor show,' but they did not contest the basic premise that a woman should pay to be married, whereas a man need not. Some men stated that excessive displays of dowry made them feel uncomfortable. An owner of a mobile phone shop said: 'If someone has made a big display and everything is very *jigganah* (flashy), then normally I criticise those people, because they're making an advertisement of it. It's vulgar in my opinion.'

If disapproval of 'flashy' behaviour may be considered an early stage of recomposition, other men's beliefs moved further along the continuum. Some said that dowry might be undesirable in itself, regardless of whether the dowry is 'moderate' or not. A Muslim man said: 'It would be nice if the practice didn't exist, but it does, and it happens in all communities.' It seems that men might be *in the process of* recomposing their attitudes to dowry, but its all-pervasiveness proves a stumbling block against the possibility of forming alternative positions. The men asked: 'When everybody is doing it, how is it possible to avoid it?' A sense of dowry's ubiquity was equalled by protests of there being 'no option.' Stories of parental pressure were a common theme. Blaming parental control represents an abdication of responsibility and, one suspects an element of disingenuousness among those who claim a filial 'helplessness'. Yet, many of them protested that the pressure they felt was real and not some imaginary construction behind which a full-blown support for dowry was hiding. It was widely discussed that in India, parental pressure is a force to be reckoned with. Nor was it confined only to the young, as one 73-year old man said: 'I think it is the parents who push for this, not the children.'

In a culture that strongly emphasises filial duty, it is not surprising that young men might be reluctant to counter their parents' wishes. Thus, although their personal support for dowry was in *recomposition*, they could not guarantee that their dowry *practice* would follow, and that it would not, in fact, *intensify* in line with their parents' wishes. As one young dalit student said hesitantly:

> Although I like to think that I wouldn't ask, I know there are lots of things that could change. I think my parents will definitely say something ... Circumstances are such that, if you've found a girl, there's lots of pressure from the outside, and you have to accept it.

However, it was not only parental pressure under which the young men labour but also the notion that a range of people may be disappointed in them should they fail to claim what was 'rightfully' theirs. Dowry is associated with manliness, as significant as those other markers of hegemonic masculinity which we have come to know, such as being a provider, a migrant, or being able to manage money (Osella and Osella 2000). Dowry, viewed as a financial asset in itself, is intricately woven into an intangible fabric of 'manliness' involving money—the ability to earn it, command it or manage it. A man dressed without such a fabric is disrobed, 'naked', a weakling, not a real man. A notion repeatedly used by

the men is 'suspicion': 'They will suspect me if I don't take it,' or
'A man who doesn't take will be suspected.' One young student
said: 'There's always the possibility that if the boy doesn't take
the dowry or ask for it, then people will think there's something
wrong with him. Neither the boy's family nor the girl's family
wants that.'

That the bride's family may be complicit in perpetuating
dowry was a topic liberally discussed by the men. Although men
might *wish* to re-evaluate hegemonic attitudes to dowry, it was
very difficult to do so when: 'These days too, even if the boy isn't
asking, the parents give it anyway.' As with the issue of parental
control, this theme also requires a cautious approach. Yet it is
widely known that many families do willingly give dowry, and
that many young women themselves support it. As Osella and
Osella (2000) found, the giving of generous dowries among
returning Gulf migrants is a substantial marker of masculinity
which in turn bolsters the status of the family and the bride.
From this perspective, confused by status-seeking moves from the
bride's family, the groom feels efforts to recompose his attitudes
are futile. Status-seeking is but one of a multiplicity of factors
prompting families to give dowry. Dowries given 'in love and
affection' was a much used phrase. Just as *taking* a dowry boosts
the groom's potential role of provider, *giving* a dowry becomes
another commodity which the bride's father, uncle or brother needs
to 'provide' in order to fulfil his role.

In an attempt at progress, many recomposing fathers claimed
that although they would provide a dowry for their daughter,
they would refrain from asking one for their sons. This was met
with derision by a working class man from a rural area who said:

> If someone has three daughters and then a son, he will ask for the son's
> dowry. It's like he has stood in the queue and paid—so why would he
> give his son away for free? Generally if they give, they will expect. In fact,
> they will want double the money.

The situation that presents itself is cyclical and cycles, as is widely
known, are difficult to break. A man may be against the idea of

dowry in principle, but society compels women to be married, and he is unable to see his daughter married without one. Such recomposers feel that dowry is somehow 'wrong' and yet are unable to envisage a solution. By way of reconciling the seemingly intractable, many respond by dissociating themselves from the problem. The construction of dowry as a women's problem (aided by the government, media, and NGOs) enables the men to perceive that, as a 'woman's concern', they might recompose their attitudes to dowry in sympathy but not in empathy. As a 'woman's concern', it is not something they feel qualified to advise upon or to act to change.

Certainly, many recomposers attributed a dislike of dowry as being wasteful and unfair on the poor. Yet disapproval of dowry as a financial liability is not the same as disapproval of it in the name of gender justice. A distinction must be drawn, and there was often much ambiguity here. Indeed, recomposers inhabited a highly uneven terrain. Many men seemed to teeter on a see-saw of beliefs, lurching toward an anti-dowry stance, on the one hand, only to revert back to more hegemonic beliefs, on the other. One young rural electrician seemed in a good deal of confusion. He said, 'It's not correct. It's not faulty also.' Such men seemed most troubled by a lingering sense that, in the final analysis, men occupy a privileged position. 'This may not be fair, but that's the way things are and women's lot is unfortunate.' A dalit youth voiced this internal debate:

> I've come to the city and now I'm aware that there are other ways of doing things. I'm aware that there can be a marriage without dowry. I know it's possible. But I also think that the parents of the girl should feel that they haven't done anything wrong and they shouldn't feel guilty later. I think that the girl has a responsibility to look after the family as well ... she'd want to come to a nice home and to feel happy and secure and she'll also want people to look up to her.

His tone sounds empathetic to women, yet, in spite of being 'aware' of alternatives, his reasoning for dowry stems from old forms of patriarchy, a dressing-up of the notion that a bride must pay to ensure better treatment and her worth equates to her wealth.

Men with wavering beliefs may ultimately choose to defend dowry, as this student did. An over-riding characteristic of most recomposers, however, was an attitude of heavy resignation, rather than total acceptance. Yet it is this resignation that perpetuates dowry. By failing to defy the practice, dowry becomes the norm and resistance more difficult for the generation to follow. In a common scenario, one Roman Catholic man suffered hardship selling his house to fund three dowries. At the age of 70, he continues to work and live in penury. Yet rather than express an ideological resistance to dowry, he stops short of condemning it outright, preferring to see that it could have been worse:

> There are plenty of people who have also had this happen to them—at least God had blessed me with work and also with a house in the first place. Had I not had a house to sell then I would have been in trouble.

In keeping with Christian theology, it is also possible that he viewed his struggles as a test of his faith. Yet religious beliefs did not factor heavily among the majority of Christian or Hindu men when they talked about dowry.[15] Religion came into real significance in conversations with Muslim men only. It was stated by many that dowry is un-Islamic and a contravention of that which is stated in the Quran, though it was argued there is room for interpretation. Another Muslim man stated simply: 'The Quran says that you shouldn't take dowry. But people still do it because they like having money.'

A young member of the Church of South India summarised the position of recomposers of all faiths when I asked him: 'What do you think your sister thinks about her forthcoming dowry?' He was fairly disdainful of dowry himself, his beliefs in an advanced stage of recomposition. But his personal beliefs lay in opposition to his behaviour. He was *intensifying* the dowry practice of his community, unable and unwilling to resist the system, and preparing to assemble his sister's dowry:

> What is there to think about? I'm the one who has to do the thinking. If my sister likes the boy and the dowry is too high, I will just have to give it. What is asked for must be given.

74

The recomposers may be characterised by an ideological struggle between misgivings over dowry and a practical unwillingness or inability to resist it. The young Christian's, 'What is asked for must be given', is the typical response of the reluctant dowry giver. The reluctant dowry taker, conversely, may be typified by the following student's response:

> I wouldn't ask for anything that they couldn't give. I wouldn't really want to ask anyone. But I say that now. There might be a time in the future when I'm in difficulty. I might need the money. When it comes to the crunch, it might be difficult not to ask.

Decomposition of support for dowry

If ambivalence or ambiguity characterises the recomposers, there is little equivocation in the men's stated beliefs here. Though this group was smaller in number, firm beliefs were stated that no dowry should take place at the wedding or afterwards at functions or ceremonies. It was claimed that no dowry was given for daughters and no dowry taken for sons. As one man explained of his son's marriage: 'I took care of all the expenses, and as far as taking any gifts, forget it. I have always had this conviction.' But from where does the decomposer find his 'conviction'? Kodoth (2006) elucidates two typical anti-dowry perspectives: the liberal sees it as a 'social evil'; the feminist sees it as an affirmation of patriarchy. It may be supposed that most media over the years have gathered support for the former. A perhaps surprising number of men, however, espoused the views of the latter. Such men were not limited to cosmopolitan settings, but came from different social strata. A poor village watchman said:

> When people are educating their daughters and giving utensils and jewellery and all of that, I don't understand why it is not in the groom's mind to give something back too. But when the parents offer such big things, I think the grooms are still not treating the daughters well. So personally, I don't support this dowry system. How can I?

A young student said: 'I think dowries are a waste. You don't need to have one. If a girl is happy to come and marry me, that's enough.'

The men of this group were united in their disdain. Yet there was debate regarding why other men might support dowry. Like the intensifiers, globalising processes were seen to feed notions of money-love. But whereas the intensifiers claimed that modernisation was causative of dowry (and men themselves could not be blamed), the decomposers asserted that each man must take responsibility himself. *Gouravam* (prestige) was the key. One dalit student said: 'Earlier people were satisfied with what they had, that you had food, that your family was well, and that everyone was getting along. Now, the more you get, the more you want.' Another said: 'It's become an ego clash between the bride and the groom. Who asks for more, who gives more.' The growth in hypergamy was seen as critical, as well as the notion that the man must assume the position of dominant provider. Another student said: 'Nobody thinks, "Let me get my daughter married to a nice person and let them both go forward in life together happily". They only seem to think, "Let me get my daughter married to someone better off than me".'

Adherence to caste, as rigid as ever in rural areas, was identified as the key in perpetuating dowry in both rural and urban settings. In the city, a wealthy Brahmin man dismissed claims by 'sophisticated' people that it was lessening in importance. He argued that an underlying 'preference' remained, thus narrowing the pool of potential partners, creating an environment favourable for dowry. Similarly, the recomposers' protests that 'the family always give' was met with some scorn. One urban dalit youth said: 'The bride's family may well decide just to give. But the guy never says no. He never says, "No, I don't want it".' Some decomposers felt that rather than embody some kind of hyper-masculinity, a man who takes a dowry is not strong, but 'weak', 'a coward', 'foolish' or 'lazy'. One working class Christian youth said: 'They're mad! I won't take it, nor will I let my children take it.' Another rural dalit youth said bluntly: 'I don't need a dowry to feel secure.' A poor labourer from a nearby village emphasised that his antipathy to dowry did not arise from the fact that he did not receive one. He said: 'I'm not jealous about others. I just think they're being spoilt. Why can't they spend their own money?' Meanwhile, privileged and educated college boys in the city talked of infanticide, foeticide, and other 'ills' of which they had read. Rich or poor, the decomposers were often (though by no means always) young. Position in the kinship hierarchy brings different demands, and ideas may change. We must factor in the idealism of the young and be cautious with assumptions of a paradigm shift.

Decomposers liked to speculate on the future of dowry. A few were of the opinion that it would decrease with education. Others rubbished the idea, citing a positive correlation between education and dowry. This troubled many men, and there was little sense of resolution. As one agricultural labourer said: 'There are more educated people now. They are the ones who should be changing this system. But even the educated people are taking dowry.' Some men proposed love marriages and the formation of nuclear families as possible means of tackling dowry. Others refuted these arguments, giving examples they knew of where dowries persisted even in these.

Whilst the men were at variance over the likely trajectory of dowry, there was wide agreement that the position of the decomposer was a difficult, often lonely one. One elderly villager had even adopted the role of campaigner, 'poking' his nose as he put it into any 'wrongdoings' that he sensed going on. But he was a senior and respected figure in the village. What was the ordinary man to do in the face of such overwhelming social sanction of dowry? In frustration, one youth articulated the absurdity of the situation by suggesting: 'Maybe you could take the money at the wedding to keep people satisfied, then give it back afterwards?' A rural auto-rickshaw driver said: 'I won't be needing any dowry. I'll make sure I'm in a strong position before I get married. By that time, if I want something, I should very well be able to afford it myself.' His friend sitting next to him objected to this claim. He pointed out that the driver had two elder married brothers, who had both taken dowries. The friend argued that he would be seen to enjoy the fruits of his brothers' dowries—the fridge, the TV, the bike. Then, at a time of crisis, the family may turn to him and ask why he won't bring his share. The friend mocked: 'Will you then stand there like some big social reformer, this hero, and say you won't take dowry?' The young man withstood the teasing, but it did cause him to pause, and reflect a little sadly: 'Is it a choice between heroism or haggling for Hondas? There must be another way.'

Mixed messages from men: what can be learned?

What can be learned from such discordant voices? It must be established that a continuum is not a precisely graded scale. It allows for overlap, shades of grey and movement from left to right. Though the majority of men's views were more static, a few adopted a number of different positions—intensifying, recomposing and decomposing stances from one minute to the next. The tension between degrees of personal support for dowry and their actual dowry behaviour was always in evidence. In any analysis, it is important to acknowledge that masculinities are a product not only of socio-economic and cultural change but one's 'own life course, organisational experience, own experience in gender relations and particular life histories' (Pineda 2001: 76). In turn, 'the processes of development impinge upon class, caste, and gender identities, constantly redefining needs, levels, and measures of what is condoned' (Srinivasan 2005: 608). Under such circumstances, it is unrealistic to expect men's narratives to conform to rigid typologies. On the contrary, it is ill advised, for, as Pearlman notes, men may undergo a process of so-called 'code switching' (Pearlman 1984 in Connell 2005: 80). As men move through life, they may adopt different perspectives, yet retain old allegiances and move from 'code' to 'code'. Connell elaborates that a situation may arise where 'different patterns of masculinity are enacted with different audiences' (Connell 2005: 80). How much of these narratives could be repeated in front of strangers, relatives or friends? Connell goes further, suggesting that men might even 'strategically

78

adopt or distance themselves from the hegemonic model, depending on what they are trying to achieve at the time' (2005: 80). Whilst this could prompt endless second-guessing, it is sufficient to note that men are unlikely to be 'permanently committed to a particular model of masculinity' (Connell 2005: 80). Certainly, some men may have lines of work that might presuppose a decomposed support for dowry. Their practice, however, may reveal quite the opposite. (An NGO worker and even a man studying for a Masters degree in Women's Empowerment, both confessed that they would take a dowry). However, it must be noted that though an 'anti-dowry' outlook may be counter-hegemonic, this does not automatically mean a man is pro-gender justice. Men may say they object to dowry but may find little wrong in patrilocal residence, the early marriage imperative, restrictions on women's labour, or any other issue intricately linked to dowry and detrimental to women's empowerment. Some devout Muslim men, for example, objected to dowry, but their attitude to gender equity in general was ambivalent. One man from a Scheduled Tribe community still strongly against dowry, proudly noted that anyone caught taking one would be 'thrown out of the community'. Yet when asked whether he thought women in his community had more power than in others, he looked surprised. 'Of course not,' he said. 'Man is still king.'

Policy considerations

This study examines the link between the growing hold of dowry practice and the current socio-economic context from the perspective of men. It was found that men with an intensified support for dowry depicted their support within two types of narrative (one in which men benefit, the other in which they suffer from globalising processes). It is not sufficient, however, to accept these as finally *causative* of dowry, thus absolving the men of responsibility. On the contrary, although globalising processes undoubtedly shape the men's experiences and provide markers for possible choices of action, what is borne out by the narratives is the tenacity with which patriarchal notions persist, transform and *intensify* in conditions of socio-economic change. Though marriages in India today may come with modern, consumerist trappings (motorbikes, widescreen TVs, foreign visas), or take place between software engineers and MBAs, or among farmers whose livelihoods have collapsed, this does not mean that 'the dowry problem' can be attributed only to modernisation or that it is a *result of* modernity. Men may claim this, but on the contrary, modern dowry is the successor of persisting patriarchal norms and 'old-fashioned' values that go back for centuries (Gupta 2000). Such traditionalist or hegemonic values may simply assume new guises within new locales (ibid.). Men (and women) who support dowry are not off the hook by blaming 'the new'. On the contrary, the neo-liberal agenda has nicely preserved what Connell would call a 'patriarchal dividend'.

When dowry is viewed as an unavoidable fall out of modern life, forming policy is difficult. It is a challenge to inspire action when people are of the view that 'nothing can be done' or 'what is asked for must be given.' Current approaches to dowry are diverse and often contradictory. The law is accused of both under- and over-zealousness. Favouring dowry in lieu of functioning property rights is a highly optimistic (some would say misguided) approach. The men in this study were in wide agreement that equal inheritance would not persuade men to forgo their 'right' to dowry. Others cite abstention from marriage, but, in the current context, this is one of the most difficult and idealistic of policy suggestions for the majority of India's women. Practical, workable solutions are sought, and those that make attempts to work with women and men collaboratively will serve the interests of both genders best. Working with young men and boys with films, theatre and gender sensitisation workshops is often advocated, but this must be followed through to adulthood, as the sheen of idealism may fade over time. Certainly, an end to the emphasis on dowry as a 'women's problem' is called for. From the young man compelled to pay for his sister's dowry, to the old man working to pay his debts, to the idealistic youth who claims that dowry is not required although nobody is listening—dowry is far from simply 'a women's problem', and men have their own gendered vulnerabilities. Similarly, it should no longer need stating that men are not a homogenous group. Yet concerted policy efforts are required in order to create an environment in which men are supported in their efforts to become 'counter-hegemonic'. Critically, as feminists have long argued, we must replace the symbolism of 'man as provider'. A reconstruction of gender identities is required, though paradigmatic change is slow. Despite changes in opinion, practice often remains the same. It is also true that attitudinal change at the individual level may not bring any change in the structure. Notions of 'death by culture' are unpopular (Narayan 1997), and these often cause some circumspection on behalf of those trying to act. Yet many activists in India argue that as far as gender justice is concerned, fears of criticising local culture should be over-ridden (Bhasin 2001). In the final analysis, however, when government or NGO officials continue to give and take dowry themselves (both male and female), any attempts at policy are rendered uniformly weak. The difficulty of a move from theory to practice is presented clearly in this example.

Conclusions

The above analysis points to the dangers of essentialising men's attitudes to dowry, and a number of competing voices were heard. However, if the men who we might call the 'intensifiers' believe that marriage *should* be contingent on dowry, that a daughter *should* be accompanied by a dowry to her marital home, that a man has a *right* to a dowry, or that a bride who is earning well should *still come to the marriage with a dowry*, it seems a conservative prediction to say that this group will only grow, soon to be joined by many others. Because as globalising processes bring an increase in men's incomes, we saw those men ask for dowry. But when globalising processes bring a decrease in incomes, those men also asked for dowry. It is unsurprising that under this set of circumstances, the majority of men were of the opinion that support for dowry would increase over time and the problem worsen overall. In the struggle for gender justice, however, it was encouraging to find that intensified support for dowry was not the only expression of masculinity. The narratives that support, condone and adhere to the dominant dowry ideology are but one end of the continuum. Further along are those that reassess, re-evaluate and question the ideology. Moving on again, quite contrasting voices disapprove of, contest and—at the farthest end—defy the ideology. The challenge now is to understand how these alternative masculinities might more easily emerge. It is undesirable that, rather than being an acceptable course of action for many, a rejection of dowry currently represents 'heroism' by the few.

Notes

[1] This data was collected as part of a larger study. Interviews were conducted with 69 men from a wide range of backgrounds and using a number of research variables. Three major religions (Hinduism, Islam and Christianity) were represented and there was wide differentiation by caste and class. Half the men lived and worked in a rural district (Pudukkottai) and half in a metropolitan city (Chennai). To gauge possible change in either beliefs or practice over time, three generations of men were interviewed in both rural and urban areas. The interviews were conducted by the author in English where the interviewees were fluent in that language or translated into Tamil by interpreters. The methodological literature concurs that the foreign researcher may experience advantages and disadvantages by their 'outsider' position. One of the key disadvantages is their language limitation. Power imbalances are also discussed, though as the foreigner is considered outside of the usual hierarchy, problems of caste may be removed. The foreign researcher is also often assumed to be ignorant of most cultural issues. One advantage of this is that more openness may occur as a readiness and willingness is shown to educate the researcher in these matters.

[2] The origins of more equitable gender relations in India's southern rice growing regions as compared with the majority of the North have been analysed as a result of the contrast between the labour needs for rice and wheat, and the value placed on women's labour (the former relying on women for transplanting, the latter relying on male muscle power) (see endnote 19 in Srinivasan 2005: 610). Basu (1999) notes that the North/South disparity in gender equity is now so institutionalised, however, that it is largely divorced from its supposed origins.

[3] Although Caplan notes that dowry payments in some form have been 'long-established in India' (1984: 216), Oldenburg (2002) emphasises the introduction of land revenue systems by the British colonisers as the key in reinforcing dowry in India. Srinivas cites monetisation, education, and the introduction of the organised sector as key catalysts under British rule that forged modern dowry (2006 [1984]: 8).

[4] Structural adjustment commonly refers to the International Monetary Fund's preconditions for loan or debt relief entailing economic restructuring in the borrower country. India began a period of structural adjustment after its balance of payments crisis in 1991.

[5] The state ranks third in terms of Foreign Direct Investment (FDI) approval, with an eight per cent share of total FDI in India (Government of Tamil Nadu 2008).

[6] Agricultural output has decreased from 53.27 per cent of Net State Domestic Product in 1950–51 to 16.65 per cent in 2001–02 (Government of Tamil Nadu 2003: 5).

[7] The number of marginal workers has increased from 1.4 million in 1991 to 4.1 million in 2001 (Government of Tamil Nadu 2008).

[8] The literal Tamil word for dowry is *varadakshanai*, though some respondents considered this a more abstract word and used *seeru* to relate more specifically to the goods exhanged.

[9] As most changes to the dowry system are perceived to have occurred in recent decades, the age groups in this study were categorised as 18–30, 31–45 and 46+.

[10] Add to this the generally more equitable status South Indian wives were accorded, and the historically lower preference for dowry in the South may be understood.

[11] As with Brahmins in the North, South Indian Brahmins adhere as closely as possible to *gotra* exogamy (the need to ensure marriage is outside one's own *gotra,* a group in which members are believed to share a common ancestor) (Beteille 1966). Close-kin marriage is therefore discouraged amongst Tamil Brahmins (see Caplan 1984).

[12] The idea that landowning castes practised dowry, and labouring castes practiced bride price (a payment given by the groom's family to the bride's) suggests that women's labour was valued in the latter castes and was considered a commodity worth purchasing (Banerjee 2002). This commodification of women's labour throws some doubt on the debate that bride price is necessarily more 'empowering' than dowry.

[13] Kishwar (1988, 2005) and Oldenburg (2002) have argued that in lieu of functioning property rights for women, dowry presents the 'best chance' for them to gain access to property or other assets. This view has been rejected

by many feminists who argue that dowry should be fought *in tandem* with efforts to promote equal inheritance rights. There is a strong debate regarding the extent to which dowry might be viewed as a pre-mortem inheritance. According to the men in this study, a proper implementation of equal inheritance rights would not eradicate dowry, as it was viewed not as an inheritance for women but as capital for men and it was unlikely that they would give up their 'privilege' of dowry, regardless of whether women were given separate inheritances, or not.

[14] See Robert Wade (2001) for a discussion of the notion of 'winners' and 'losers' in globalisation.

[15] Among five Hindu temple priests interviewed (some Iyer, some Iyengar Brahmin), one was strongly pro-dowry, three were ambivalent and one was strongly against.

References

AIDWA. 2003. *Expanding Dimensions of Dowry*. New Delhi: All India Democratic Women's Association.

Banerjee, N. 2002. 'Between the Devil and the Deep Sea: Shrinking Options for Women in Contemporary India' in *The Violence of Development: The Politics of Identity, Gender & Social Inequalities in India*. ed. K. Kapadia. London: Zed Books.

Basu, A.M. 1999. 'Fertility Decline and Increasing Gender Imbalance in India, Including a Possible South Indian Turnaround'. *Development and Change*. vol. 30. pp. 237–63.

Beteille, A. 1966. 'Caste in a South Indian Village' in *Social Stratification*. ed. D. Gupta. 1991. New Delhi: Oxford University Press.

Bhasin, K. 2001. 'Gender training with men: Experience and reflections from South Asia' in *Men's Involvement in Gender and Development Policy and Practice*, ed. C. Sweetman. Oxford: Oxfam.

Caplan, L. 1984. 'Bridegroom Price in Urban India: Class, Caste and "Dowry Evil" Among Christians in Madras'. *Man*. New Series. vol. 19(2). pp. 216–33.

Cleaver, F. 2002. 'Introduction' in *Masculinities Matter! Men, Gender and Development*. ed. F. Cleaver. London: Zed Books.

Connell, R.W. 2005. 'Globalization, Imperialism, and Masculinities' in *Handbook of Studies on Men & Masculinities*. eds. M.S. Kimmel, J. Hearn and R.W. Connell. London: Sage Publications.

Elson, D. & R. Pearson. 1980. 'The Latest Phase of the Internationalisation of Capital and its Implications for Women in the Third World'. IDS Discussion Paper. Brighton: Institute of Development Studies.

Geetha, V. 2006. *Gender*. Kolkata: Stree Publishing.

———. 2007. *Patriarchy*. Kolkata: Stree Publishing.

Government of Tamil Nadu. 2003. *Tamil Nadu Human Development Report*. New Delhi: Government of Tamil Nadu Social Science Press.

——. 2008. Website: www.tn.gov.in/ (4 March 2008).

Gupta, D. 2000. *Mistaken Modernity: India Between Worlds*. New Delhi: HarperCollins Publishers.

Kandiyoti, D. 1988. 'Bargaining with Patriarchy'. *Gender and Society*. vol. 2. no. 3. pp. 274–90.

Karanth, G.K. 1997 'Caste in Contemporary Rural India' in *Caste: Its Twentieth Century Avatar*. ed. M.N. Srinivas. New Delhi: Penguin Books India.

Dishware, M.P. 1980. 'Beginning With Our Own Lives: A Call For Dowry Boycott' in *Dowry and Inheritance*. ed. S. Basu. 2006. New Delhi and London: Women Unlimited and Zed Books.

——. 2005. 'Destined to Fail: Inherent Flaws in the Anti-Dowry Legislation'. *Manushi*. no. 148. May-June. pp. 3–12.

Kodoth, P. 2006. 'Producing a Rationale for Dowry? Gender in the Negotiation of Exchange at Marriage in Kerala, South India. Asia Research Centre: Working Paper no.16. LSE Website. http://www.lse.ac.uk/collections/asiaResearch Centre/ (3 April 2008).

Narayan, U. 1997 'Cross-Cultural Connections, Border-Crossings, and "Death by Culture" in *Dislocating Cultures*. New York: Routledge.

Oldenburg, V. 2002. *Dowry Murder: The Imperial Origins of a Cultural Crime*. New York: Oxford University Press.

Osella, F., & C. Osella. 2000. 'Migration, Money and Masculinity in Kerala'. *The Journal of the Royal Anthropological Institute*. vol. 6. no. 1. pp. 117–33.

Palriwala, R. 2006 (1989). 'Reaffirming the Anti-Dowry Struggle' in *Dowry and Inheritance*. ed. S. Basu. New Delhi and London: Women Unlimited and Zed Books.

Pearson, R. 2001 'All Change? Men, Women and Reproductive Work in the Global Economy' in *Men at Work: Labour, Masculinities, Development*. ed. C. Jackson. London: F. Cass.

Pineda, J. 2001. 'Partners in Women-Headed Households: Emerging Masculinities?' in *Men at Work: Labour, Masculinities, Development*. ed. C. Jackson. London: F. Cass

Reddy, G. 1993. *Marriage Practices in South India: Social and Biological Aspects of Consanguineous Unions*. Madras: University of Madras.

Srinivas, M.N. 2006 (1984). 'Some Reflections on Dowry' in *Dowry and Inheritance*. ed. S. Basu. New Delhi and London: Women Unlimited and Zed Books.

Srinivasan, P. & G. Lee. 2004. 'The Dowry System in Northern India: Women's Attitudes and Social Change'. *Journal of Marriage and Family*. vol. 66. no. 5. pp. 1108–17.

Srinivasan, S. 2005. 'Daughters or Dowries? The Changing Nature of Dowry Practices in South India'. *World Development*. vol. 33. no. 4. pp. 593–615.

Sunder Rajan, R. 2003. *The Scandal of the State: Women, Law and Citizenship in Postcolonial India*. Durham: Duke University Press.

Vera-Sanso, P. 2001. 'Masculinity, Male Domestic Authority and Female Labour Participation in South India' in *Men at Work: Labour, Masculinities, Development*. ed. C. Jackson. London: F. Cass.

Wade, R. 2001. 'Global Inequality, Winners and Losers'. *The Economist*. 28 April.

The Interfaces between Gender, Religion and Dowry

TAMSIN BRADLEY

Introduction

Considerations of religion and culture have tended to be absent from research into dowry. Instead the focus has been upon the ways in which modern dowry practices are a product of various interconnecting social and economic factors including modernisation, Sanskritisation and the patriarchal family. Narayan is famously critical of attempts to reduce modern dowry to cultural or religious explanations because in doing this we are effectively guilty of assigning South Asian women 'death by culture'. By contrast, when western women are victims of domestic violence, this is never seen as a cultural issue. This, Narayan argues, is an overhang from the colonial tendency to exoticise Asian women as cultural products and to fail to see that their gender oppression has similar roots to women globally (1997).

While I agree with Narayan that we should not reduce Third World women to 'culture', as an anthropologist who works closely in the field of religious studies, I find a lack of discussion in the scholarly literature concerning the ways in which religion and/or culture might feed into the dowry problematic. The purpose of this paper is not to review the reasons for social science research to ignore the role that religion and culture play in shaping key institutions in society (such as the family, the economy or the

87

state) or the impact of these institutions upon practices, such as dowry but to provoke discussion of whether religion should be brought more frequently into such research on dowry. The norms of social science often reject religion as a way of understanding social processes. Resistance to including religion within wider analytical frames is partly due to the difficulty researchers perceive in accessing its impact on peoples' lives. Adherents largely experience religion privately and internally and making this visible is difficult. Many social scientists are not comfortable with data unless it is clearly apparent to their eyes and ears. Another reason is their widespread belief, that with modernisation religion would be replaced by a more 'rational' secular way of seeing the world (Beyer 1994). Although the prominence of religion globally has now been accepted as a trend not likely to reverse, this acknowledgement has been slow to filter into research across the social sciences (Thomas 2005).

However, to argue that religion and culture have been sidelined in social science research, including that on dowry, does not in itself mean that they are necessarily relevant factors in understanding the dowry problematic. It is this link that this paper seeks to investigate. In a deeply religious culture as in India, where notions of female roles and responsibilities are engrained in many people's religious belief and practice, the interfaces between religion, gender and dowry need investigation as they might be important strands in understanding the web of interconnecting factors that sustain abusive dowry practices. This could help us more fully understand the cultural underpinnings of the dowry problematic as well as influence forms of activism to curb dowry. In particular, I am interested in the ways in which culture and religion help shape and sustain gender hierarchies in India and their potential to challenge patriarchy. While much western feminism has been deeply suspicious of religion in women's lives and has tended to reflect the secularist/modernist assumption that religion should/would disappear (Mathur 2004), some feminist activists in developing countries argue that secular feminism is less appropriate in religious contexts. This does not mean rejecting feminist calls for gender equality, but instead finding resources within patriarchal religious traditions that promote women's empowerment (Kwok Pui-lan 2002; Tomalin 2006). This can be particularly effective in contexts where oppressive gender regimes find explicit support from within religious traditions.

Before discussing the extent to which religion and culture are relevant to the analysis of dowry I will first draw on the work of Julia Leslie. She was one of the first scholars of Indian religions to argue that religious texts have an impact on the cultural and social environment in which they are read and interpreted. I therefore focus on the influence that one of the most popular Hindu texts, the *Ramayana*, has had in shaping gender ideology and social relationships. The model for wifely devotion central to most Hindu texts has helped to endorse patriarchal heterosexual marriage which supports dowry. Although the *Ramayana* does not talk about dowry explicitly it does endorse a model of wifely submission within which the role and status of men over women is promoted. This in turn has led to son preference and an array of socio-cultural practices that exist because boys are considered of higher value than girls (Knott 1996). The projection of patriarchal gendered ideals also leaves women exposed to mistreatment ranging from limited life opportunities to emotional and physical abuse. Texts such as the *Ramayana* promote marriage as central to a woman's religious role making it hard for her to choose not to marry and thereby escape dowry. This association between religion, patriarchy and dowry leaves women vulnerable to dowry-related violence and other forms of domestic violence.

Religious texts are examples of authoritative sources of values and beliefs which help to form the foundation sustaining patriarchy. Anthropologists working in religion and South Asian studies such as Flueckiger (1996) and Richman (1992) return to texts such as the *Ramayana* in order to understand why patriarchy continues to be passed down by generations of men and women. The constant anthropological interest in religious texts is partly due to ways in which they adapt themselves to changing social contexts. As such they can be used as part of a critical social commentary. Religious texts are not static but ever-changing. Over time new narratives are produced and promoted. Different versions of the text emerge in response to shifts in the surrounding social, political, economic and cultural climate (see Hess 1999; Kishwar 1996; Bose 2004; Richman 2000; Sutherland 1992). Recent versions of the *Ramayana*, for example the televised series of the epic, have a more conservative depiction of Sita as a devoted and loyal wife than Valmiki's *Ramayana* (Pauwels 2004). Scholars analysing these narratives argue that they serve to promote the model of wifely submission as still relevant in today's world. These contemporary versions help to maintain the link between patriarchy and marriage despite the strength of the women's movement in India and the many successful community level initiatives and programmes. Dowry has emerged in many parts of India as part of the ideology that denies women independence from birth through to marriage.

This paper shows how the impact of text is more than 'theoretical' and presents evidence of the influence of such imagery upon women's lives by ethnographic data documenting the attitudes and experiences of three Rajasthani women who believe this model of wifely devotion and the associated son preference has negatively impacted on their lives. Dowry is one outcome they link to a system that privileges sons rather than daughters. Two of the women said that the obligations of wifely duty attached to marriage promoted through dowry left them susceptible to other forms of domestic violence. These women do not abandon religion because of its role in sustaining an oppressive system but use it as a means of understanding it. I therefore look more broadly at research conducted by feminist scholars of Hinduism who are concerned with the various ways in which women could and do use religion to voice concerns over oppressive practices such as dowry.

This paper is arranged in three sections. The first examines the link between religion, culture and dowry. The second looks at the relationship between religious texts and the social reality of Hindu women and considers how texts might help to shape social and cultural environments. The third section takes a closer look at the impact religion has on women's lives specifically in the context of dowry and considers religion as both part of the problem and the solution to dowry. The conclusion in part considers how this paper feeds into some of the work presented in this volume.

The link between religion, culture and dowry

Finding the balance

The argument for including religion within an analytical frame for the study of dowry and dowry-related violence first requires a response to Narayan's concerns over the way in which dowry murders are understood in comparison to western instances of domestic violence. Narayan (1997) states that oppressive practices in the developing world are often explained away as products of an underdeveloped society. Moreover, religion is focused on more to understand cultural practices in the developing world than it is in studies of domestic violence in the so-called 'developed' nations. In her chapter 'Thinking about Dowry Murders in India and Domestic Violence Murders in the United States, she writes:

> I intend to argue that when such 'cultural explanations' are given for *fatal* forms of violence against Third World women, the effect is to suggest that Third World women suffer 'death by culture'. I shall try and show that fatal forms of violence against mainstream Western women seem interestingly resistant to such 'cultural explanations', leaving Western women seemingly more immune to 'death by culture'. I believe that such asymmetries in 'cultural explanation' result in pictures of Third World women as 'victims of their culture' in ways that are interestingly different from the way in which victimisation of mainstream Western women is understood (1997: 84–5).

Moreover, dowry-related violence is placed alongside sati, both given as examples of distinctly Indian forms of violence and the explanation for both is the same—Indian culture. Hindu culture is taken to represent Indian culture which, as Narayan points out, is grossly inaccurate given the diversity of the country. To be clear, this paper only discusses the impact of Hinduism on the lives of Hindu women. To illustrate how culture is deployed in explanations of dowry murders in India Narayan draws on the example of Elizabeth Bumiller's book, *May You Be the Mother of a Hundred Sons: A journey among the women of India*. Although Narayan acknowledges this book is not uniquely problematic it has been hugely popular and she focuses on its third chapter, 'Flames: A Bride Burning and a Sati.' Overall Narayan states, that Bumiller describes how Hindu women are victims of their culture and makes sweeping and inaccurate links between dowry violence and sati with Sita's ordeal as she is driven to prove her chastity after being kidnapped by Ravana. Narayan affirms that the conflation of sati with dowry is also problematic: 'Dowry-murder can hardly amount to the victimisation of Indian women by Hindu tradition when there is no tradition of burning women to death for dowry' (1997: 107). As highlighted by Dalmia and Lawrence; and Subramaniam, Remedios, and Mitra in this volume, dowry is not and cannot be described as a pan Hindu practice. Narayan states:

> Hindu religion, mythology, and tradition make very poor explanations for dowry murders, since dowry murders have not been [a] widespread social phenomenon before the late 1970s. Hindu myths and traditions have been around considerably longer. It is therefore hard to see that they have serious explanatory value with respect to the contemporary phenomenon of dowry murder' (1997: 107).

Narayan is clear that although religion may have some relationship to dowry, the rise of dowry-related violence is a recent phenomenon and religion/culture cannot offer an explanation of this disturbing pattern. The marriage practice of dowry must be separated from the violence that often surrounds it. However scholars from within the study of religion argue that religion plays a part in both sustaining heterosexual marriage practices and also the normalisation of violence against women (Bradley 2006, 2009; Hawthorne 2004; King and Beattie 2004; Puttick 1998; McIntosh 2007). These scholars would therefore be critical of Narayan's claims that religion has little if any part to play in violent acts against women. I believe that marriage as a patriarchal institution and violence as a misogynistic act carried out against women occur because of embedded gender values that sanction them. Religion cross-culturally in both western and non-western contexts has played a part in sustaining these gender values. Religion and those values and beliefs attached to it are not static but evolve with time. To argue that religion plays no part in dowry violence because dowry is a recent phenomenon ignores the extent to which religion adapts itself and reshapes its gender ideology causing the emergence of new forms of female oppression. The rise of conservative and nationalist Hinduism has seen a more intense promotion of patriarchal values that target women in a drive to ensure their continued or renewed domesticity (Rajagopal 2001; Sarkar 2001; Sarkar and Butalia 1995; Dhruvarajan 1996; Froerer 2007; Kapur and Crossman 1994; McKean 1996). Religion must therefore form part of the critical analysis of all forms of oppression against women. King is convinced that religions operate in very similar ways and create environments that support the elitism and authority of men over women even in societies that might regard themselves as largely secular. She asserts that religious beliefs, thoughts and practices are not only profoundly patriarchal but often thoroughly androcentric. Religions are predominantly if not exclusively shaped by male perspectives and experiences (2005: 3298). In order to understand the subordination of women from within the worlds' faiths and the normalisation of male experiences religion must be viewed through a critical gender lens because:

> Religion and gender are not simply two parallel categories that function independently of each other; they are mutually embedded within each other in all religions, suffusing all religious worlds and experiences. It is because of this deep hidden embeddedness that gender is sometimes so difficult to identify and separate out from other aspects of religions until one's own consciousness is trained into making a gender critical turn. (2005: 3299)

Once the analytical eye is trained to see religion as gendered the next step is to examine its far-reaching effects on wider society and human relationships. I believe that it is short-sighted for religion to be left out of the analysis into patriarchy in both western and non-western societies.

Feminist scholars of religion have highlighted how Hinduism is not an exception in the way in which it projects misogynistic ideals which in turn sustain an often hostile environment for women. Similar arguments have been made in regard to all world religions by King (1995), Young (1995), Young, Sharma and Young (1991), King and Beattie (2004) who have pointed out the degree to which religions are both gendered and patriarchal. The shape and dimensions of this gender ideology will differ from religion to religion and across cultures. In the case of Hinduism its patriarchal values has produced son preference and male succession which clearly privilege the male subject. Women are designated the role of looking after them. Dowry is one product of these traditions which ensures that male needs and desires define and dominate women's lives and roles (see also Knott 1996). These particular dimensions so prominent in Hinduism can be identified as having contributed towards the creation of dowry. Hindu texts are founded on the idea of a male lineage which in turn is founded on male authority and superiority. Wifely submission and compliance are necessary to secure the continuation of this male lineage and to deter any challenge to the authority of men. Dowry should be seen as one product of this distinct ideology.

Narayan outlines where she does see 'culture' not religion as having some impact:

> while explanations for Indian women's vulnerability to dowry murder might meaningfully refer to some aspects of 'culture', such as underlying marriage and family arrangements that contribute to women's powerlessness, neither dowry murders nor women's vulnerability to dowry murder seem explainable as simply the outcome of a specific set of 'religious' views (1997: 113).

The experiences and views of some Rajasthani women I have spent time with contest aspects of Narayan's argument acknowledging a link between Hinduism and the oppression they have suffered. Some Hindu women acknowledge the centrality of religion in their lives and draw on it not just to seek explanations for the injustice they suffer but also as a way of coping with it. The views expressed by women within religious spaces may not represent outward challenges but should be understood as the first step in resisting the dominance of patriarchy. Anti-dowry activists could use such spaces to generate further momentum turning the resentment expressed into defiant actions calling for change.

A balance needs to be found that understands the way in which religion and culture weave together and help to create and support a gendered chain that begins with a patriarchal environment and ends in violence against women. The chain begins in Hinduism with son preference, heterosexual marriage and wifely submission and then leads to dowry in many parts of India, finally leaving women vulnerable to dowry-related violence and also other forms of violence. Religion plays a part in securing the first links of this chain and this is clear from textual analysis of Hindu epics and also through anthropological studies of the role of women in Hindu society.

Narayan's work has made a significant contribution in making researchers more sensitive and self-critical in their writings on dowry. Particularly those outside India need to both challenge their own motivations and also ensure their representations of other women are founded on what they witness and hear women articulating for themselves and not their own exotic imaginings. Without being informed by face to face dialogues researchers cannot be confident they understand the processes that produce dowry and the violence often emerging because of it (see Tomalin's Introduction to this volume).

The core premise of this paper can be described as follows: dowry is at the root of many acts of violence against women, but the ways in which it is symbolic of deeper systemic structures that perpetuate gender inequality must also be considered. Dowry, dowry-related violence and other forms of violence against women come out of the same gendered ideology. It is the role of religion and culture in producing aspects of this ideology that I wish to draw attention to.

Many sources writing on domestic and dowry violence do not consider religion as a contributing factor in producing this patriarchal ideology (see Emerson Dobash and Dobash 1998; Garg 2001; Joshi and Hooja 1997; Kelkar 1992; Mathur 2004, 2007; Perez 2002). Although patriarchy is seen as the foundation of women's oppression its roots are left relatively unexamined. I argue that the inclusion of religion and its relationship to culture can help to develop this theoretical stance by adding a further, carefully balanced dimension to help understand misogynistic practices such as dowry as well as dowry-related and domestic violence. But this requires an examination of the relationship between religion and culture to show that both need to be included together in research on dowry. Narayan, as is often the case, does not clearly delineate between religion and culture in her work. I believe it is important to understand the differences between religion and culture and how they interrelate as this helps to provide further insight into the patriarchal foundations of dowry and dowry-related violence. As stated in the introduction the social sciences generally exclude religion. Outside of religious studies, social anthropology is an exception in which 'religion' and 'culture' represent popular research themes. Since I am an anthropologist working within religious studies it is appropriate to detail how the relationship is understood within anthropology.

The anthropological view on religion and culture

A review of key texts on the anthropology of religion highlights how culture and religion underpin dowry by legitimising patriarchy. Practices such as dowry rest within broader religious ideals about the role of men and women which can and are used to justify it. The anthropological view generally states that religion is inextricably linked to culture (Angro 2004; Bennett 1996; Bowen 2002; Bowie 2000; Crapo 2003; Glaizer 2003; Hicks 2002; Lambek 2002; Morris 1987; Scupin 1999; Whitehouse and Laiulaw 2004). Religion is regarded as providing a conceptual framework for understanding the world and the place of humans within it. Culture is the mechanism by which these beliefs are translated into social structures and practices shaping behaviour and determining how people relate to the world and to each other. Bowie (2000) defines religion as a supernatural realm to which people look for explanations for why and how human life came to be and the arena through which spiritual and practical guidance is offered. Religion is one source of authority used by culture to assert control over human perceptions and actions. Activists and researchers express frustration at the seemingly impenetrable nature of the patriarchal gender ideology responsible for dowry. The role religion plays in sanctioning patriarchy can in part help us to understand the embeddedness of dowry.

Male religious teachers and leaders interpret and translate religious ideas into everyday life. In South Asia this has helped patriarchy to remain thereby supporting dowry by promoting the domination of men over women in marriage which has also led to violence against women both dowry-related and other forms. Hinduism existed before dowry and indeed the patterns of dowry observances suggest that other socio-economic factors have strongly influenced and steered its development. My argument that religion should form part of the analysis of dowry should not be confused with the suggestion that without religion dowry would not occur. Religion shapes world views and is therefore linked to matters of what it is to be human, including kinship, life cycles and environmental beliefs, ideals of a human society, dignity, exchange, well-being, values and beliefs (Geertz 1973a, 1973b; Rappaport 1999; Bloch 1986; Asad 1987). However, alongside, and at times instead of, religion secular dimensions operate. Economic, social and political factors combine in different configurations at different moments in history with or without religion to produce socio-cultural practices. However, in regard to dowry religion must be considered because of its connection to marriage. Marriage is a central religious ceremony and rite of passage strongly promoted through Hindu texts, oral traditions and rituals. Religion therefore must have some bearing on dowry in promoting the patriarchal marriage values which underpin it.

Religious beliefs and practices are not static and change with history. The authority of religion is ensured through the adaptation of beliefs and practices, in order to suit the needs of a new emerging order (Asad 1993). The adaptability and ever-changing nature of religion could well account for the reason why dowry has emerged in different ways and at different points in history across South Asian communities. In section three I examine specific changes and evolutions in how religious texts such as the *Ramayana* are retold and used as a mechanism through which gendered ideals are transmitted to men and women. Later versions of this text pull out Rama and Sita as role models. Other narratives focus on Sita's duty as a good and loyal consort strengthening over time the model of wifely devotion (Pauwels 2004). The differing and changing patterns of dowry could be partly influenced by changes in the way in which dominant religious narratives are told. For example, the message of wifely devotion has solidified conventional gender paradigms which will have compromised the effectiveness of anti-dowry activism.

The relationship between text and social reality

The links between religion and culture in the context of dowry need more research. Religion appears in some research papers on dowry and women's subordination as one of the causes of the problems women face (Vohra 2003; Johnson and Johnson 2001; Chacko 2003; Prasad 1999). The chain as I see it is as follows: religion operates to produce codes of conduct projected through textual images of the ideal woman that support patriarchy and specifically son preference promoting women's marginalisation through numerous socio-cultural practices, such as purdah, female infanticide, child marriage and dowry. India's economic, cultural and social diversity means this chain ends differently hence the lack of uniformity in the emergence and observation of such practices. Child marriage for example occurs in rural Rajasthan where poverty makes the possibility of raising dowry impossible

(Miller 1981; Sagade 2005). Marrying a daughter as a child avoids the need for dowry.

Many scholars such as Basu (in this volume) understand dowry as symbolic of systemic gender inequalities. Gender is therefore crucial as a methodological tool to unpack this patriarchal ideology but cannot on its own explain its pervasiveness. As already argued in section one religion creates authoritative world views about how men and women should live. Religious texts or specifically dominant narratives on texts are powerful sources of authority. This authority is shaped by patriarchy and feeds into gender relations which marginalise women.

One of the first scholars to argue that texts have an impact on social and cultural reality was Julia Leslie. A classical Indologist working with Sanskrit texts, one of Leslie's most cited works was *The Perfect Wife* (1989) in which she translates the *Stridharmapaddhati of Tryambakayajvan,* a text that outlines the role of 'orthodox' Hindu women. The term 'orthodox' used here denotes the dominant prescriptive view on how Hindu women should behave and the roles and responsibilities they should take on. This role is domestic and means being a dutiful and loyal wife and nurturing mother (see also Leslie 1991). Texts both impact on social life and give a commentary on it. Within Hinduism some texts offer guidance and knowledge on how to live and the purpose of life to help individuals find their place within it. While dowry itself is not a religious practice sanctioned by Hindu texts and traditions, Leslie was interested in the ways in which patriarchal religion establishes gender inequalities that can then allow dowry and dowry-related violence to flourish.

An example of this patriarchal gender ideology specifically through son preference can be seen in the differentiation between the purpose of women's and men's lives which strictly binds women's roles to the domestic sphere. Dowry can be understood as a mechanism used to further embed this ideology in the lives of women. Texts such as the *Laws of Manu* (Doniger 1991) and the *Stridharmapaddhati of Tryambakayajvan* directly list the roles and responsibilities of women. In *The Perfect Wife* Leslie stresses the importance of linking texts to the social reality existing both at the time the texts were produced and their relevance for today. In her last published article, 'Gender and Hinduism' Leslie (2005) affirms that religious texts hold significant influence in shaping cultural and social environments and ancient Hindu texts clearly promote a gender ideology which is still in existence today. Although many texts may have diminished in prominence, they have left a lasting imprint on the social and cultural fabric of women's lives.

The relationship between religion and culture emerges in Leslie's analysis. She believed Hindu texts on the role of women prescribe a cultural environment in which they were expected to live. They were not assigned a spiritual or religious path but were positioned by their *stridharma* squarely in the domestic sphere. Marriage was endorsed within these texts as a rite of passage that cements women into their cultural role. Dowry was seen by Leslie as a necessary means of ensuring women made this transition from daughter to married life. The gender ideology emerging out of these ancient texts has been shown by anthropologists and sociologists to exist today. Leslie (2005) argued that scholarly interpretations of religious texts and ideas have now expanded to include more nuanced socio-cultural and gendered understandings of the prescriptive roles assigned to men and women (Gold and Raheja 1994; Feldhaus 1995; Good 1991; Kapadia 1995). Although sufficient evidence exists that the patriarchal ideology present in the ancient texts lives on in the socio-cultural lives of South Asian women Leslie was adamant that it should not be assumed that women feel oppressed. She argued that individuals and groups will take different meanings from texts and negotiate different social cultural realities. Leslie agreed that *The Perfect Wife* can be read fundamentally as a patriarchal text that constrains women, but she also believed that the image of docile, oppressed women depicted in it is not one shared by Indian women themselves. She states:

On psychological grounds alone it is hardly likely that half the population of India actually regarded (or regard) themselves in the negative terms outlined by the other half. It is far more probable that they either resisted altogether the interpretations foisted on them or created their own positive construct—for Indian women rarely want to be men; nor as a general rule do they seek the 'freedoms' of western women (1989: 328–9).

Texts may help to explain the origins of social systems which at different points in history legitimise practices such as dowry, but they cannot lead to an understanding of women's experiences of patriarchy. Few people today read texts such as the *Stridharmapaddhati of Tryambakayajvan* but they have contributed to the creation of a lasting social environment within which female oppression has become normalised. For adherents it is within the experiential and personal aspects of religion that patriarchal ideals become internalised and normalised but also challenged. My case study of three women shows how they are resigned to patriarchy accepting that texts such as the *Ramayana* help to endorse it. However, they also use particular narratives of the same text to question their marginalisation. It is difficult to offer clear empirical evidence of what occurs within private spaces of an individual's religious life but research on ritual suggests that the experiential dimension is hugely powerful as a means through which certain values and beliefs become normalised (Van der Veer 1994; Bell 1997) and can also explain why someone might both challenge and accept patriarchy. Basu (2001) describes how her informants perceived their own subjectivity as part of a 'collective Indian subject' and used the plural 'we' when talking about Indian tradition, thus including themselves in the patriarchal subject position. Yet, the process of self-identification is more complex. Indian women simultaneously associate with the patriarchal male subject constructed partly through religious images such as that of Rama, whilst holding on to their position as women subjugated by this system, which helps explain the alignment of some Hindu women with Sita. All Basu's female informants also acknowledged the grave injustices women suffer because of their tradition. Through religious ritual women contest but also uphold patriarchy. This complex subject positioning makes anti-dowry activism difficult. Basu argues that the removal of dowry increases women's vulnerability because they no longer carry the same economic value. Many women are acutely aware of this and hold on to the patriarchal aspects of their cultural identity as a guarantee of their economic value. Marriage without dowry is not attractive to many families who resent accepting an additional member who does not bring sufficient economic gain and turn violently against this outsider. Basu asserts that the eradication of dowry can only be achieved if deeper gender inequalities that reduce women to economic commodities are also dealt with. It must also be acknowledged that some women continue to support dowry because they can rely upon it to avoid mistreatment in their married lives.

The impact of religion on women's lives

One of the most commonly researched Hindu texts analysed by textual scholars, sociologists and anthropologists is the *Ramayana*, a good example of how some religious texts have an impact on and contribute towards shaping and sustaining social relations. In my own field research (Bradley 2006, 2009). I have documented numerous women who were subjected to dowry yet also honoured Sita daily in rituals created by them for this purpose. The women whose lives have informed my research argue that they can see the negative impact that religion has had on their lives specifically in regard to compulsory heterosexual marriage and dowry. However, it is their religion that they turn to in an attempt to make sense of the suffering they have endured as a result of being devalued, marginalised and often beaten. One example of such a case study provides further evidence of the link between religion, culture and dowry.

Gaytri[1] is a Rajput woman who married into a prominent landowning family. She lived in strict purdah and hardly left her home which was a crumbling fort on the edge of a small town in Rajasthan. Her husband is a businessman and local councillor.

Though she was physically confined behind the fortress walls she knew much of what went on outside through frequent visits from other women, mostly from a lower caste than her own, since mobility for women of her status was limited. I visited her accompanied by two local women, Parvati and Devi, who worked for a Gandhian community organisation. Both women had left their husbands after their marriages became violent and took employment with this organisation. Despite her high caste status, Gaytri had no problem in meeting these two women who sat for hours drinking tea and exchanging news. Through their visits the outside world became accessible. Their unhappy marriages were a frequent topic of conversations and their circumstances could be traced to the economic situations of their respective families who were unable to give them much of a dowry. Both women were married to much older men who drank and beat them regularly. The domestic violence they suffered was not described by them as directly related to the issue of dowry but they recognised that because of their families' lack of money they were unable to secure a good match and were left vulnerable in relationships with men who did not respect them. Although Gaytri was not violently abused she was physically secluded. All three women used the Rama and Sita story to explain why marriage so often resulted in women being marginalised and abused. Just as with Rama and Sita, men control women which was the normal state of gender relations. Women need to find strength to endure this inequality and religion is one source of motivation for these three women at least. Although the *Ramayana* does not specifically talk about or prescribe dowry it does promote the dominance of men within heterosexual marriage and for many women represents the first link in the chain that leads to dowry and then to dowry-related violence and other forms of violence against women.

The link between the *Ramayana* and dowry may appear tenuous to those outside the feminist study of religion but in my case studies it is made by women who have suffered because of dowry and also describe themselves as religious. Leslie's view that Hindu texts set out clearly defined roles for men and women can be seen in the Rama and Sita story. Most versions delineate between the domestic social role of Sita and the religiously authoritative role of Rama as the exiled future king. Sita's marriage to Rama is presented as fundamentally important not just to the couple but also to the nation. The stability of Hindu society is shown to rely upon the fidelity of the woman. Rama may not want to force Sita into the fire to test her faithfulness but he must prove her innocence in order to reinstate her as a symbol of purity and female perfection in the eyes of his subjects. If Sita's fidelity cannot be assured Rama's authority and judgement may be questioned for marrying a woman who is less than virtuous. Sita's dependence on her husband is also exposed. She cannot escape her husband's accusations and harsh treatment except through the drastic route of suicide. The story emphasises the practical and symbolic importance of marriage and the high level of scrutiny of female behaviour. Dowry is a mechanism through which women are bound into heterosexual marriage unable to live as single women or in other partnerships. Dowry forms part of the transition from daughter to wife which increases a woman's vulnerability by reducing her economic, cultural and social independence. If a woman does not conform or submit to the transition into marriage and the roles of a wife and a mother of sons, violence is used to enforce her compliance. The following passage taken from the *Ramayana* by Tulsidas highlights women's vulnerability to physical abuse should they make any attempts to resist this path:

> If women became independent, it would lead to evil ... The drum, the village fool, the shudras, animals, women ... all these are fit to be beaten.

The normalisation of violence as central to male/female relationships is built into certain narratives of the *Ramayana*. The critical analysis of these narratives can be described as anti-*Ramayana* as they challenge the misogynistic aspects of the patriarchal message so firmly embedded in many versions. Sita is often presented in these versions as courageous and defiant (see Bradley 2006; Kishwar 1996; Hess 1999; Sutherland 1989, 1992, 2000; Suthren Hirst 1997). Some narratives reveal Rama's less than honourable behaviour towards Sita but do not articulate a new paradigm in gender relations as Sita remains a loyal wife until the end. As my case studies show the process of critically challenging dominant narratives and creating new ones represents a possible coping strategy and perhaps could even be regarded as a form of activism for women who have suffered through dowry and/or violence.

Despite the pro-Sita line in some *Ramayana* versions the patriarchal underpinning of Rama and Sita's relationship has not diminished and can be used to partly explain the gender inequalities that shape the lives of many Indian women (see also Diesel 2002; Fruzzetti 1990; Agarwal 2000; Kakar 1981, 1993). These Sita-focused narratives can help to support anti-dowry activism. Kishwar (2000) looks at how Sita as a symbol of strength has been used by Sharad Joshi (leader of the Lakshmi Mukti campaign in Maharashtra) in his efforts to make fathers hand over land to their daughters as inheritance and break their dependence in marriage because of practices such as dowry. Joshi recounts the injustices that Sita suffered at the hands of her husband and asks his audience if this is a humane way to treat women. He states that villagers must right the wrongs committed by Rama and repay a long overdue debt. His narration of the Rama and Sita story makes links to cultural practices such as dowry as he asks communities to critically reflect on the effects that women's economic status as dependents has on their lives. This example highlights that although patriarchal narratives of Hindu texts endorse dowry, if other interpretations of popular texts such as the *Ramayana* are promoted they may chip away at the dominance of patriarchy. Although there are no easy or quick solutions religious studies scholars such as King and Leslie argue that religion should be seen as both part of the problem and the solution (see also Bradley 2006, 2009).

Literature within the feminist study of Hinduism highlights the different paths scholars have taken in trying to establish the existence of this link between religion, patriarchy and women's oppression and strategies to challenge it. Some scholars such as

Hiltebeitel and Erndl (2000) have produced volumes focusing on the goddess images of Kali and Durga, heralded as examples of female power and dominance. Explorations have often been deeply personal involving the scholar seeking embodied experiences of the Goddess through ritual and pilgrimage (Dobia 2000; Erndl 1992). These studies seek to highlight the transformative potential of certain goddess images contrasted against examples of the dutiful Hindu woman. The intended outcome seems to be a desire to challenge and subsume patriarchy within an oppositional female image that represents gender equality. These works emphasise the positive images and symbols of femininity present in Hinduism and challenge views that religion brings only negative effects.

Scholars such as Diesel (2002) argue that Hinduism supports cultural and social norms that marginalise women through the sanctioning of practices such as dowry, but at the same time other aspects of the tradition support gender equality. Hinduism should be examined carefully and not just dismissed as a source of disempowerment. She focuses on the image of Kali as a powerful and fearful Hindu goddess that can offer Indian women a strong role model. If activists were to emphasise Kali's self-determination and autonomy as admirable qualities, then perhaps more women would adopt these characteristics in their own behaviour and do more to challenge the structures that repress them. Although Diesel does not touch directly on dowry she is clear that this approach holds potential as a means of eradicating gender injustices, dowry being a prominent example. However, she overlooks the possibility that Hindu women may see these same courageous attributes, portrayed so vividly through Kali and Durga, in other less obvious goddess images such as Sita (see Bradley 2006).

The texts by Hiltebeitel and Erndl (2000), Dobia (2000), Erndl (1992), and Diesel (2002) can be labelled as feminist studies of Hinduism. Collectively they point to an alternative social and cultural vision in which women live free from misogynistic practices such as dowry by rejecting patriarchal models of the feminine such as Sita. This viewpoint is problematic; women are not choosing to worship Kali and Durga in huge numbers. Contemporary work on the *Ramayana* provides an explanation. This research documents how the epic continues to be revised and new narratives written because the core message still reflects the gender ideals shared by many. Narayana Rao (2004) examines different versions of the *Ramayana* and asks the question, 'What makes Sita, Sita?' Her conclusion is that Sita's loyal devotion to Rama is her central characteristic and as soon as she rejects her wifely position she ceases to be Sita. This aspect of the narrative has remained despite the rise of 'anti-*Ramayana*' narratives. As already stated, although more recent versions challenge Sita's mistreatment, women still hold on to the model of wifely devotion represented through her. Narayana Rao believes that the continued popularity of the epic shows that it carries values that are important to many. It also shows that there is a limit to how far men and women wish to challenge patriarchy. For example the traditional role of women may still be desired by some and anti-dowry activism is facing this possibility. Pauwels (2004) makes a similar argument to that of Narayana Rao in relation to the popularity of the television adaptation of the *Ramayana* which she believes carries an even more conservative gender message than early narratives. She claims the television version is responding to a need. Women want to be empowered but on their own terms. This echoes Leslie's much earlier statement that Indian women want to create their own positive construct and not necessarily embrace western concepts of 'freedom' (1989: 328–9).

If the general trend seems to be that at least some aspects of a patriarchal gender ideology are desired and perpetuated by both men and women how can religion support more radical anti-dowry activism? Closer studies of women's rituals (Pintchman 2007) reveal the complex process of reinterpretation and social networking that takes place through and around women's religious activities. Although this volume does not deal directly with dowry or approaches to gender justice, it does feed into the wider anti-dowry agenda. The domestic obligations attached to marriage and the behaviour of husbands are highlighted as issues of concern to Hindu women. The contributors point out that religion has both negative and positive impacts on women's lives and emphasise how religion, specifically ritual, can be used as a vehicle to assert counter ideals that challenge the oppression of patriarchy. Rituals often provide forums and spaces for reflection and strategy building. Dialogues across castes and ages take place within these spaces that reveal an awareness of gender injustice (Harlan 2007; Erndl 2007).

Rituals may always have existed in the lives of many Hindu women but their contents or specifically how women experience them is understudied. Women-only rituals provide useful insight into how religious women perceive and are often critical of practices such as dowry. Erndl identifies social spaces existing before and after the ritual possession of a woman known as a *Mataji*. During these moments women from different age groups, castes and social positions sit and chat freely. Erndl states that in lives where very few opportunities for social interaction exist because time is largely used to perform domestic tasks limiting women's movements outside the home, rituals present important opportunities for female collectivity. Out of these moments of sharing and social intimacy can emerge possible solutions to the challenges women face as is also shown in my case studies presented here. Erndl gives an example of a woman who is helped by the time she spent with other women in these pre-ritual spaces to work through a course of action to confront her husband's violent behaviour. Such spaces are missed by non-governmental organisations (NGOs), yet hold a wealth of insights into the lives of women. The social spaces created by rituals are, as she describes them, cracks in the patriarchal system which offer NGOs the opportunity to appreciate the experiences and agency of women whose lives they hope to affect and can also enable more effective communication between those active in anti-dowry campaigning. Informal spaces could work alongside those publicly created spaces used in female empowerment and self-help strategies in South Asia. For example the Mahila Samakhya programmes throughout India begin with the creation of female-only spaces within which women can feel safe talking about and sharing experiences of abuse (Subramaniam

2006). The inclusion of religious spaces could draw in more women to wider transnational anti-dowry campaigns. Research such as that cited here has made women's religious lives more visible and has highlighted the potential such spaces could offer activists working on dowry. More research could be useful on the role that religion can play in empowering women to eradicate dowry.

Conclusion

In this paper I argued that religion is largely absent from research into dowry and dowry-related violence and when it is cited as a factor the link is not sufficiently thought through. Religion should occupy one strand of an interlocking multi-disciplinary approach to the study of dowry, dowry-related violence and other forms of violence against women. This approach can help to avoid overly simple and inaccurate perceptions of why dowry happens, but does not help activism to end dowry. For example, some literature has tended to over-focus on legislation as the primary route through which dowry could be eradicated (see Basu in this volume). Palriwala in her paper presents dowry as a spider's web. It is now accepted that dowry continues to exist because of a deeply embedded gendered ideology that considers women to be inferior to men. I have argued that religion is one aspect that contributes to sustaining a particular cultural and social environment that allows dowry to flourish. As this volume shows the reasons for dowry's embeddedness in South Asia continue to be researched. It is in understanding the pervasiveness of dowry that this notion of a spider's web is important. However, the strands that comprise it must draw on a range of social science disciplines. Evidencing the link between religion and dowry is difficult because religion's impact is largely invisible, penetrating the fabric of people's lives through spoken but also unspoken normative values and ideals. The strength of this link is determined by how powerful religion is thought to be as a force shaping socio-cultural relations and practices. My paper is also in part a critique of social science disciplines that in general do not often include religion in their analysis. Here I have argued that although its role should not be overstated, religion through its relationship to culture has contributed to the existence of dowry and dowry-related violence and that the pervasive nature of the religious patriarchal environment within which dowry exists must have some bearing on how and why it has evolved and continues to exist. The inclusion of religion can help researchers and activists understand the pervasive nature of dowry and the gender ideology on which it depends. In furthering knowledge on dowry perhaps religion can also help bring to the fore anti-dowry strategies practised by some women but not visible to the wider activist network.

Notes

[1] I have changed the names of my informants and restricted the amount of detail I give about them in order to ensure their disguise. Although this case study may lack detail I believe it is still of value as an illustration of how some Hindu women reconcile different aspects of their own tradition.

References

Agarwal, B. 2000. 'Two Poems on Sita' in *Questioning Ramayanas: A South Asian Tradition*. ed. P. Richman. Delhi: Oxford University Press.

Angro, M. 2004. *The Culture of the Sacred: Exploring the Anthropology of Religion*. Prospect Heights: Waveland Press.

Asad, T. 1987. 'Are There Histories Without People? A review article'. *Society for Comparative Society and History.* pp. 594–97.

———. 1993. *Genealogies of religion: Discipline and reasons of power in Christianity and Islam*. Baltimore: Johns Hopkins Press.

Basu, S. 2001. *She Comes to Take Her Rights. Property and Propriety*. New Delhi: Kali for Women.

Bell, C. 1997. *Ritual Perspectives and Dimensions*. New York and Oxford: Oxford University Press.

Bennett, C. 1996. *In Search of the Sacred: Anthropology and the Study of Religions*. London: Cassell.

Beyer, P. 1994. *Religion and Globalization*. London: Sage.

Bloch, M. 1986. *From Blessing to Violence: History and Ideology in the Circumcision Ritual of the Merina of Madagascar*. Cambridge and New York: Cambridge University Press.

Bose, M. ed. 2004. *The Ramayana Revisited*. Oxford: Oxford University Press.

Bowen, J. 2002. *Religions in Practice. An Approach to the Anthropology of Religion.* Boston and London: Allyn and Bacon.

Bowie, F. 2000. *The Anthropology of Religion: an introduction.* Oxford: Blackwell.

Bradley, T. 2006. *Challenging the NGOs: Women, Religion and Western Discourses in India.* London and New York: IB Tauris.

———. forthcoming January 2009. 'Physical Religious Spaces in the Lives of Rajasthani Village Women: The ethnographic study and practice of religion in development'. *Journal of Human Development.*

Chacko, E. 2003. 'Marriage, development, and the status of women in Kerala, India'. *Gender and Development.* 11(2).

Crapo, R. 2003. *Anthropology of Religion: The Unity and Diversity of Religions.* Boston and London: McGraw Hill.

Dhruvarajan, V. 1996. 'Hinduism, Empowerment of Women, and Development in India.' *Labour Capital and Society.* 29. pp. 1–2.

Diesel, A. 2002. 'Tales of Women's Suffering: Draupadi and other Amman Goddesses as Role Models for Women'. *Journal of Contemporary Religion.* 17(1). pp. 5–20.

Dobia, B. 2000. 'A garland of talking heads for the goddess: some autobiographical and psychoanalytic reflections on the western Kali' in *Is the Goddess a Feminist? The Politics of South Asian Goddesses.* eds. A. Hiltebeitel and K. Erndl. New York: New York University Press.

Doniger, W. 1991. *The Laws of Manu.* London and New Delhi: Penguin Classics.

Emerson Dobash, R.E. and R.P. Dobash. 1998. *Rethinking Violence against Women.* London: Sage.

Erndl, K. 1992. *Victory to the Mother: The Hindu Goddess of North West India in Myth, Ritual and Symbol.* New York: Oxford University Press.

———. 2007. 'The Play of The Mother: Possession and Power in Hindu Women's Goddess Rituals' in *Women's Lives, Women's Rituals in the Hindu Tradition.* ed. T. Pintchman. Oxford: Oxford University Press.

Feldhaus, A. 1995. *Water and Womanhood: Religious Meanings of Rivers in Maharashtra.* New York: Oxford University Press.

Flueckiger, J. 1996. *Gender and Genre in the Folklore of Middle India.* Delhi: Oxford University Press.

Froerer, P. 2007. 'Disciplining the Saffron Way: Moral Education and the Hindu Rasthra'. *Modern Asian Studies.* 41: 5.

Fruzzetti, L. 1990. *The Gift of a Virgin: Women, Marriage and Ritual in a Bengali Society.* Delhi: Oxford University Press.

Garg, A. 2001. 'Countering Violence against Women in Rajasthan: Problems, Strategies and Hazards'. *Development.*

Geertz, C. 1973a. 'Deep Play: Notes on the Balinese Cockfight' in *The Interpretation of Cultures.* New York: Basic Books.

———. 1973b. 'Thick Description: towards an interpretive theory of culture' in *The Interpretation of Cultures.* New York: Basic Books.

111

Glaizer, S. 2003. *Selective Readings in the Anthropology of Religion: Theoretical and Methodological Essays*, Westport, CT: Praeger.

Gold, A. and G. Raheja. 1994. *Listen to the Heron's Words. Re-imagining Gender and Kinship in North India*. Berkeley, CA: University of California Press.

Good, A. 1991. *The Female Bridegroom: A Comparative Study of Life Crisis Rituals in India and Sri Lanka*. Oxford: Clarendon.

Harlan, L. 2007. 'Words That Breach Walls: Women's Rituals in Rajasthan' in *Women's Lives, Women's Rituals in the Hindu Tradition*. ed. T. Pintchman. Oxford: Oxford University Press.

Hawthorne, S. 2004. 'Rethinking subjectivity in the gender-orientated study of religions: Kristeva and the subject in process' in *Gender, Religion and Diversity: cross cultural perspectives*. eds. U. King and T. Beattie. London and New York: Continuum.

Hess, L. 1999. 'Rejecting Sita: Indians Respond to the Ideal Man's Cruel Treatment of His Ideal Wife'. *Journal of the American Academy of Religion*.

Hicks, D. eds. 2002. *Ritual and Belief: Readings in the Anthropology of Religion*. Boston and London: McGraw Hill.

Hiltebeitel, A and K. Erndl. eds. 2000. *Is the Goddess a Feminist? The Politics of South Asian Goddesses*. New York: New York University Press.

Johnson, P. and A. Johnson. 2001. 'The Oppression of Women in India'. *Violence Against Women*. 7(9).

Joshi, V. and R. Hooja. 1997. 'Popular Vrats and Vrat Kathas: Women and Patriarchy'. *IDSJ Working Paper Series*. no. 079.

Kakar, S. 1981. *The Inner World A Psychoanalytic Study of Childhood and Society in India*. Delhi: Oxford University Press.

———. 1993. *Identity and Adulthood*. Delhi: Oxford University Press.

Kapadia, K. 1995. *Siva and her Sisters: gender, caste and class in rural south India*. Boulder, CO: Westview Press.

Kapur, R. and B. Crossman. 1994. 'Women and Hindutva'. *WAF Journal* 5. http/waf.gn.apc.org/j5p42.htm.

Kelkar, G. 1992. 'Stopping the Violence Against Women: Fifteen Years of Activism in India' in *Freedom Violence: Women's Strategies from Around the World*. ed. M. Schuker. Washington DC: OEF International.

King, U. 1995. *Religion and Gender*. London: Wiley Blackwell.

———. 2005 'Religion and Gender' in *Macmillan Encyclopaedia of Religion*. ed. L. Jones. USA: Macmillan Reference Books.

King, U. and T. Beattie. eds. 2004. *Gender, Religion and Diversity: cross cultural perspectives*. London and New York: Continuum.

Kishwar, M. 1996. 'Yes to Sita, No to Ram! The continuing popularity of Sita in India'. *Manushi*. Jan-Feb.

———. 2000. 'Yes to Sita, No to Ram: The Continuing Hold of Sita on Popular

Imagination in India' in *Questioning Ramayanas: A South Asian Tradition*. ed. P. Richman. New Delhi: Oxford University Press.

Knott, K. 1996. 'Hindu Women, Destiny and Stridharma'. *Religion*. 26.

Kwok Pui-lan. 2002. 'Unbinding Our Feet: Saving Brown Women and Feminist Religious Discourse' in *Postcolonialism, Feminism and Religious Discourse*. eds. Laura E. Donaldson and Kwok Pui-lan. NewYork and London: Routledge. pp. 62–81.

Lambek, M. ed. 2002. *A Reader in the Anthropology of Religion*. Oxford: Blackwell.

Leslie, J. 1989. *The Perfect Wife (Stridharmapaddhati)*. Delhi: Oxford University Press.

———. ed. 1991. *Roles and Rituals for Hindu Women*. London: Pinter Publishers.

———. 2005. 'Gender and Hinduism' in *Macmillan Encyclopaedia of Religion*. ed. L. Jones. 2nd ed. USA: Macmillan Reference Books.

Mathur, K. 2004. *Countering Gender Violence: Initiatives Towards Collective Action in Rajasthan*. New Delhi: Sage.

———. 2007. 'Body as Site, Body as Space: Bodily Integrity and Women's Empowerment in India'. *IDSJ Working Paper Series*. no. 148.

McIntosh, E. 2007. 'The Concept of Sacrifice: A Reconsideration of the Feminist Critique'. *International Journal of Public Theology*. 1.2.

McKean, L. 1996. *Divine Enterprise: Gurus and the Hindu Nationalist Movement*. Chicago: University of Chicago Press.

Miller, B.D. 1981. *The Endangered Sex: Neglect of female children in rural North India*. New York: Cornell University Press.

Morris, B. 1987. *Anthropological Studies of Religion: an Introductory Text*. Cambridge: Cambridge University Press.

Narayan, U. 1997. *Dislocating Cultures: Identities, Tradition and Third World Feminism*. New York: Routledge.

Narayana Rao, V. 2004. 'When does Sita cease to be Sita? Notes towards a Cultural Grammar of Indian Narratives' in *The Ramayana Revisited*. ed. M. Bose. Oxford: Oxford University Press.

Pauwels, H. 2004. 'Only You: The Wedding of Rama and Sita, Past and Present' in *The Ramayana Revisited*. ed. M. Bose. Oxford: Oxford University Press.

Perez, R. 2002. 'Practising Theory through Women's Bodies, Public Violence and Women's Strategies of Power and Place' in *Feminist Post-Development Thought Rethinking Modernity Post-Colonialism and Representation*. ed. K. Saunders. London: Zed Books.

Pintchman, T. ed. 2007. *Women's Lives, Women's Rituals in the Hindu Tradition*. Oxford: Oxford University Press.

Prasad, S. 1999. 'Medicolegal Response to Violence Against Women in India'. *Violence Against Women*. 5(5).

Puttick, E. 1998. 'The Problem of Sexual Abuse in New—and Old—Religions' in

Religion and Sexuality. eds. A. Hayes, W. Porter and D. Tombs. Sheffield: Sheffield Academic Press.

Rajagopal, A. 2001. *Politics after television: Hindu nationalism and the reshaping of the Indian public.* Cambridge: Cambridge University Press.

Rappaport, R. 1999. *Ritual and Religion in the Making of Humanity.* Cambridge: Cambridge University Press.

Richman, P. ed. 1992. *Many Ramayanas: The Diversity of a Narrative Tradition in South Asia.* Delhi: Oxford University Press.

———. ed. 2000. *Questioning Ramayanas: A South Asian Tradition.* New Delhi: Oxford University Press.

Sagade, J. 2005. *Child Marriage in India. Socio-Legal and Human Rights Dimensions.* Oxford: Oxford University Press.

Sarkar, T. 2001. *Hindu Wife, Hindu Nation: community, religion and cultural nationalism.* New Delhi: Permanent Black.

Sarkar, T. and Butalia U. 1995. *Women and right-wing movements: Indian experiences.* London: Zed Books.

Scupin, R. 1999. *Religion and Culture and Anthropological Focus.* New Jersey: Prentice Hall.

Subramaniam, M. 2006. *The Power of Women's Organizing: Gender, Caste, and Class in India.* Lanham, MD: Lexington Books (imprint of Rowman and Littlefield).

Sutherland, S. 1989. 'Sita and Draupadi: Aggressive Behaviour and Female Role-Models in the Sanskrit Epics'. *Journal of the American Oriental Society.* 109(1).

———. 1992. *Bridging Worlds. Studies on Women in South Asia.* Delhi: Oxford University Press.

———. 2000. 'The Voice of Sita in Valmiki's Sundarakanda' in *Questioning Ramayanas: A South Asian Tradition.* ed. P. Richman. Delhi: Oxford University Press.

Suthren Hirst, J. 1997. *Sita's Story.* Norwich: Religious and Moral Education Press.

Thomas, S. 2005. *The Global Resurgence of Religion and the Transformation of International Relations.* New York: Palgrave Macmillan.

Tomalin, E. 2006. 'The Thai Bhikkhuni Movement and Women's Empowerment'. *Gender and Development.* 14(3). pp. 385–97.

Van der Veer, P. 1994. *Religious Nationalism: Hindus and Muslims in India.* Berkeley, CA: University of California Press.

Vohra, S. 2003. 'The Practice of Dowry from the Context of Hinduism'. *Critical Half.* 1(1).

Whitehouse, H. and J. Laiulaw. 2004. *Ritual and Memory: Toward a Comparative Anthropology of Religion.* Walmtcreek, CA: Alta Mira Press.

Young, K. 1995. 'Introduction' in *Women in Worlds Religions.* ed. A. Sharma. Albany, NY: State University of New York Press.

Young, S., A. Sharma, and K. Young. eds. 1991. *Annual Review of Women in World Religions.* vol. 1. Albany, NY: State University of New York Press.

Trends and Patterns in Dowry Transactions
Evidence from North and South India

SONIA DALMIA and PAREENA G. LAWRENCE

1. Introduction

The transfer of wealth at the time of marriage in the form of bride price or dowry is known to have varied regional distribution in India. Social scientists, for instance, have often pointed to the long-standing history of distinctness between North and South India with respect to their kinship organisations, structural patterns of inheritance and the resulting types of monetary transfers at marriage. While most of North India is typified by a patrilineal inheritance system and the exclusion of women from property rights, a patrilocal residence system with exogamy,[1] hypergamy[2] and the unilateral flow of gifts from the bride's family to the groom's family (or dowry) (Trautmann 1993), states in the South are characterised by a recognition of women's rights to land, small distances of marriage migration with endogamy,[3] isogamy[4] and a prevalence of bride price and/or reciprocity[5] (Kolenda 1984; Dyson and Moore 1983; Miller 1981; Dumont 1966).

Although the heterogeneity in factors influencing marriage transactions in North and South India have been widely discussed in the literature, a large number of the studies are based on ethnographies of single villages or districts that are now over 35 years old (Srinivasan 2005; Epstein 1973; Goody 1973; Tambiah 1973; Boserup 1970; Karve 1953). In addition, surveys of villages and districts as part of particular ethnographic studies and of households (AIDWA 2002) describe a community's norms and not the actual functioning of the marriage markets. Moreover, in the past several decades marital transfers in India have experienced a number of changes including the adoption of dowry as the mandated form of marriage payment for a marriage to occur in both the North and the South, and an increase in the magnitude of payments across regions and communities. Changing demographics of the marriage markets, increased heterogeneity amongst marriageable men, wealth dispersion with modernisation and Sanskritisation[6] are some of the reasons provided in the literature for the consequent dissolution of a North-South dichotomy in marriage payments (Edlund 2006; Anderson 2001; Bhat and Halli 1999; Rao 1993; Caldwell, Reddy and Caldwell 1983; Srinivas 1984). Therefore, data from a large survey of a representative sample is essential to provide not only a more inclusive picture of the regional socio-cultural variation in marriage payments in India but to also document the theoretically debated switch in dowry from its primary historical role of an intergenerational wealth transfer to its contemporary role of a marriage payment.

In this paper, we take a step in that direction. We combine unique retrospective data on marriage transactions and on the personal and family traits of marriage partners collected from the states of Uttar Pradesh (North India) and Karnataka (South India) with demographic data on the size of the marriageable population from the Indian Census.[7] This secondary data set is unique because it is one of a kind both with respect to its size and the level of detail it provides on the variables required for the analysis. Our objective is to examine the patterns and variations in dowry transactions based on cultural, social, demographic and economic organisation of each region in North and South India.

While the data used in this study reflects marriages that occurred between 1956 to 1994 in rural India, and it is likely that some of the traditional practices referred to are undergoing change in contemporary urban India, the fact that traditions and practices are relatively slow to change in rural India means that we are confident that regional differences in kinship organisations, cultural and social practices that are discussed here are still applicable and worth exploring.

This paper is arranged as follows. Section 2 reviews the most widely accepted explanations for the regional distribution of marital transactions in India and changes in their practice over time. Section 3 describes the data and the research methology employed; Section 4 outlines the results; and Section 5 concludes the paper.

2. Regional distribution of marital transactions in India: practice and debate

Hindu custom in India historically prohibited daughters from inheriting land, particularly in the presence of a male heir and this practice still dominates in North India. A daughter's right to her parental property was instead restricted to *stridhan* or dowry, paid at the time of her marriage in the form of moveable assets. Consequently, dowry in India came to be viewed as a pre-mortem inheritance of a female progeny (Carroll 1991; Sharma 1984).

While the nature of marriage transactions in India is largely driven by the strict limitations on women's access to parental property, the regional distribution of monetary transfers, particularly the contrast in marriage payments observed between North and South India, is attributed to the differences in the prevailing kinship organisations. Consequently, the magnitude and frequency of dowry payments in the North is explained by its preference for exogamy, marriage with non-kin of the same or higher social status and the exclusion of women from property rights. In contrast, South India is characterised by marriage between close relatives (preferably cross-cousins), status equity between the 'bride givers' and the 'bride takers,' and recognition of women's right to parental property. The practice of bride price and the tendency towards equal sharing of marriage expenses by the families of the bride and groom are a reflection of these features of mate selection in the South (Dyson and Moore 1983; Miller 1981; Dumont 1966; Karve 1953).

Though organisation of kinship, exogamy and hypergamy may have an impact on the size of dowry payments, they constitute too small a proportion of dowry-paying marriages to serve as the only explanation for the existence and regional variations in marriage transactions in India. Goody (1973) suggests that women's role in production and hence their contribution to subsistence can also shed light on the type of marriage and marriage payments existing in a society. Accordingly, dowries in North India are sometimes explained by its plough-based agricultural production of wheat (primarily), which excludes women from production, while bride price in the South is explained by the region's intensive rice-growing economy, which is dependent on women's labour (Miller 1981; Boserup 1970).

However, Gulati (1975) and Schlegel and Eloul (1987) find that even regions such as Kerala, Assam and Orissa that are characterised by low woman labour contribution sometimes exhibit bride price as the common form of marriage payment. Moreover, the area of low woman labour force participation stretches from Punjab to Assam (North India to East India). The southern state of Kerala also falls into this category. What is surprising about these states is that they include both wheat-producing areas (theoretically low woman labour demand) as well as rice-producing areas (theoretically high woman labour demand) (Harrell and Dickey 1985). This suggests that there are other factors that affect woman labour from participating in agricultural activities and therefore broad conclusions about geographical distribution of bride price and dowry cannot be totally derived from the dominant mode of production in a society.

Perhaps the explanation lies in the close correlation between class, caste or socio-economic position and marriage transactions in India. For instance, Goody (1973), Miller (1981) and other researchers have observed that the custom of dowry is more prevalent in the upper castes and classes, while bride price or reciprocity is more frequent in the lower castes and lower income segment of society. Consistent with this argument is the notable pattern of exclusion of women from economic production roles by caste/class. Women of lower caste/class are less subject to restrictions concerning employment outside the realm of production and reproduction within the household (Van Willigen and Channa 1991). With land tenure patterns showing a higher percentage of landless population in the South, reciprocity in the region may just be an outcome of there being relatively more lower class families compared to the North (Schwartzberg 1961).

Miller (1981) found dowry payments to be more common among both upper and lower castes and classes in the North. In the South she found reciprocity among propertied groups and bride price among the non-propertied groups. However, casting doubt on claims that class or caste can explain marriage transactions are the findings by Caplan's (1984) study that focused on southern India. It revealed an equal sharing of wedding costs by the households of the bride and groom at lower levels of caste and class compared to the wealthy and prominent and no evidence of bride price payments, irrespective of class affiliations.

Compounding a clear understanding of the regional variations in marital transfers are two important changes observed in the marriage markets over the last several decades that are claimed to have reduced the regional differences in India. First, dowry has progressively replaced other forms of marriage payments particularly in communities and castes that traditionally paid a bride price. Second, this switch has been accompanied by a significant increase in the value of dowry payments over time (Bhat and Halli 1999; Rao 1993; Billig 1991, 1992; Caldwell, Reddy and Caldwell 1983).

Researchers have speculated that the diffusion and inflation of dowry is a result of the changing demographics of marriage markets that has led to a numerical surplus of marriageable women over men, also called the 'marriage squeeze' argument in India. This phenomenon reverses the overall sex ratio that reflects more men relative to women. Caldwell, Reddy and Caldwell (1983) cite population growth, an ever increasing supply of young men

119

and women, with the cultural prescription of older men marrying younger women as the primary reason for the observed changes in marriage payments. Because of population growth there are always more young people than older people in any particular age group band, and because men are marrying younger women there are always more women of marriageable age for them to choose from: thus young women are literally 'squeezed' from the marriage market and have to compete for husbands with ever increasing dowries. This argument will be further developed and explained with the use of Census data from India later in this paper.

Although the marriage squeeze argument offers a compelling theoretical explanation for the rise in contemporary marriage payments in India, it has not received strong and consistent empirical support. For instance, Rao (1993), using data on 141 marriages for the period 1923–1978 from a retrospective survey in 1983 conducted by the International Crop Research Institute for the Semi-Arid Tropics (ICRISAT), finds empirical support for the marriage squeeze as a primary cause of dowry inflation in three districts of South Central India.[8] But he does not explain why the average monetary transfers in one of these districts are negative in spite of an increase in the number of marriageable women compared to men in the region. Moreover, in an attempt to replicate Rao's methodology and results by employing the same ICRISAT data set, Edlund (2000) could not replicate his results nor could she find any statistical support for his marriage squeeze argument. Casting further doubt on his own marriage squeeze argument, Rao (2000) was unable to replicate his 1993 results in his response to Edlund's findings. In this paper we empirically investigate the marriage squeeze argument and its impact on dowries in both North and South India.

Social anthropologists on the other hand describe rising dowries as a consequence of Sanskritisation, a term used by Srinivas (1984) to explain the adoption of upper-caste patterns of behaviour by members of lower castes as a means of acquiring higher social status. Sanskritisation explains the observed shift in marital payments from bride price to dowry in all castes as upwardly mobile behaviour. However, since real dowries (payments adjusted for inflation) have increased even in castes that historically paid a dowry (Rao 1993) a supplementary explanation by some researchers links these changes to new economic opportunities concomitant with modernisation (Anderson 2001). A person's occupation, education and hence potential wealth were traditionally determined by caste in India. With a breakdown of traditional caste barriers that followed modernisation and growth, economic opportunities became available to all and increased the dispersion of income within caste groups. In the resulting wealth-based society, a groom's income-earning potential replaced caste (Anderson 2001). The changes in marriage payments are conjectured to be an outcome of economic growth and development, which has increased wealth heterogeneity within each caste and resulted in a class system based on wealth (see Palriwala in this volume).

Moreover, with modernisation, grooms become a more heterogeneous group (better educated, higher incomes, better health) relative to brides due to a male bias in the development process that increases gender inequality within a stratified society such as India (Anderson 2001). Consequently, equilibrium marriage payments[9] emerge to offset quality differences between the grooms and the brides and the spread of dowry is associated with a growing necessity to compete for 'desirable' men in the marriage market (Lindenbaum 1981).

Theoretically multiple factors such as cultural, economic, social and demographic differences determine the regional distribution of marriage transactions in India. While individual factors have received significant attention in the socio-economic literature on marriage transactions in India, their individual and combined effects in a multivariate regression analysis are not as well documented by economists and other social scientists (Agarwal 1995). The intensity and inter-relationship of individual factors vary across regions with differences for example in their kinship organisation and mode of production.[10] The multivariate analysis in the next section incorporates these factors and tests the arguments with data on marriage transactions and the personal and family traits of marital partners.

3. Data and methods

The data is obtained from two secondary sources. The 1995 retrospective survey[11] of rural households in regions of North and South India provides information on heterogeneity in individual and household characteristics and on marriage transactions. The Indian Census data from 1951–1991 is used to reconstruct the marriageable age gender ratios to provide a more accurate measure of the 'marriage squeeze' variable than a simple sex ratio construct.

To distinguish between several interpretations of dowry, we follow a simple multivariate regression analysis that models it as a function of (i) the individual and household characteristics of the bride and groom such as age, height and education and their family's landholdings; (ii) control variables such as caste, region, year of marriage and (iii) the marriageable age gender ratio that represents the size of the marriage squeeze. This framework allows us to empirically examine and analyse the impact of these individual variables on dowry payments in both North and South India and explain these payments as rational human behaviour.

Additionally, we disaggregate our data by decade, and by region, and compute simple cross tabulations and correlations to explore the prevailing conditions in these marriage markets.

Retrospective sample data

Data regarding individual and household characteristics and associated marriage transactions were obtained from the retrospective household surveys from a 1995 study titled 'Poverty, Gender Inequality and Reproductive Choice' undertaken by the National Council of Applied Economic Research (NCAER), New Delhi, between July and September 1995. Seventy rural villages representing five districts of Uttar Pradesh in North India (henceforth North) and five districts of Karnataka in southern India (henceforth South) were chosen to represent the agroclimatic diversities of each state resulting in a sample size of 1878 households. In Uttar Pradesh, the districts were Almora, Faizabad, Ghazipur, Mathura and Muzaffarnagar, while those in Karnataka were Bidar, Dakshin Kannad, Kodagu, Kolar and Mysore. The study covered 35 villages in each state averaging 7–9 villages per district. The total numbers of rural households included in our study are 465 in Uttar Pradesh and 572 in Karnataka. This is because only Hindu households, where both spouses responded to the questionnaire and no relevant data were found to be missing, were included.[12] We excluded non-Hindu households from our analysis because, having very diverse cultures and traditions with respect to marriages, they represent a small part of our data set and could distort the analysis. This allows us to focus our attention on Hindu families that comprise 80 per cent of the Indian population and among whom dowry has become a persistent problem.

While questions about the accuracy of retrospective data can always be raised, a person's memory of a marriage transaction is likely to be more accurate than of other events, as marriage is the central event in the life of most women/families in India, and the exchange of a dowry is a planned event that usually has a substantial impact on a household's assets. However, it is interesting to note, then, that most couples in the survey disagreed on the amount of dowry/bride price exchanged. Women in general reported higher amounts compared to their husbands from a minimum of Rs 6,000 to a maximum of Rs 200,000. To correct for this discrepancy we consider an average of the exchange reported by the husband and wife in each household.

Most marital transactions at the time of marriage occurred on both sides reflecting ritual gift exchange between the families of the bride and groom. The households reported amounts both received and paid in cash and in kind, including transfers of gold and silver, land, livestock and consumer durables, valued according to prices prevailing during the year of marriage. The term total dowry, refers to the monetary value of all gifts including cash and gifts in kind made from the bride's household to the groom's household. To isolate the 'price' component of the marriage transaction or the transfers, the net value of the transfer, net dowry, is considered. Net dowry deducts the monetary value of all gifts made from the groom's household to the bride's household from total dowry. If net dowry is positive, the transaction is a dowry and if it is negative, the payment is a bride price.

One problem with the total and net dowry variable is that the dowries in the sample were made at vastly different points in time, since the earliest marriage dates in 1956 to the most recent in 1994; these are referred to as nominal total dowry and nominal net dowry. All nominal dowry values were then converted to constant 1994 prices or to real total dowry and real net dowry. In addition, the transfer of cash between families as part of the marriage transaction was also looked at. The nominal net cash transfers were calculated and converted to constant 1994 prices (or real values). These figures are reported in the next section. Nominal net cash transfers refer to the value of all cash transfers made from the bride's household to the groom's household minus the cash transfers, if any, made from the groom's household to the bride's household.

Also, data on pre-marital incomes of bride's and groom's households were not available in the secondary data set, but are likely to be highly correlated with parental household wealth just prior to the time of marriage and thus that is used as a proxy for pre-marital income. In addition, it is important that the wealth variable reflects the bride's and groom's household wealth positions before or at the time of marriage and not at the time the retrospective survey was undertaken (which was several years and sometimes decades later in 1995). This is because, for households whose children married before 1995, the 1995 wealth assessment of the groom's household would be an overestimate and that of the bride's household would be an underestimate, of the actual amount, given that a dowry had already been transferred from the bride's to the groom's household before that year. Fortunately, the 1995 retrospective survey did obtain information on parental household wealth (in terms of cultivable land owned in acres) of both marriage partners just before they were married.

Further, we use the bride's and groom's age at marriage in years), height (in centimetres) and education (years of schooling completed), with the landholding variable described above to represent their individual and household traits. To examine if the size of dowry provided to one daughter decreases with the number of daughters in the household (due to resource constraints), the percentage of daughters in the bride's household is included to measure the proportion of female children in the household. Moreover, to examine if the practices of exogamy or endogamy affect dowry payments, the variable 'distance of marriage migration (in kilometres)' is included in the multivariate regression analysis as a measure of the distance between the bride's parental household and her marital household.

To control for cohort-specific trends in the choice of a spouse and marital transfers the year of the marriage is included as an independent variable. Finally, since caste in India is positively related to the socio-economic standing of a household it is included in the regression analysis as a dummy variable taking the values 0 or 1 to estimate its impact on the size of dowry transferred from the bride's household to the groom's household. The caste variable, ranging from upper, middle to lower, is generally indicative of a household's relative hierarchical status and rank within the community. The term upper is used to represent the two highest castes, which include the Brahmans (priests and educated) and Kshatrias (rulers and aristocrats); middle to represent Vaisia (landlords and business men) and Sudras (peasants and working class); and lower to represent the Scheduled Castes (untouchables), Scheduled Tribes (aboriginals) and Other Backward Classes.

Marriage market gender ratios

Marriage transactions signal a gender bias in the intensity of competition for marital partners. Men are the competitors when bride prices are observed and women are the competitors when they bring dowry into the marriage (Becker 1991). The observance of escalating dowries in India would, thus, lead to the conclusion that women are in competition for 'available men.' While it is true that the ratio of women to men in the total population has been steadily falling since the beginning of the century, suggesting an advantage for women in the marriage market which should result in women being paid to marry, it is important to recognise that cultural and social norms in India dictate that women marry at younger ages than men (Goyal 1988). Therefore, the overall women to men ratio would not be a very accurate measure of the availability of potential spouses in the marriage market. A more precise measure of surplus brides or grooms and the resulting 'marriage squeeze' would be to consider the ratio of women of marriageable age to men of marriageable age and the trend of this ratio (Rao 1993). To indicate the relative numbers of men and women who attain marriageable age in a particular cohort data were compiled on age and gender composition for the period 1951–1991 from the Indian Census reports of 1961, 1971, 1981, 1991. The ratio of women in the 10–19 age group and men in the 15–24 age group was used to construct the marriage squeeze index for North India, and the ratio of women in the 15–24 age group and men in the 20–29 age group was used for South India to correspond with the age brackets in which the largest proportion of women and men marry in the two regions.

Figure 1 presents the overall ratio of women to men (sex ratio) in the total population of India and the marriageable age sex ratio in the North and South using data from the Indian Census. Comparison of these figures exhibits the ability of age hypergamy and population growth to reverse a woman marriage market advantage. So what was originally a surplus of men in the general population (sex ratio below 1) turns into a surplus of women after age hypergamy and population growth is factored in (sex ratio above 1).

The next section discusses the general social and demographic characteristics of the study population and analyses the data to understand regional variations in the extent and type of marriage payments in India.

Figure 1: Women to Men Sex Ratio and Marriageable Age Gender Ratio

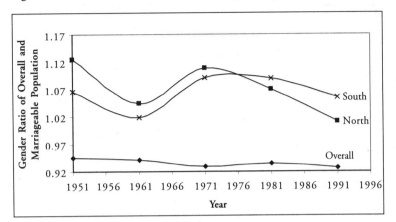

4. Results

Summary statistics for the two regions are reported in Table 1. Real monetary transfers, whether they are in the form of total dowry, net dowry or net cash transfers, are significantly higher in the North compared to the South indicating different patterns of gift-giving and dowry payments in the two regions. Moreover, even with the large time span over which marriages occurred in our data, we find no evidence of a pure bride price payment in the South. Thus, we find consistent support for the anthropological findings of a decline in the practice of bride price in South India.

In comparing the individual and household characteristics of the groom and the bride, it is interesting to note that while grooms are older, taller and more educated than their brides in both regions, the parents of the brides owned more land than the parents of the grooms. This indicates a fair degree of male hypergamy in the sample. Furthermore, the bride's household has a larger percentage of daughters compared to the groom's household in both regions, which is intriguing but we cannot find any reasonable explanation for this.

Contrary to popular belief, with respect to exogamy in the North and a taste for endogamy in the South, the sample statistic

Table 1: Summary Statistics of the Sample

Variable	North Mean	South Mean
Real total dowry (constant 1994 rupees)	189406.2 [273416.3]	131490.8 [137684.7]
Real net dowry (constant 1994 rupees)	169053.3 [200001.8]	124526.5 [130641.2]
Real Net cash transfer (constant 1994 rupees)	37555.2 [170801.6]	19863.1 [114830.6]
Distance of marriage migration	30.64 [83.1]	27.58 [51.19]
% of daughters in the bride's household	57 [19.99]	61.26 [20.13]
% of daughters in the groom's household	36.04 [23.47]	34.19 [22.54]
Groom's age at marriage	19.06 [5.04]	24.78 [4.09]
Bride's age at marriage	14.93 [3.99]	17.26 [3.13]
Groom's schooling (years)	5.94 [4.99]	3.77 [4.34]
Bride's schooling (years)	1.53 [3.14]	2.48 [3.79]
Groom's height (cms.)	163.35 [6.62]	163.98 [6.52]
Bride's height (cms.)	150.92 [6.17]	152.98 [8.67]
Groom's father's landholdings (acres)	2.74 [5.33]	3.40 [7.32]
Bride's father's landholdings (acres)	3.34 [9.57]	3.39 [9.23]
Year of marriage (19__)	78.26 [8.95]	80.28 [8.41]
% of high caste.	35	51
% of medium caste	47	35
% of low caste	18	14
Sample size (N)	465	572

* Standard deviations in parentheses

reveals no significant difference in two regions as both have similar distance of marriage migration. Next, looking at marriage and caste, in rural India virtually all marriages are arranged within caste and sub-caste boundaries. This is also true of our data as we find no inter-caste marriages in the sample. This is perhaps reflective of the rural nature and the time period, 1956–1994, covered by our data set and not of marital patterns observed in contemporary urban India.

Figure 2: Average Real Net Dowry by Region and Year of Marriage

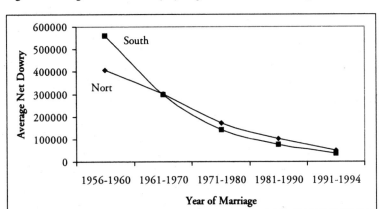

Figure 3: Average Real Net Cash Transfers by Region and Year of Marriage

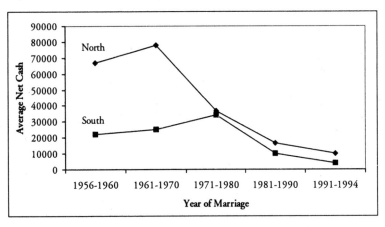

A look at the trend in real marital transfers over time in Figures 2 and 3 reveals that both net dowry and net cash payments have fallen significantly over time on average in the two marriage markets. While the net dowry transfers for the most part are slightly higher in the North than in the South, a breakdown of dowry down to its cash component exhibits a significant gap in cash transfers in the two regions particularly before 1971. Although the North leads the South in the average amount of cash transferred to the groom's household at the time of marriage, the huge lead it had in the period before 1971 narrows substantially thereafter.[13]

The decline over time in these real net dowry and real net cash transfers is indeed a surprising result as one often hears of escalating dowry payments and the consequent domestic violence against women associated with it. These results do not diminish the reality of the heavy financial burden that dowry imposes on families with daughters. Indeed if one looks at nominal net dowry payments over time (Figure 4), the increase is clearly evident in the North while it has stayed fairly constant in the South, even though in real terms these marriage transfers show a decline in both rural North and South India.[14]

Next we examine the patterns in real net dowry transfers and cash transfers in the two regions by caste. The patterns reported

Figure 4: Average Nominal Net Dowry Transfers by Region and Year of Marriage

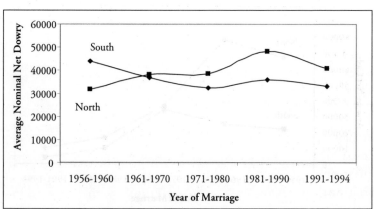

Table 2:   Average Real Net Dowry Transfers and Real Cash Transfers
by Region and Caste

Caste	N	*North*		N	*South*	
		Real net dowry	*Real cash transfer*		*Real net dowry*	*Real cash transfer*
1956-1994						
Lower	83	143708.5	34192.14	82	98773.85	688.759
Middle	220	140287.6	42862.57	199	124017.6	10221.76
Upper	162	221103.1	31960.04	291	132131.2	32091.14
1956-1960						
Lower	4	208333.3	29487.18	0	0	0
Middle	6	334935.9	92202.56	1	608974.4	32051.28
Upper	2	1017628	32051.28	1	512820.5	17948.72
1961-1970						
Lower	20	318446	93317.22	11	187476.9	84.17508
Middle	54	246418.1	76017.19	28	285548.1	13268.85
Upper	18	453211.6	69185.27	24	343864.5	43771.04
1971-1980						
Lower	26	120069.5	10808.87	31	133428.3	880.7558
Middle	68	122651.2	52528.33	72	136928.5	18688.85
Upper	65	244471.4	32275.47	102	149188.9	55708.09
1981-1990						
Lower	27	54247.54	12656.44	28	53901.65	880.5823
Middle	69	93336.47	14312.43	67	76921.9	2331.627
Upper	66	131997.2	20292.08	121	79465.37	15801.85
1991-1994						
Lower	6	23176.52	16256.13	12	32640.43	427.3504
Middle	23	33329.64	5406.11	31	34276.2	1476.563
Upper	11	93017.37	15177.12	33	42830.14	9010.539

in Table 2 reveal the strong hold that caste affiliation has on net dowry transfers in the two regions. Irrespective of the period in question, upper caste households pay higher dowries. This relationship echoes conclusions in the literature that finds increasing dowries associated with stratified societies, which emphasise preserving of status through marriage (see Anderson 2001). The pattern of net cash transfers is not as consistent indicating that they are not as clearly related to caste affiliation of marital households.

Table 3 examines the relationship between average dowry and education of the bride and the groom by region. As expected, education enhances the value of a groom to the family of the prospective bride, though more so in the North than in the South. The effect of a bride's education on dowry, although ambiguous, does indicate that her higher education fails to have a negative impact on the amount of real net dowry transferred. Even though the sample size (see N in Table 3) shows relatively more educated women in the South than the North, the education level of the bride is not negatively related to real net dowry transfers in the two regions. In fact the data in Table 3 show no consistent pattern between education of the bride and real net dowry payments.

The data in Table 4 display the relationship between familial landholdings, an indicator of household wealth in rural India, and real net dowry. There are no consistent patterns between real net dowry and landholdings indicating weak support for the inheritance role of dowries in either regions or what is referred to in the literature as *stridhan*.

Table 3: Average Real Net Dowry by Education of the Bride and Groom

	Groom			Bride	
Education	North	South	Education	North	South
0	138109.4 (N=152)	117177.8 (N=243)	0	162878.2 (N=354)	109482 (N=345)
1–5	147116.3 (N=65)	148298.8 (N=164)	1–5	174866.3 (N=65)	172400.6 (N=117)
6–8	166335.6 (N=66)	129415.6 (N=71)	6–8	266533.2 (N=23)	130598.2 (N=49)
9–12	191513.5 (N=152)	84964.43 (N=72)	9–12	147053.2 (N=20)	100094.3 (N=50)
>12	265546.9 (N=30)	142182 (N=22)	>12	171089.4 (N=3)	171177.5 (N=11)

Table 4:   Average Real Net Dowry by the Groom's and Bride's Father's Landholdings

Groom's Father's Landholding			Bride's Father's Landholding		
Landholdings (acres)	*North*	*South*	*Landholdings (acres)*	*North*	*South*
0–5	141906.2 (N=384)	127406.3 (N=440)	0–5	157459.3 (N=398)	123382.8 (N=477)
5–10	247300.3 (N=50)	94836.68 (N=72)	5–10	242232.5 (N=32)	99362.39 (N=51)
10–15	301986.3 (N=16)	130672.8 (N=35)	10–15	305752.6 (N=6)	163632.3 (N=17)
>15	461401.6 (N=15)	150743.8 (N=25)	>15	219138.7 (N=29)	167641.6 (N=27)

The Pearson correlation coefficients between bride and groom characteristics[15] are reported in Table 5. They reveal a highly significant and positive association between the individual traits of the groom (age at marriage, schooling and height) and the respective traits of the bride. The correlations, thus, reflect positive assortative mating across all traits of the bride and groom in the two regions. They also reveal that grooms from wealthy families in the North are successful in obtaining brides with more family wealth. Although positive in the two regions, the correlation between the landholdings of the bride and groom households is significantly stronger in the North than in the South. This therefore, casts doubt on claims in the literature that status equity with respect to wealth in the South, between 'bride takers' and 'bride givers' is an important consideration in arranging marriages (Goody 1973). In addition, we find a number of significant cross-assortative mating effects. For example, grooms with more education are matched with brides from wealthier family backgrounds, and wealthier grooms marry older, taller and more educated brides.

Table 6 reports on the average difference in groom and bride characteristics by region. Of utmost interest here is the large and persistent age gap between brides and grooms in the South in contrast to a similar large and persistent education gap in the North.

Table 5: Pearson Correlation's between Bride and Groom Traits in the North and South

Characteristics	North	South
Age/Age	0.7859	0.5747
	[0.000]	[0.000]
Education/Education	0.4324	0.6490
	[0.000]	[0.000]
Height/Height	0.3224	0.5643
	[0.000]	[0.000]
Landholding/Landholding	0.1502	0.0751
	[0.001]	[0.072]
Upper/B. Landholding	0.2234	0.1762
	[0.000]	[0.000]
Upper/G. Landholding	0.3692	0.2429
	[0.000]	[0.000]
G. Edu/B. Landholding	0.0928	0.1677
	[0.045]	[0.000]
B. Edu/G. Landholding	0.1329	0.1417
	[0.004]	[0.001]
B. Height/G. Landholding	0.1485	0.0524
	[0.001]	[0.211]
B. Age/G. Landholding	0.0574	0.0828
	[0.217]	[0.047]

P-values in parenthesis (The p value represents the probability of obtaining a value that is different from 0, so the lower the number the more statistically significant the relationship between the two variables)

Table 6: Average Difference in the Traits of the Groom and Bride in the North and South

Period	North			South		
	Edu. (years)	Landholdings (acres)	Age (years)	Edu. (years)	Landholdings (acres)	Age (years)
1956–60	3.25	6.01	4.08	0	1.01	7.5
1961–70	3.64	−0.67	4.41	1.29	−0.25	8.3
1971–80	4.72	−0.89	4.63	1.06	−1.02	7.73
1981–90	4.68	−0.72	3.69	1.69	−0.05	7.38
1991–94	4.15	−0.86	3.32	0.77	−0.56	6.53

Finally, we use Ordinary Least Squares (OLS) regression to estimate the dowry function for the two regions to examine how real monetary transfers differ and vary by the characteristics of the bride and the groom. The regression analysis helps in two ways: (i) to establish causality and (ii) to estimate independently the impact of individual characteristics such as education, age and height on net dowry while holding the influence of other factors, such as caste or wealth of bride's household, constant. The results presented in Table 7 reveal that while the North places a premium on male education, the groom's age, which perhaps reflects stability in career and income, is valued more in the South. Although his height makes him significantly more marketable in the North, it has little impact in the South. For the same characteristics in a bride, her educational attainment raises the amount of dowry slightly more in the South than in the North, but her age at marriage has no significant impact in the two regions. Interestingly, the coefficient on her height is negative and statistically significant for the North and positive and statistically significant for the South. This suggests that a taller bride brings a higher dowry in the South and a lower one in the North. Thus, height penalises brides in the South but is an asset for brides in the North.

The impact of the bride's father's landholdings, a proxy for rural household wealth, on net dowry is not significant in the North, suggesting that dowry does not serve as a pre-mortem inheritance of the bride in the region. The landholding variable on the other hand has a marginally negative and significant impact in the South indicating that dowry does not serve as a pre-mortem inheritance but perhaps the negative sign reflects the recognition of a woman's right to land in the southern region compared to the North. While membership in the upper caste, which reflects status, has a positive and significant impact on marriage payments in the North, it fails to have a significant effect in the South. This result is contradictory to prior research on South India, according to which, while groups at the top of the hierarchy tend to follow dowry customs, those at the lower end of the spectrum practise bride price (Tambiah 1973). Our results however, concur with

Table 7: Ordinary Least Squares Estimates of the Net Real Dowry Function for North and South India

Variable	North 1	South 3
Intercept	11.969* [0.023]	6.027 [0.108]
Groom's age at marriage	.1470719 [0.508]	.507770* [0.016]
Bride's age at marriage	.2290148 [0.305]	.201364 [0.986]
Groom's schooling (years)	.135002* [0.000]	.0214213 [0.537]
Bride's schooling (years)	.0838999* [0.044]	.2635736* [0.000]
Groom's height (cms.)	1.553278** [0.065]	1.204951 [0.128]
Bride's height (cms.)	−1.334937** [0.093]	1.146777* [0.030]
Groom's father's landholdings (acres)	.034531* [0.012]	−.041908* [0.000]
Bride's father's landholdings (acres)	.0081906 [0.478]	−.0218448* [0.040]
% of daughters in the bride's household	.0009352 [0.560]	−.0005726 [0.669]
Middle caste	.0808465 [0.379]	−.0470961 [0.583]
Upper caste	.371403* [0.001]	.0994498 [0.236]
Year of marriage	−.0707493* [0.000]	−.0788966* [0.000]
Distance of marriage migration	−.0004071 [0.285]	.000733 [0.162]
Marriageable age gender ratio (woman/man)	2.1459** [0.061]	−1.8186 [0.191]
Sample size (N)	465	572
The variation in real net dowry from its mean explained by the regression (R^2)	0.5338	0.5452

Table 7: *contd.*

	North	South
The variation in real net dowry from its mean explained by the regression adjusted for degrees of freedom (Adjusted R²)	0.5193	0.5337
F-statistics	36.80	47.69

P-values in parenthesis (This represents the probability of obtaining a value that is different from 0, so the lower the number the more statistically significant the variable)
* Significant at the 5 per cent level
** Significant at the 10 per cent level

more recent work that found dowry to be an all-caste phenomenon in South India (Srinivasan 2005). In our results we find no practice of bride price in the South and caste does not appear to have an impact on dowry payments either. This could be because other individual and household characteristics of the bride and groom besides status measured by one's caste may be relatively more important in determining dowry payments in the region.

The groom's household wealth, measured by his father's landholdings, has a positive and significant effect on dowry in the North, thus confirming the claims that female hypergamy is widely practised in the North (Billig 1992; Miller 1981; Srinivas 1984). In the South, on the other hand, the groom's father's landholdings have a significant negative effect on the net dowry transfer suggesting that reciprocity is more prevalent among the propertied groups in the region. Overall, it appears that there is a dominant urge to contract a desirable marriage in the North, one in which the status of the groom and his family is higher than that of the bride and her family with respect to education, income and wealth.

The percentage of daughters in the bride's household had no significant impact on dowry in either region, as one might have suspected that fathers with more daughters may pay a smaller individual dowry because of resource constraints. The distance of marriage migration variable also has an insignificant impact on net dowry, thus providing no statistical support for the claim that practices of exogamy or endogamy influence marital payments in India.

The marriageable age gender ratio, a measure of the degree of the marriage squeeze, has been singled out by researchers as having the most influence on the diffusion and inflation of dowry payments and hence contemporary marriage behaviour in India. Our results indicate that this variable has a positive and significant impact on net dowry in the North but no impact in the South. Thus, the evidence to support the marriage squeeze argument is mixed at best.

The estimated coefficient on year of marriage reiterates what we see in Figures 2 and 3 that there has been a significant decrease in real net dowry over time in both rural North and South India. This contradicts not only a large body of evidence obtained from ethnographic studies of the Indian marriage market, but also prior analysis of these markets, with an emphasis on rural South-Central India (Rao 1993). The consensus in the literature has been that real dowry payments have increased across India over the last four decades (Epstein 1973; Lindenbaum 1981; Caldwell, Reddy and Caldwell 1983; Srinivasan 2005), but we find evidence to the contrary.[16] There are several reasons that could support our findings. First, our study reflects practices in rural India and not urban India where the escalation of dowry has been severe. Second, we look at dowry as net transfers and not as total transfers and third we look at real dowry values and not nominal dowry. Based on our definition of dowry and the size of our sample compared to other ethnographic studies we find the real value of net dowry to be declining marginally in the regions of both North and South India.

5. Conclusions

The regional distribution of marriage transactions in India is determined by a myriad interactive factors that include cultural norms, economic, social and demographic factors. The nature of residence, inheritance system, kinship organisations, personal and household characteristics of the bride and the groom and prevailing market conditions with respect to availability of a suitable groom all affect the dowry payment.

Overall, the results do support the ethnographic evidence pointing to a broad North-South dichotomy in marriage transactions in India. Although our results provide strong evidence that real net dowry and cash payments are significantly lower in the South compared to the North, no evidence of a pure bride price payment in the South is borne out by our data. Furthermore, the practice of making cash transfers at the time of marriage is more common in North India and relatively less of a tradition in the southern part of the country. Irrespective, in both rural North and South India, a significant downward trend in real net dowry payments is clearly evident over the entire time period of our data (1956–94).

As far as specific factors that affect variations in dowry payments in both regions are concerned, our results suggest that dowry should not be viewed as the pre-mortem inheritance of a bride. We also find no evidence that the size of dowry depends on the distance at which marriages are contracted from the natal home of the bride. We do, however find evidence to indicate the existence of strong patterns of female hypergamy in the North and reciprocity among propertied groups in the South. Hierarchical status as measured by caste also appears to have a significant positive impact on the size of dowry for the North.

The marriageable age gender ratio, which has been championed by several demographers and researchers as being the primary cause of dowry inflation in India, is found to have inconclusive or mixed effect on marriage transactions in the two regions. This variable is found to be positive and significant for the North but insignificant for the South leading us to question the overall validity of the marriage squeeze argument. The results do however support the theory that dowry acts as an equilibrium marriage payment and is partially determined by quality differences between brides and grooms and their respective families. Evidence indicates strong regional differences in the valued traits of bride and groom such as education, age and height.

In summary, while it is impossible to single out a set of factors that explain the regional variations in dowry payments in India, this paper allows us to systematically examine the variation in marriage transactions across four decades and shed important light on the different theories and explanations that prevail in the literature on the North-South dichotomy in marriage transactions in India. A better understanding of different theories and identification of the factors that contribute to the prevalence and the escalation of dowries is crucial if we are to suggest effective policy recommendations that will curb the spread and growth of the practice of dowry in India.

Appendix

Model specification

The dowry function that is estimated in this chapter can be specified as:

$$Ln(D) = \alpha + \sum_{i=1}^{n} \beta_i Ln(G_i) + \sum_{i=1}^{m} \gamma_i Ln(B_i) + \sum_{i=1}^{k} \phi_i(R_i) + \varepsilon_i$$

where D is dowry, the G_i's are the measure of the groom's individual and family attributes, B_i's are the measure of the bride's individual and family attributes, R_i's are the exogenous dowry shifters such as caste and region to capture the endogamous nature and customs of the marriage markets and ε_i is the error term. Also, since theory does not suggest a preferred functional form and given the expected non-linear relationship between the attributes of the bride and groom and dowry we use a double-log specification based on fit and significance to estimate dowry as a function of the groom's individual and family attributes, the bride's individual and family attributes, and exogenous dowry shifters such as caste and region to capture the endogamous nature and customs of the marriage markets.

Notes

[1] Marriage involving a larger distance of marriage migration and taking place outside kin group.

[2] Marriage of a woman to a man of the same or a higher social status.

[3] Marriage between consanguines (of the same kin or lineage), which often results in a short distance of marriage migration.

[4] Marriage between partners of equal status.

[5] Reciprocity in marriage refers to gift-giving on both sides of approximate equal value such that the net gift is zero.

[6] Sanskritisation refers to the adoption of upper-caste patterns of behaviour by members of lower castes as a means of acquiring higher social status (Srinivas 1984).

[7] Retrospective data is from a 1995 study titled 'Poverty, Gender Inequality and Reproductive Choice,' undertaken by the National Council of Applied Economic Research, India. Details about the data are presented in Section 3.

[8] The districts surveyed were Akola and Sholapur in the state of Maharashtra and Mahbubnagar in the state of Andhra Pradesh.

[9] Price paid by the bride's parents to cement a good alliance for their daughter.

[10] Multivariate analysis allows us to estimate the impact of a particular factor, e.g. education of the groom, on dowry holding the impact of all the other variables, e.g. caste of groom, constant.

[11] See Note 7.

[12] Hindu households comprised 87 per cent of the total households in both states, 12 per cent of the households in Uttar Pradesh and 11 per cent of the households in Karnataka were Muslims, with Christians and Sikhs representing the remaining one per cent and two per cent respectively (*Report on Poverty, Gender Inequality and Reproductive Choice*, vol. I, II, III [1996]. Delhi: Institute of Social Studies Trust).

[13] We must caution that the period 1956-60 witnessed only 12 marriages in the North and two in the South, thus the data for those particular years should be interpreted with care.

[14] It is possible that we find a decline in dowry payments due to systematic underreporting of dowry and cash transfers as individuals may fear investigation led by women's groups which have become increasingly more active in prosecuting dowry related activities.

[15] The Pearson correlation coefficient or the sample correlation coefficient is standardised and ranges between 1 and −1 and measures the degree of association, positive or negative between two variables (call them X and Y). A positive value for the correlation implies a positive association (large values of X tend to be associated with large values of Y and small values of X tend to be associated with small values of Y). A negative value for the

141

correlation implies a negative or inverse association (large values of X tend to be associated with small values of Y and vice versa).

[16] We could not effectively test the argument in the literature related to a region's relatively low woman labour force participation and its impact on marriage transactions. The primary occupation of women in rural areas is working on the family farm. Unfortunately we do not have information on woman labour force participation before marriage, after marriage or at the time marriage transactions were made.

References

AIDWA (All India Democratic Women's Association). 2002. Report on the workshop on expanding dimensions of dowry. 1–2 Sept. New Delhi, India.

Agarwal, B. 1995. *A Field of One's Own: Gender and Land Rights in South Asia.* New York: Cambridge University Press.

Anderson, S. 2001. 'Why Dowry Payments Declined with Modernisation in Europe but are Rising in India'. *Journal of Political Economy.* 111(2). pp. 269–310.

Becker, G.S. *A Treatise on the Family.* Cambridge: Harvard University Press.

Bhat, P.N.M. and S.A. Halli. 1999. 'Demography of Brideprice and Dowry: Causes and Consequences of the Indian Marriage Squeeze'. *Population Studies.* 53. pp. 129–48.

Billig, M.S. 1991. 'The Marriage Squeeze on High Caste Rajasthani Women'. *Journal of Asian Studies.* 50. pp. 341–60.

———. 1992. 'The Marriage Squeeze and the Rise of Groomprice in India's Kerala State'. *Journal of Comparative Family Studies.* 23. pp. 197–216.

Boserup, E. 1970. *Women's Role in Economic Development.* New York: St. Martin's Press.

Caldwell, J.C., P.H. Reddy and P. Caldwell. 1983. 'Causes of Marriage Change in South India'. *Population Studies* 37. pp. 343–61.

Caplan, L. 1984. 'Bridegroom Prices in Urban India: Class, Caste and "Dowry Evil" Among Christians in Madras'. *Man.* 19. pp. 216–33.

Carroll, L. 1991. 'Daughter's Right of Inheritance in India: A Perspective on the Problem of Dowry'. *Modern Asian Studies.* 25. pp. 791–809.

Dumont, L. 1966. 'Marriage in India—The Present State of the Question. 111. North India in Relation to South India'. *Contributions to Indian Sociology.* 9. pp. 90–114.

Dyson, T. and M. Moore. 1983. 'On Kinship Structure, Woman Autonomy and Demographic Behavior in India'. *Population and Development Review.* 9(1). March. pp. 35–60.

Edlund, L. 2000. 'The Marriage Squeeze Interpretation of Dowry Inflation: A Critique'. *Journal of Political Economy.* 108(6). pp. 1327–33.

——. 2006. 'The Price of Marriage: Net *vs.* Gross Flows and the South Indian Dowry Debate'. *The Journal of the European Economic Association, papers and proceedings.* 4(2–3). pp. 542–51.

Epstein, T.S. 1973. *South India: Yesterday, Today and Tomorrow.* London: Macmillan.

Goody, J. 1973. 'Bridewealth and Dowry in Africa and Eurasia' in *Bridewealth and Dowry.* eds. J. Goody and S.J. Tambiah. New York: Cambridge University Press.

Goyal, R.P. 1988. *Marriage Age in India.* Delhi: B.R. Publishing Corporation.

Gulati, L. 1975. 'Woman Work Participation: A Study of Inter-State Differences'. *Economic and Political Weekly.* 10. 1&2. pp. 35–42.

Harrell, S. and S.A. Dickey. 1985. 'Dowry Systems in Complex Societies'. *Ethnology.* 24. pp. 105–20.

Karve, I. 1953. *Kinship Organization in India.* Bombay: Asia Publishing.

Kolenda, P. 1984. 'Woman as Tribute, Woman as Flower: Images of "Woman" in Weddings in North and South India'. *American Ethnologist.* pp. 98–117.

Lindenbaum, S. 1981. 'Implications for Women of Changing Marriage Transactions in Bangladesh'. *Studies in Family Planning.* 12(11). pp. 394–401.

Miller, B. 1981. *The Endangered Sex: Neglect of Female Children in Rural North India.* Ithaca: Cornell University Press.

Rao, V. 1993. 'The Rising Price of Husbands: A Hedonic Analysis of Dowry Increases in Rural India'. *Journal of Political Economy.* 101. pp. 666–77.

——. 2000. 'The Marriage Squeeze Interpretation of Dowry Inflation: Response'. *Journal of Political Economy.* 108(6). pp. 1334–35.

Schlegel, A. and R. Eloul. 1987. 'Marriage Transactions: A Cross-Cultural Code'. *Behavior Science Research.* 21. pp. 118–40.

Schwartzberg, J.E. 1961. *Occupational Structure and Levels of Economic Development in India: A Regional Analysis.* Census of India. Monograph no. 4, Delhi: Office of the Registrar General.

Sharma, U. 1984. 'Dowry in North India: Its consequences for Women and Property' in *Women and Property: Women as Property.* ed. Renee Hirschon. London: Croom Helm. pp. 62–74.

Srinivas, M.N. 1984. *Some Reflections on Dowry.* Delhi: Oxford University Press.

Srinivasan, S. 2005. 'Daughters or Dowries? The Changing Nature of Dowry Practices in South India'. *World Development.* 33(4). pp. 593–615.

Tambiah, S.J. 1973. 'Dowry and Bridewealth and the Property Rights of Women in South Asia' in *Bridewealth and Dowry.* eds. J. Goody and S.J. Tambiah. New York: Cambridge University Press.

Trautmann, T.R. 1993. 'The Article of Dravidian Kinship' in *Family, Kinship and Marriage in India.* eds. P. Uberoi et al. New Delhi: Oxford University Press.

Van Willigen, J. and V.C. Channa. 1991. 'Law, Custom, and Crimes Against Women: the Problem of Dowry Death in India'. *Human Organization.* 50(4). pp. 369–77.

The Spider's Web
Seeing dowry, fighting dowry

RAJNI PALRIWALA

Political action and social activism against the practice of dowry has varied in scope, form and language over the centuries in the Indian subcontinent. There is evidence from Chola inscriptions in Tamil Nadu and from 18th century edicts from the Maharaja of Jaipur (following petitions from 'respectable' families to control prestations around marriage) that dowry and related marriage expenses were viewed as pernicious as they pauperised such families. It is only in the last century, however, that political action on the issue mobilised people beyond the court and elite[1] and a discourse emerged linking dowry and women's emancipation. During the social reform movements of the late 19th and early 20th centuries, the national movement and the pre-Independence women's movements, dowry did not attract the attention that the issues of child marriage, widow remarriage, women's property rights, and women's right to modern education and employment did. With the faith in legislation held by the leaders of the newly independent nation and their aversion to radical measures, the 1961 Dowry Prohibition Act and other 'women-friendly laws' were considered sufficient to the purpose.

By the late 1970s, and with the Report of the Committee of the Status of Women in India (CSWI), this was no longer considered to be true by activists and women's studies scholars. This was a result of various factors discussed in the CSWI report: flaws in the

144

law itself; the spread and intensification of dowry; growing socio-economic and gender inequalities after Independence rather than a transformed society/economy/polity; and the radicalisation of the women's movement with a critique of the liberal feminism of the mainstream national movement (Agnihotri and Palriwala 2001; Kapur and Cossman 1996; Kumar 1993). A more complex web of interrelated factors emerged revealing dowry to be an embedded part of a much deeper structure, to break which would require multiple interventions.

In the 1980s, dowry, but more so what came to be named as dowry deaths, became one focus of a renewed women's movement, which variously questioned aspects of family, personal life, violence against women, and governance (Palriwala 1985/forthcoming). The symbol of the young, burning wife whose dowry had not satisfied the greed of her husband and in-laws for material goods in life came to the fore in public discourse. The Dahej Virodhi Chetna Manch, a platform of more than 25 organisations, was formed with a central focus on amendments to the 1961 Dowry Act. The amended Dowry Prohibition Act was passed in 1984 and became effective in 1985.

In 2002 the All India Democratic Women's Association (AIDWA), the largest mass organisation of women in India today and which had been at the forefront of the 1980s anti-dowry campaign, decided to conduct a large-scale, all-India survey on dowry.[2] This paper presents the findings of that survey as one aspect of the movement against dowry. To understand why AIDWA decided to conduct that survey requires a brief consideration of the nature and outcomes of the earlier mobilisation of the 1980s and the critiques raised of it as well as issues of perspective and strategy from within the Indian women's movement. Some of the findings of the survey for selected states are presented here and show the changes in the practice of dowry and its implications. An analysis of these findings returns us to the debates over perspectives within the women's movement. The survey was stimulated by the need to rethink strategies in furthering the struggle against dowry. I conclude with the metaphor of dowry as a spider's web to capture its numerous threads and peoples' multiple encounters with dowry, which point to the need for an equally complex set of responses to eradicate it.

In keeping with the theory/practice theme of this volume, this paper looks at both the changing dimensions of dowry as well as strategies to eliminate the practice, asserting that despite difficulties the last must remain a goal. Other papers in this volume (Rozario; Jehan; Dalmia and Lawrence) also show that dowry is deepening rather than weakening through processes of globalisation, while some (Bradley; Basu) urge that anti-dowry campaigns be strengthened. The volume emphasises that not only is research able to highlight and make visible the continued injustices caused by dowry, it thence becomes a significant tool in the formation and practice of social activism.

Rethinking the campaign against dowry

Questions have been raised if, rather than dowry, the 'distortions' of dowry, had been central to the 1970s-80s movement.[3] In various fora of AIDWA it was suggested that rather than the structural causes of violence, it was violence alone and its policing that had come to the fore.[4] A close study of the anti-dowry movement shows that the analyses and the extent to which dowry itself was at issue varied with organisations and time, even as campaign 'messages' were read and circulated unevenly (Palriwala 1985).[5] After two decades and more, it is evident that dowry deaths and domestic violence, and the need for concerted legal and administrative action against the taking of dowry, were the visible components of the public campaign in the 1980s.[6] Individual case work, vital to the movement, centred on the retrieval of dowry as a woman's property. While the work of some organisations and institutions could be described as marriage counselling, others aimed to provide support to women to restart their lives away from their grasping husbands and in-laws. The 'politically correct' stance in public discourse became one of opposing dowry (Kishwar 1988), more so in regions where the impact of mass women's organisations had been wider.

Yet, large numbers of people in their everyday lives, and also those in the police, judiciary and government, continued to insist that it was 'dowry demands' and not the practice of dowry which presented the problem and must be opposed.[7]

In the subsequent period, five critiques of the anti-dowry movement of the 1970–80s and the 1985 law were raised by various individuals, including feminist scholars, anti-feminist commentators as well as newly formed men's groups which led to ongoing, high voltage, and intricate debates. Only a broad overview of these critiques is provided here. One critique was that dowry was in fact a woman's right to property, her only property right, which had been wrongly undermined in the campaign (Kishwar ibid.; Bradley this volume). The second was that 'dowry violence' had come to subsume all forms of domestic violence and oppression that women experienced, to the detriment of the larger feminist struggle (Agnes 1992; Kishwar ibid.; Bradley ibid.) The third was that women, their natal families, and activists were misusing the anti-dowry law (Kishwar 2000; Basu, this volume), a proposition put forward not only by the families and men accused of dowry crimes, but also by judges in the sessions and high courts. The fourth was that hoping to fight dowry through law and in particular criminal law was itself a misplaced strategy (Agnes 1992; Menon 1999). The fifth, and obverse thread of the above four, voiced at various fora and in the media, argued that evidence of the spiralling spread of dowry was an indication of the failure of the women's movement to fight dowry and in that failure was its culpability (Bradley ibid.; Basu ibid. on the limitations of anti-dowry campaigning).

Women's organisations and activists have countered these views along various lines.[8] Given the content, form, compulsions, and common sense perceptions of dowry, viewing it as an alternative to women's rights to natal and conjugal property, albeit transitory, reinforced the perception of daughters as burdens and marginal members of the family as well as their lack of economic rights (Palriwala 1989, 2003). Hence, while property rights were at issue, dowry could not be accepted as even an interim right. It was closely intertwined with women's social and economic dependence on marriage, their self-perceptions, and their vulnerability to domestic controls (Kapur and Cossman 1996; Agnihotri and Palriwala 2001; Bradley ibid.; Basu ibid.). The anti-dowry movement had never suggested that dowry violence was the only form of domestic violence or gender oppression. In their campaigns, some women's groups and the Dahej Virodhi Chetna Manch had emphasised the links between dowry and multiple aspects of women's inequality and oppression (Palriwala 1985/forthcoming; 1989). The very success of the 1980s anti-dowry movement in bringing it to public notice and condemnation became a problem as it became the language in which women could draw attention to the violence they experienced within their conjugal families (Kapur and Cossman ibid.). That did not mean that dowry-related violence should not have been attacked, but that the attack had to be widened. Law by itself could not change society and polity, but could be an instrument in that struggle even as misuse of law and state machinery by the powerful was evident in many contexts in India (Mazumdar 2000; Kapur and Cossman ibid.). When existing power equations were threatened, those who were least able to use, let alone misuse, the law were accused of malfeasance by those whose position and assertion of right was being questioned. This was evident when Dalits demanded the registration of cases under the Anti-Untouchability laws and women under pro-women laws. It also had to be recognised that the women's movement, alert and dynamic though it was, could not transform structures of gendered inequality in which dowry was embedded without a much larger socio-political movement which addressed a range of socio-economic inequalities and the very raison d'être of the state (Karat 2005).[9]

These debates brought into relief the need for the women's movement to readdress and rethink its strategy around dowry and the legal and social means to tackle it. Dowry had become a central factor in a range of social abuses as well as new forms of gendered violence, in particular sex selective abortion. Ongoing discussions within AIDWA emphasised the need to go beyond a focus on violence and the recording of or response to violent incidents, to the factors behind the violence and the links to other forms of discrimination and subordination. The experiences of the organisation's vast membership (nearly 10 million covering 20 states in 2001) and multiple, local-level activities suggested that dowry had spread with a new intensity and virulence since the early 1990s, with 'dowry rates' growing exponentially, while opposition to it was increasingly muted. Its national conference in 2001 raised questions on the effects on dowry and related social practices of the rapidly changing socio-economic dynamics of a post-liberalisation India and globalised world. How were the links between dowry and a range of anti-women social practices, including son preference rituals and caste discrimination, shifting or being reinforced? AIDWA members had found that the available material was either a couple of decades old, or limited in its scope and geographic coverage, or did not go beyond figures of dowry-related violence from police records or burns wards of hospitals. Bradley (ibid.), in a review of the early work of the dowry project, also finds this to be so. This volume addresses these gaps of regional coverage and the methodologies used to collect contemporary data on dowry, as in the presentation of economic data by Dalmia and Lawrence mapping north/south regional differences. The question of how dowry and its repercussions were to be addressed in the current struggle for gender equality and emancipation so as to draw not just women but also men into the struggle was important for AIDWA (AIDWA 2003; Karat 2005). The necessity for the last is also argued by Jehan (this volume).

From these discussions three conceptual themes can be highlighted. These are the entanglement of gender oppression and other social oppressions; the dialectic between gender relations and apparently non-gendered social, economic, and political processes; and the relationship between various types of law and society. These issues emerged from specific questions regarding the past and future praxis of a movement against dowry. The charge of misuse of law had to be answered concretely. Basu (this volume) relates the feminist movement's loss of focus on dowry to the failure of legislation to stop the practice. Were lacunae in the law the problem or was its implementation at fault? Was a civil law required in addition to the criminal law? Was dowry to be addressed as a moral issue in the manner of earlier social reform campaigns or as a gender and feminist concern? As in those earlier campaigns, was there again a mistake of universalising women across class and caste from the experience and practices of particular sections?[10] The last question reflected a continuing stream in the women's movement in India, articulated now in the post-colonial critique of over-simplified representations of women and various 'others', both in academia and activism. This methodological critique frames the present volume also. Not only was a new description of the practice required, it was time to restudy what dowry did, what it reflected, and what it realised in daily social relations, in the economic and political life of the nation and the people who made it up. Only then could the strategy for gender equality as related to dowry be charted out.

Restudying dowry: the 2002 AIWDA survey

The decision by AIDWA in 2001 to undertake a massive, all-India survey has to be related to a development in its own activism. In the late 1980s, its Delhi unit, Janwadi Mahila Samiti, (JMS) had planned to undertake a large study of dowry, both to deepen its understanding of the phenomenon and to examine the impact of the anti-dowry movement. Initial work was begun, but the study did not take off. From the mid-1980s onwards, there were repeated discussions in its various state units as well as in its all-India fora of the need to undertake studies on problems which the organisation confronted in the course of its mass-based activities. Not only was there little knowledge or experience of these issues in the movement, they were often not being addressed in research in the detail and manner which AIDWA activists sought in the particular locations that they worked in. There had been a massive, quantitative growth in gender-related research, but not necessarily on the issues or experiences which poor and working class women brought to the organisation or on the questions which it was asking about these issues (Karat 2005). Further, AIDWA had a responsibility to place the experience of its vast membership and myriad activities and the understanding drawn from these within the larger arena of feminist knowledge and activism. Readings of feminist movements in India as well as analyses of gender issues were flawed by the silencing of this perspective and experience (see Note 2). Activists, who were also social science researchers, and other scholars were drawn into this discussion and in the early 1990s they set up a research centre, the Indian School of Women's Studies and Development (ISWSD), with which AIDWA collaborated. However, the demands of research had continually to be balanced with the exigencies of everyday struggle and the demands of immediate issues, in which time for research received less priority.

The dowry survey was the first research activity in which urban and rural AIDWA members across the country were involved in large numbers. The investigators were not trained researchers, but women with experience in organising poor women, in legal counselling, and interventions in cases of dowry and dowry deaths. An epistemological point was at issue here. The involvement of local level activists, familiar with the issues, areas, and possibly with the people who they surveyed, gave the survey the insider's advantage. This meant a more immediate connection with informants and thence a closer insight into women's experiences of dowry than the micro-level methodologies, however sensitive, (employed by Basu, Jehan, Rozario, and Subramaniam) available to outsider academics. At the same time, the activists were critical of the gender and social relations of their context, which gave them an 'outsider's' view. Their activism had also given them the skills needed to conduct a survey sensitively on issues, which could not be understood through numbers alone or the immediate conversation through which data was usually collected in large surveys. The idea of praxis—of theory and political practice clarifying and building on each other—was central to the idea of the survey. Thus, it was hoped that there would be a synergy of knowledge-creation, awareness-generation, mobilisation and refinement of the politics and actions of struggle.

Regarding the survey itself, the list of questions included the location, caste, religious and economic background of the respondents, their age at marriage as well as type of marriage (whether it followed or violated any expected norms). It covered their own experience of giving and taking dowry: the occasions and moments when 'gifts' were asked for and/or given; the sorts of 'gifts' asked for or given; wedding expenses and the style of celebration; financing sources (including sale of assets and loans); and its economic repercussions. Questions were also asked about the role of boys/grooms; the attitude of girls; perceptions of the impact of education, especially girls' education; the general practice of dowry and differences between groups; changes and emerging trends in dowry; links with other social practices or trends; views on ending a bad marriage or when dowry demands were made. Information was also collected on son preference rituals and attitudes. Case studies of extreme dowry demands as well as refusals to give dowry and alternative marriages were documented.

The respondents were from two broad categories: potential givers of dowry—the parents/guardians of daughters (both female and male)—and young girls of 'marriageable' age. In a couple of states, a sample of young men was also interviewed (see also Rozario; Jehan, this volume). There was no attempt at a 'representative' sample, but a cross-section of caste, class/income, and religious groups were included in each state. The bias was towards the poor and the lower middle classes, the sections among whom AIDWA was most active, with purposive samples of Dalits and religious minorities who till recently had been marginal in much social science research. In all, there were more than 10,000 respondents from over 18 states. AIDWA activists found that in many parts, but especially in regions where there has been a history of radical and social reform movements, people were not ready to admit that they had taken or given dowry and certainly not that they had demanded it. However, there was gossip and discussion of dowry given by kin and neighbours or demanded of them by their sons-in-law. In many places, responses were very emotional and highly charged with women crying about their daughters or raging at their 'in-laws' and investigators had immediately to take on the role of counsellors and/or organisers of protest demonstrations.

In tapping the enthusiasm generated at its 2001 national conference, AIDWA rushed to undertake the survey, but did not plan adequately for the processes of collation and analysis. Only after large amounts of information came in to be put together at the various state offices was this organised, with the help of members of the ISWSD. Unfortunately, this meant that not all the questions that had stimulated the study could be addressed through the quantitative data. Another factor was the unevenness in the data, which correlated to some extent with the regional unevenness of the development of the organisation and of literate activists who could conduct the survey. In large part, this was offset by the illuminating case studies and the narratives that had been recorded with the survey. These reflected what made the AIDWA survey different from the usual large-scale surveys. The 'investigators' were committed to the study, had a long acquaintance with the areas and at times the particular informants, and were known to them.

The main findings are summarised in the following section. While some recent studies of dowry practices are drawn on, this section largely limits itself to discussions at the national workshop held to present the findings (in Delhi in September 2002) and the 2003 publication of the survey findings and workshop proceedings.[11] This enables an exploration of the knowledge-creation process and the resulting activism which the survey was embedded in and engendered.

The findings of the survey: the spread and increase in dowry

In the mid-1970s, the CSWI Report, some sociologists, and the women's movement noted that dowry had spread beyond the Hindu upper castes—the groups among whom it had traditionally been practised and restricted to as a mark of their status. The 2001 survey found that by the end of the 20th century, dowry marriage was practised among more groups of middle and lower castes of Hindus, as well as among Christians, Muslims, animists and other tribal groups, who had earlier practised bride price, bride service, or forms of bride price given the garb of dowry.[12] However, there were still groups 'on the margins' of the dominant Hindu cultural ethos, particularly tribal groups, among whom the practice was uneven.

Looking first at the surveys of guardians, respondents from middle and low ranking castes in state after state (AIDWA 2003)[13] indicated that not so long ago marriage prestations were of a different order—in quality and quantity. Apart from a few designated items, there had been no prestations at the time of their parents' marriage and in a large number of cases in their own marriage. This may be illustrated from the findings in a few regions and communities on the margins of or outside the dominant Hindu order. In Assam, the common and dominant practice had been of bride price paid by the groom or his family in kind and money (*gadhan*), as well as in labour on the farm or house of the future father-in-law (*jamai khatani*). Over 80 per cent of the guardians interviewed (in a sample of 237) said that there had been no dowry at the time of their own marriage, but at the time of their daughter's marriage 45 per cent had given dowry gifts. The giving of cash was the newest phenomenon, while jewellery and other gifts in kind were the most common. Dowry was still absent in tribal communities. Respondents suggested that dowry as a cultural phenomenon emerged in the 1960s. Its beginnings lay in the gifts given by middle class parents to daughters, in imitation of the practice among groups from other parts of the country. In the course of time, people, including girls, started to see these gifts as a daughter's legitimate right over parental property and later dowry took on a compulsory character. Some suggested that it had now become the primary requirement for marriage. For groups and regions where dowry marriage has long been the norm, respondents spoke of competition in dowry leading to rejection of prospective brides, divorce, or more harassment and that dowry gifts were seen as enhancing the status and dignity of brides at their in-laws' house.

In Tripura, as in Assam, the practice had been limited to upper caste and well-to-do families. It had been more or less absent among the middle-income and poorer families and among the middle and lower castes (Schedule Castes, Schedule Tribes and Other Backward Classes), with the groups of OBCs reporting a nominal *aashirwad* or 'blessing'. The practice of *jamai patha* or labour service by the prospective groom for his possible in-laws, which was meant to demonstrate the fitness of the groom to be a husband, had been prevalent among tribal communities such as the Jamatia, the Reang, and the Noatia. It had been 'abolished' said informants. Almost 50 per cent of upper caste Hindu guardians reported dowry at the time of their own marriage, as did Muslim parents. Dowry had now become a part of the lives of all communities in both towns and villages, but was not yet a universal practice. All upper caste parents and more than a quarter of all other groups—SC, ST, OBC, and Muslims—reported giving dowry at the time of their daughters' marriage.

In the hill regions of northern India, the prevalence of the practice varied and in many parts, informants, largely urban-based and educated, were divided on its historicity. In Simla district in Himachal Pradesh and in various districts of Uttarakhand, most argued that the practice was just over a decade old. Yet, it already had a 'compulsory' character among the Vaishnavs and Muslims. It had also emerged among poor Scheduled Castes. The emulation of caste-like behaviour and practices, including that of dowry marriage, was evident among various tribal communities. Among the Bhutias whose economic position had improved dramatically with secure government jobs, dowry had gained ground with unimaginable speed, but it was still not the common practice and there was no dowry system as such. Among specific castes as in the Jaunsar Bawar region, bride price rather than dowry, and polyandry, divorce and remarriage rather than monogamy continued to be the practice.

Among the Warli tribals of Maharashtra too, bride price remained the prevalent practice, with wedding expenses borne by the groom and his family. These costs on entertainment, food and drink had increased, however, going up as high as Rs 70,000, and there were cases where the bride's family had also spent a large amount. The sample sizes in Maharashtra (and in the hill districts of North India) were relatively small and the information has to be read qualitatively. The common opinion was that among the middle and lower ranking Hindu castes, the practice of *daez*—a cash sum given by the bridegroom to the bride's father to perform the ceremony—had been the common practice traditionally. The shift to dowry had begun at least two or three decades ago, such that only one of the respondents had been married with *daez*. However, dowries were modest, consisting of a few household utensils and jewellery. While in their own marriages, *daez* had been replaced by dowry, it was only with their own daughters' marriages in the last few years that cash sums were given to the groom.

In the states of South India, again one finds the spread of dowry in recent years to low ranking castes, tribal communities and Muslims. Scheduled Caste respondents said that in their parents' marriage, a bride price made up of clothes, animals, silver and money had been prevalent. With their own marriages, the shift to dowry was evident, but its value had been 'nominal'. Now, cash and gifts in kind were demanded and had to be given. Among Christians in Kerala it has been a long-standing practice, but Muslims of North Kerala saw the recent adoption of the custom within their own community.

In West Bengal, nearly 60 per cent informants said that marriage without dowry was impossible, but more than 40 per cent said the opposite, an even smaller percentage admitting to dowry in their own marriage and less than seven per cent in their daughters' marriages. Activists learnt of many more dowry marriages than were admitted to and some informants blatantly asserted that they would recoup the expenses of a daughter's dowry and wedding at their son's marriage. The figures from the Bengal survey reflect the nature of public discourse in the state, following the widespread mobilisation by women's organisations and the Left, attaching political stigma to dowry marriage. They also suggest, however, that those who argue for tradition and the impossibility or undesirability of change continue to be strong voices within the public discourse and a significant presence in socio-cultural practices even in states marked by a history of widespread radical mobilisation.[14] Conflict over culture, values, practices, and ideas of equality and emancipation are part of everyday life of local communities, rural and urban, and of local politics. This is entangled with conflict over immediate political and material interests and access to benefits. Thus, the struggle for gender equality and emancipation has to be continuously waged.

The findings in the geographic and political centre of the country was in keeping with that found among Hindu upper castes in most regions, but a step ahead. Almost all the respondents in the six districts of Uttar Pradesh covered in the survey had given or were planning to give dowry, though the proportion who asserted that it was a tradition was lower among 'lower' castes and Muslims than among upper and middle castes. Dalits reported that the practice had become common in the last 10–15 years. In Old Delhi, Muslims suggested that though dowry had existed 25–30 years ago it was not compulsory. It used to be simple and parents gave what they wished to and could afford. The change was visible in the period between the marriages of their first and last child with dowry amounts doubling and tripling in this time.

These and other findings of the survey suggest that not only had dowry been absent among many communities in the recent past, there are still some communities among whom it is absent or not compulsory. In other areas and groups, the spread of dowry practices and the spiralling of dowry amounts has been marked in the last 10–15 years—the years of economic liberalisation and identity politics, themes I return to later. Two aspects are to be noted of this spread. First, the time span over which the shift to dowry practices has taken place among many groups has been very short. Second, the amount being spent has significantly increased (Rozario, this volume, reports similarly in relation to Bangladesh).

Two more trends are noticeable from the narratives and other studies. One is that the amount of money that is to be spent on the marriage and the content of dowry is increasingly central to 'fixing a match'. The negotiations are conducted in myriad and subtle ways and insufficient promises of dowry lead to the breakdown of marriage discussions. Dowry has shifted from being a sign of marriage to being both an incentive and obstacle to marriage. It is the major criterion of a girl's eligibility and compatibility and certainly as critical as the marriage ritual itself. Second, as much if not more than the 'gifts', the wedding itself has become a focus. The survey questions did not allow for a specific calculation of the proportion of the non-'gift' expenses in the total wedding expenses. The burden of the former, however, was evident in the differences in scale in what people reported as expenditure on dowry and on the wedding, in people's conversations among themselves, and in the case studies. Statements like 'we do not want dowry, give your daughter what you wish. Only treat us with respect at the wedding' were often heard. In a middle class family, the groom's party/invitees may include hundreds to be fed over two days, if not also housed. It is not just the generosity, but also the creativity of the bride and her family during the marriage preparations and ceremony (to give it a 'special' character) that display the suitability and status of the match. The variety in the bride's trousseau, the food, facilities, entertainment, and 'thank you' gifts all become the markers by which the marriage and the bride are judged. Even where dowry in the strict sense may be absent, as among the Warlis of Maharashtra and the Bhutias of Uttarakhand, there has been a great increase in the cost of the wedding relative to annual income and resources of the bride's/groom's parents.

It is critical to recognise that in the description and structure of contemporary dowry, no clear distinction can be made between dowry as gifts and elaborate weddings. They are part of the same phenomenon—a daughter's marriage—and are stimulated by the same concerns of familial status and her well-being. The family of the bride has to fulfil the expectations of her in-laws and of their own families with appropriate entertainment and gift-wrapped expenditure, not only for the couple, but also for the man's parents and siblings, and for public display.

Particularly among those communities with a longer history of dowry, its structure has changed in at least three further ways. The first and most recognised change, which respondents repeatedly bemoaned, was that dowry had come to encompass and dominate the entire life of a proposed and existing marriage. Expenses on prestations and rituals were incurred from the time the match was finalised, then at the engagement and the wedding, and continued at the birth and marriage of sons and daughters. In short, 'gifts' were expected from a woman's natal family to her in-laws at every major familial event—social and/or ritual. The second shift is in the relative importance of the various life cycle rituals. From being one among a number of critical rites of passage, marriage has come to overshadow all others. In the past, among many groups funerals were more marked in terms of community involvement and feasting and hence expenditure and had been a concern for local social reformers. Dowry and marriage have pushed funerals and death aside. The third shift is in the significance of the core wedding ritual, *kanyadan*—the gift of a girl in marriage with accompanying gifts. Many no longer think of it as a ritual that every Hindu must perform at least once in his/her lifetime, even if by temporary adoption of a girl. The merit earned seems now to be outweighed by the necessary and growing costs of the wedding/dowry of a daughter. Some informants suggested that this merit can be earned through much less expenditure—donations to organisations that undertake mass marriages.

Liberalisation, identity politics, and the intensification of dowry

The survey explored the experiences of activists and the impressions of many observers regarding the spread of and inflation in dowry.

The plurality of marriage and family practices among various castes, classes, regions, and religions, particularly among Dalits, Adivasis, and Muslims were shifting, albeit unevenly, in favour of a homogenous, Hindu, upper caste model encompassed by the giving and taking of dowry and patrivirilocal[15] marriage. Earlier analyses (Srinivas 1984; Palriwala 1985; Sheel 1999) have shown that dowry in India was tied to a particular gender and caste ideology summed up in the idea of hypergamy—that a woman must marry into a family of equal or higher status rather than one that is lower than her own. In marriage, the bride and bride-givers are placed in the position of supplicant and their lower status is reaffirmed through the giving of dowry. The power of the dowry system rests also on the idea that marriage is a compulsory ritual in an individual's life and a social institution vital to the cultural and social order. Therefore, marriage cannot be left to individual choice, but has to be arranged according to appropriate norms of endogamy and exogamy of caste, clan, and village. This may vary with caste, religious community and region. The public celebration of the wedding calls the community to witness the ritual and to sanction it as a correct marriage. The pomp of the celebration also expresses the status of both sets of affines vis-à-vis each other and their wider social world.

These analyses also suggest that as mobility and liquid wealth increased due to various factors, first under colonialism and then after India's independence in 1947, all avenues to assert status, including dowry, were fostered or co-opted. In the post-liberalisation period, downward and upward mobility has intensified, while liquidity in the economy has increased. Status and economic position, whether apparent or secured, are affirmed through weddings and public displays of wealth (See also Dalmia and Lawrence, this volume). The range of goods making up dowry have long seen changes with shifts in cultural styles and consumption patterns made possible and desirable by industrial, technological and market conditions (see also Rozario, this volume). Since the late 1980s, the world of consumption has dramatically expanded and there is an unprecedented circulation of images of desired lifestyles by the media. Weddings and dowry, implicitly or explicitly, frame many advertisement campaigns of luxury and consumer goods.[16] For many in the middle and lower middle class, dowry is the means to acquire desired consumer goods, capital for investment, bribes to 'buy' secure jobs, or an investment which may draw in further wealth. To varying extents, these threads ran through the narratives of many of the respondents.

What was not so explicit in the responses, but can be inferred, is the link between the aggressive assertions and claims of 'primordial' identities—caste, clan, religion, region—and the strengthening of practices cast as tradition, including the public celebration of identity and status. Weddings and dowry are among these. Globalisation has fuelled fears of losing identity among the middle classes in particular and displays of cultural uniqueness through celebration are a response. Some respondents from communities where dowry has taken its present form only in the last 15 years or so frequently claimed it as religious tradition and a marker of their identity and culture, while others argued that it was a recent practice and/or a 'social evil' with no religious sanction.

Even as identity is asserted, the practice of dowry has widened marriage circle boundaries. Muslims in Old Delhi were divided as to whether marriage within the *biradari* (kinship community) meant more dowry or less and if they would be able to bypass social compulsions of intra-*biradari* marriage in order to strategise around dowry. In parts of South India, the guarantees of preferred kin marriage have given way to marriage with strangers, though of the same caste, who will bring in more dowry or whose economic futures match the dowry which can be given (Kapadia 1995). There is a duality here of change and continuity. In the midst of the insecurities of the new financial order and economic and social upheavals, traditional networks are held on to as safety networks, as markers of past status, and as a guide through strange and new life-forms. Thus respondents in Tamil Nadu said that they could not face their community if their children 'had love-marriage or inter-caste marriage'. People feared even mention of such practices. None were prepared to lose their ties with their community. Yet, dowry had led families to give particular ties the go-by to the extent of marriages outside the region and community.

Thus, dowry appears as a reflection and effect of macro trends in the economy, in culture, and in politics, a symbol and effect of widening economic disparities, a means to hedge economic and social uncertainties. In the process, however, it also underwrites these processes.

Compulsory marriage, compulsory dowry, and pauperisation

Indebtedness in order to meet the expenses of a daughter's marriage was widespread among informants, across most states, communities, and classes. A striking feature was that many poor families had taken loans and mortgaged their land and other assets and thereby their own futures to get a daughter married. The compulsions of dowry no longer operated only among upper castes and classes. Even agricultural labour families in Assam and in Tamil Nadu reported dowry requirements. In Bengal, a range of methods were adopted to pay for the wedding and dowry of daughters: sale or mortgage of land (including that received as sharecroppers under Operation Barga),[17] house, flat, jewellery or other valuable assets, or loans at a high rate of interest from moneylenders. Those in public sector employment took loans against their Provident and Pension Funds or opted for 'voluntary retirement' to obtain the linked annuity, though it meant that after the wedding they would have neither income nor savings. Some poor families went door-to-door to collect money and/or requested clubs and mass organisations for assistance. With dowry, the cycle of poverty and debt is renewed as families lose their productive assets, maybe even their homes. It adds to the assets not only of those who receive dowry, but the local elite who encourage the practice and from whom the poor take loans against their own assets, including land (Gupta 1993, 2005).

The large proportion of poor and Dalit households who took loans for a daughter's dowry was striking, indicating that the pressures of dowry now cut across class and caste and conjoined a

162

gender concern with the dynamics of poverty. Among the upper castes and the better off, those in debt formed a smaller proportion, but the amount was very high in some cases. In Kerala, debt liabilities could go as high as Rs 400,000! The age at marriage of informants in this state was high relative to other parts of the country. This was related not only to a desire to delay marriage, but also to compulsory dowry and the expenses of an ostentatious marriage (consequent to remittances from the state's large workforce in the Gulf countries), for which years of savings were necessary. Some informants from Tamil Nadu reported that kin were ready to provide them with loans at minimal rates of interest to enable their daughters' marriage, but not for their education. The extent of indebtedness for dowry reasons was comparatively the least among Muslims in most states.

That people become indebted due to marriage expenses has been noted through the last century (Darling 1947). It indicates the compulsory character of dowry, which informants linked to both the compulsory nature of marriage and to the role of community sanction, discussed in the previous section. The marriage of daughters is a primary parental duty carrying both social and ritual connotations in most parts of India and among most communities. Unmarried women are viewed with pity and sexual suspicion, a burden on their parents and on their brothers. Furthermore, social adulthood and relative 'freedom' from parental constraints depend on marriage, more so for young women. This fuels their desire for and the taken-for-grantedness of marriage and all that accompanies it—be it dowry and/or abuse in the marital home. One option before poor parents, who wish to avoid debt in the face of spiralling dowry, is to arrange a match with a man who cannot command dowry: he may be much older; this may be his second or third marriage with children from earlier marriages to be taken care of; he may have no work or income; or be known as undesirable due to his habits. A 17-year old girl in Uttarakhand, where dowry has not reached the proportions it has elsewhere, said, 'marry a poor man and do not pay.' In all these cases, the daughter is destined for a life of hardship, deprivation, and possibly violence, but this is considered preferable to her remaining single.

Dowryless marriage is also accomplished by marrying the daughter at a great distance, through a matchmaker/agent, the unsaid being that the man is not an eligible match due to the reasons given above. Most of such reported marriages, however, take a girl from a poorer region to a more prosperous region (Blanchet 2008; Kaur 2004), while also avoiding dowry. The distance weakens the possibilities of the girl turning to her natal family for help in a bad marriage. Further, on marrying into a region where dowry is otherwise prevalent, she may be made to believe that she has been 'bought' and hence cannot leave. While not many informants during the survey talked of this, the Haryana unit of AIDWA (and other reports) recorded several cases of mistreated and abused wives from other states, who had turned to local members and activists for help.

Dowry and daughters' property rights

Across the country, the larger number of parents and guardians interviewed counterposed dowry to women's rights in natal property, saying that they had spent on their daughter's marriage and she had no rights to a share in their property or that her dowry had exhausted her legitimate rights. The proportion which held this view was greater in the higher income and upper caste categories. Those who said that they would give property were often those who had no property to give! Many gave the paucity of their property as a reason why daughters would not have a share. In West Bengal, Kerala, and parts of Himachal Pradesh a substantial number of parents said they would give daughters a share over and above what they may have spent at the time of their marriage. Daughters have had rights in parental property in the latter two states, while recent campaigns have ensured knowledge of the politically correct response in the first two.

It is often only at their wedding, with the accompanying trousseau and dowry, that young girls become the centre of attention and receive articles and gifts of some value. A number of them said that they too had a right to a share in parental property and since this was all that they would receive, they would ask and expect their dowry. An educated young woman in Assam confessed, 'I do not want a lion's share of my parents' property. My brothers will enjoy everything of my parents. So when I leave this house forever (at the time of my marriage) never to return ... I feel it is the duty of my parents to give me some material things for my personal use at the time of my marriage' (AIDWA 2003: 63). 'We do not like to take dowry, we are not supporters of the practice of dowry, but if we enter our in-laws' house with nothing (no jewellery, no furniture or other material things for our personal use), whom do we ask to supply those essential requirements?' (AIDWA ibid. 62). In previous fieldwork in Rajasthan, I heard girls speak of their dowry as a measure of parental love and concern. Some middle class parents and young women said that marriage prestations ensured that young women would have some of the comforts in their conjugal homes that they had become accustomed to in their natal homes. This was not because the girls had been married down (vis-à-vis the socio-economic status of the groom), but an acknowledgement that brides may not be provided or be able to ask for their daily requirements or luxuries in their marital home, or have any say in the disposal of household income. Among more and more groups, they were expected to move to their husband's home with all their immediate requirements (other than food).

This would appear to be in tune with the view expressed by scholars, members of the judiciary, and 'opinion makers' that dowry is a form of pre-mortem inheritance and women's wealth (*stridhan*). Depriving them of dowry further deprives them (Kishwar 1988, 1989). More is being acceded to here, however, than is immediately apparent. The young women quoted earlier were in fact saying that marital prestations meant that they had no other rights to parental property. Accepting the compulsion to marry, they were not ready to question the conjugal contract or the power relations within the marital home. A substantial number of them believed that they could not have peaceful, married lives without dowry and had become party to the equation made between the dowry they take/bring and their value as family members. In various ways they said that without dowry they would be insecure, neglected, and not respected by their in-laws whose treatment depended on the quantum of their dowry. Rather than risk that, they wanted dowry. Whether in Tamil Nadu or in Assam, girls' self-respect seemed to tie in with the dowry they expected to take with them on marriage. Thus, rather than being an immediate expression of daughters' property rights, this view not only accepts patriliny, but encodes within it women's secondary position as young, powerless wives.

A literate, young woman of a poor peasant family questioned the view that 'dowry is fine, it is dowry demands that are wrong'. She said that that those who justify their dowry gifts to daughters 'because' they can afford them, should not object, on the grounds of the poverty of the parents, to others' daughters asking for gifts. 'We do not have money so we should avoid it, isn't it? But who will be there to protect me when because of lack of dowry I have to face difficult circumstances in my in-laws' house. So I need dowry, not for my own satisfaction, but to satisfy my in-laws' family. And my parents will have to bear it for the security of their daughter' (AIDWA 2003: 63). She also stated that she did not want cash in dowry, but gifts such as ornaments and furniture.

The division between dowry as daughters' rights in familial property and sons' inheritance of the ancestral patrimony reiterates the distinction between sons/men as breadwinners and economically independent and daughters/women as burdens/ dependents. Rather than dowry being her pre-mortem inheritance, increasingly her wedding expenses are an excuse not to give her a property share. The difference in the nature of material goods which are transferred also reifies the distinction between productive men and burdensome daughters. While men inherit productive and/or fixed property, dowry consists largely of household and personal articles and the expenses of the marriage—goods for immediate and conspicuous consumption. Importantly, the division between earning sons and burdensome daughters is also tied to the practice of patrivirilocal residence. Daughters will take away what they receive, while sons will remain (hopefully) with the parents. Thus more permanent assets such as land had been given in dowry only among those who practised kin marriage and among the very well-off.

The articulation and sense of daughters' dowries and daughters as burdens were evident in the responses of guardians and young girls.[18] Many of the latter spoke of their sense of humiliation, of being a burden, and their fears that lacking the means for adequate dowry their marriage could not take place. The stories, cases, and views that were heard by activists during the survey reconfirmed that dowry marriage was a central aspect of the iniquitous and oppressive nature of contemporary gender relations.[19]

Can we/should we marry without dowry?

The dowry system has received fresh life with the new religion of liberalisation, reflecting contemporary consumerist desires. It has also been fuelled by the new orthodoxies of primordial identities in which cultural practices and markers of social groups are created or revived and sanctified as right. Markers of ancestry, particularity, and roots have become ways to 'fix' and secure one's place in an increasingly differentiated, unfamiliar, 'globalised' world. Cultural identity and 'tradition' are put forward as justifications for a range of practices, though they may be anti-women and detrimental to a range of social groups. Thus, the ethnic marriage, the ostentatious wedding, dowry, and the display of status are celebrations of community and moments of enjoyment. Various reasons and justifications given by young women and their parents for dowry and the impossibility of marrying without it have been described.

At the same time, young women and their parents have experienced the compulsions of dowry as oppressive and devaluing. Voices from the women's movements, alone or in conjunction with other movements, such as those centred on social reform, have in various times and forms campaigned against dowry, against domestic violence, and against caste as concerns for women's rights and equality. It is not surprising, then, that views on dowry are not consistent and coherent, either among girls as a group or in the articulations of any one respondent. For example, some informants from Tamil Nadu said that dowry expressed the idea that men were superior to women and equated women with material goods rather than seeing their value as persons. Young women, from a range of states including Haryana and Tamil Nadu, expressed their determination to remain single rather than have a dowry marriage. By and large, however, non-marriage was not considered as an option. Further, parental approval of marriage was desired, while parents did not consider the possibility of a marriage that was obviously against local norms.

The survey showed that dowry was present as a system but was also perceived as socially pernicious and devaluing of women across strata. It was striking that across caste, religion, and region, the majority of young women felt that dowry should end and stated that they did not think that their parents should 'have to give'. As narrated earlier, it was argued that if dowry was good for the rich, it could not be said that it was bad for the poor—it was either bad for all or good for all. This is in keeping with both the moral discourse of social reform and with the stance that the gender divisions articulate with other stratifications. From the first standpoint, a range of social evils are encapsulated in dowry, and from the second, dowry reflects not only gender, but other contemporary and intensifying inequalities and oppressions such as those of class and caste.

The findings showed that the effects and hold of the dowry system were differentiated across and within economic and social strata. The proportions of young women who thought that dowryless marriage was possible are higher among Muslims and 'lower' ranking castes. Their range of views was not very different from that of their parents. It also bore some correlation with the regional and community pattern in the spread of dowry, and the strength of the women's and other social movements and Left politics mentioned earlier. Thus, the proportion of those who expressed a yearning for dowryless marriage was highest in Tripura, Assam, West Bengal, and Kerala. The first two have recently been drawn into the web of dowry, where the gap between economic realities and the desires of the consumerist economy are striking.

In Kerala, despite the matrilineal history of some castes, dowry has a long history particularly among the Christians. It has been increasing astronomically with foreign remittances. A sense of desperation and anxiety about their future was evident among young, unmarried women, who knew that their parents could not afford prevalent dowry rates. Many were angry that their marriages depended on dowry and were ready to agitate on the issue. They asserted that they would have dowryless, love marriages. With Tripura and West Bengal, Kerala has also been witness to social reform movements and radical mobilisation in which structures of social and economic inequality have been attacked and linked to caste, irrationality, 'superstition', and even 'tradition'. In that scenario, it is not surprising that informants critical of dowry saw arranged marriage, caste endogamy,[20] and dowry marriage as going hand-in-hand. While this was heard in other states also, here in particular the view was expressed that love marriage, dowryless marriage, and inter-caste/religious marriage would go together.

Young women from various parts of the country said that it was young men, the prospective grooms, even as individuals, who had to take the initiative to marry without dowry. The survey results held out little hope in this regard. A small sample of boys and young men in Agra in Uttar Pradesh appeared even more obedient to parental wishes than girls. While more than two thirds said they would not ask for dowry, almost a similar proportion said that not only was dowryless marriage not possible, but that they would marry according to their parents' wishes. This was in consonance with the view of respondents in Tamil Nadu, who said that young men are not ready to take a stand against dowry and, if they are, their parents easily dissuade them. This is tied to the nature of familial, property, and community structures in which are embedded emotion, material, and social resources, but which cannot be further explored here.

How is dowry to end?

In undertaking this survey, AIDWA and the ISWSD were not only asking questions about the nature of contemporary dowry, but also whether and how dowry practices could be challenged. They were revisiting the strategies of such a movement and reasserting an anti-dowry politics. As people spoke of their experiences of dowry, its fall out, and stories of humiliation and violence, it led to discussion on the need for urgent action. In one situation in Bengal, informants decided that they and the activists should immediately take out a demonstration regarding a particular case of dowry demands. In presenting the findings of the survey at the Delhi convention, the aim was to construct a charter for a campaign against dowry starting from whether young people were ready to reject dowry marriage.

Reading the responses of some informants, the dowry system appears as a spider's web—once you are caught in it, you cannot get out. People's lives are enmeshed in dowry. For others, however, this was not acceptable—dowry could be eliminated. One line of approach indicated in the previous section, was to slash at the very structure of the dowry web—at the system of caste-based, arranged marriage. The interweaving of gender subjugation with other oppressions was reiterated. Campaigns for inter-caste and love marriage, which would simultaneously address the caste system and gender relations, were proposed as essential to the movement. Even as examples of 'love marriage' which floundered on the issue of dowry were pointed out, a common thread that ran through the comments of many of the workshop delegates was that the ideology and institution of marriage itself had to be addressed. This meant redefining the conjugal contract on a more gender-equal basis, questioning caste-based marriage and the idea that marriage was the only life option for women.

At the convention, forms of action similar to those of earlier social reform movements were suggested. One was public protests against ostentatious weddings and conspicuous consumption. Ideals of asceticism were not the main impetus to this suggestion, but the impossibility of separating dowry from the wedding display. Another form that was proposed was that boys and girls and their parents would be asked to take an oath to refuse dowry marriage. Some young delegates from Haryana stated that girls who refuse to marry with dowry end up unmarried and become the target of gossip and slander, even if they are able to support themselves economically. 'The movement has to take this issue seriously. We take on the burden of social change—and only suffer.' Such young women spoke of the need of support and solidarity in their endeavour to remain single.

The issue of women's economic independence emerged as a major plank of any struggle against dowry. Not only would this enable them to resist oppression, it would change the conjugal contract and the way in which parents viewed daughters. This entailed women's rights in natal and matrimonial property, equal wages for equal work, and economic and social recognition of their labours. The representation of women as consumers and decorated bodies, often tied to the projection of potential dowry goods, had to be attacked. Here too, the entanglement of dowry, gender and other structures of inequality were reiterated.

A strategy which many suggested was awareness campaigns to educate people on the implications of the dowry system. Delegates observed that individuals behave as if the violent repercussions of dowry would not touch them. Some activists, however, pointed out that the innumerable awareness campaigns against dowry had had little effect. Others said that these campaigns had remained limited. They agreed that 'seeing' dowry or mere knowledge were clearly not enough. People had to be prepared to reject it in their own lives and fight it socially. Awareness and education were necessary, but through large-scale women's and social movements and the mass media that reached corners of the country they had not touched so far.

Most who said that dowry could be fought also felt that individuals did not possess the strength to break out of the web alone. Despite anti-dowry legislation, conviction rates remained low, encouraging dowry practices to grow (see Basu, this volume).

Furthermore, the web of dowry was strengthened by systemic social, economic and political processes. Social movements and other alliances should use their collective weight to enforce legislation and seek redress. Large-scale collective action could build awareness against dowry, but only government action could break the stranglehold of community elders and other advocates of dowry, who supported caste and dowry norms in marriage. Concerted anti-dowry steps by the government could stop in-laws who made dowry demands and give strength to those who wished to refuse to give dowry.

Rather than dowry demands and the 'distortions' or obvious violence related to dowry, it was the system itself which had to be addressed. If dowry was to be tackled, its multi-structural links and the network of relationships in which it was embedded had to be broken. To make these connections visible, a multi-level struggle had to be fought through a movement that encompassed community, religious, political, and mass organisations of women and of men and women, and myriad actions by state bodies and government instruments. The cultural and the normative, the material and the social, the emotional and the political had to be addressed simultaneously—a task which is co-extensive with a movement for the radical transformation of state and society.

Acknowledgements

I would like to thank the many activists and friends in AIDWA, who undertook the survey around which this paper is constructed and who discussed the issues with me over many years. Thanks also to Tamsin Bradley and Emma Tomalin for their comments and close reading of earlier drafts of the paper.

Notes

[1] This can probably be correlated to the processes that saw the spread of dowry beyond the elite

[2] Very little is written of the activities and campaigns of AIDWA and other mass organisations in most of the writings that have documented women's

movements in India, including Sen (1990); Gandhi and Shah (1992); Kumar (1993). This had much to do with the personal political position of many of the authors within the spectrum of feminist politics, their antipathy to the CPI(M), which a number of AIDWA leaders and activists were members of or in sympathy with, as well as the orality of culture and politics in India (see Note 4). The last has meant that without fieldwork or participatory research, large swathes of resistance and politics can get blanked out or misread (as in Calman 1992). A partial view of social processes is of course always the case. However, without the diversity of Indian women's organising experiences and feminist debates as well as the location of women activists entering the analysis, and given the limited reach of the trends documented, it is not possible to explain the shifts, responses and directions of the movement.

3 J.P.S. Uberoi in an oral communication.

4 More than writings in the press, in pamphlets, or in articles, much of this took place in oral discussions and campaigns. The oral is the predominant mode of argument, debate, and campaigning—of discourse—in the women's movement in India and a range of grass-roots and mass organisations, not just AIDWA. See Agnihotri and Mazumdar (1995), Agnihotri and Palriwala (2001), Palriwala (1985/forthcoming) as well as the writings mentioned in Note 2 for a documentation of some of these positions.

5 This unevenness may be related to the diversity in the orientations of the various women's groups and organisations that campaigned on the issue and their different reach and locations, the perspective of the media which tended to focus on the violent and the sensational, and the lack of access to mass media other than the radio by much of the populace in that period.

6 Writings on the anti-dowry movement also cast it as a campaign against violence rather than the practice of dowry, most evidently through placing their discussion of it in their sections on violence. See Agnihotri and Mazumdar ibid.; Kumar ibid.; Gandhi and Shah ibid.

7 This was evident in incidents after 2002 wherein young brides called a stop to the wedding and called the police to arrest their fiancé and his family when the latters' 'demands' prior to the ceremony became 'excessive'.

8 As much as the writings referenced below, the following is based on interviews with activists and participation in conventions and other fora over the period 1984–2003.

9 This was the position reiterated at every national conference of AIDWA.

10 It has been argued that issues such as the right to widow remarriage was a concern of upper caste women, but was presented as a battle for all women in pre-Independence movements, in the process undermining struggles of women of other castes (see Chowdhry 1994). Central to Kishwar's 1988 critique of the anti-dowry movement was the idea that it was the one form

RAJNI PALRIWALA

of property which many women received and hence universalising the struggle against it deprived such women of their limited rights.

11 AIDWA activists from across the country attended the workshop. Women's studies scholars and representatives of women's and other mass organisations were also invited. The subsequent publication includes the state-wise presentations of the findings and the questionnaire, as well as other presentations made at the workshop, the resolution passed, and a report on the discussions.

12 Bride price is the goods and/or money given to the parents of the bride and was found among many middle and low ranking castes across the country. Bride service took the form of labour performed by the prospective groom at the house/lands of the bride's parents, to secure the match or following the engagement and prior to the marriage. This has been recorded among many groups in the north-east. Among some castes, particularly in areas where dowry was the dominant practice traditionally, the bride price was/is given the appearance of dowry by being returned at the time of the wedding in the form of gifts and cash to the couple or the wedding feast. Mehr, the premier and sanctioned marriage prestation among Muslims, is different from all of these, being a gift from the groom to his bride promised at the time of the wedding and given at that time or later.

13 The findings are presented in state-wise chapters in the published report.

14 Though evident even in electoral figures, quick readings of events and politics in states such as Kerala, West Bengal, and Tripura obscure this and thereby the social and political dynamics in these states.

15 The practice of a newly married couple taking up residence with the father of the groom.

16 See Malhotra in AIDWA 2003 for a brief description of some of these advertisement campaigns.

17 Under Operation Barga, the Left Front government, which was elected in 1977 in West Bengal undertook a massive survey and registration of sharecroppers, who formed the bulk of cultivators in the state. Through this registration, regulation of the terms of cultivation and security of tenancy was ensured. Gupta (1993) discusses the reallocation of land and labour through dowry, including among those who gained land under Operation Barga.

18 The story of the young Tamil boy who wanted his parents to get rid of his twin baby sisters was a striking example (AIDWA 2003: 165).

19 This is evident in the declining sex ratios and in the justifications given of sex selective abortion by both the doctors who practise it and their clients. Another aspect linking dowry and gender ideology is not being discussed here—the idea of dowry as a compensation for an unproductive wife, though it came up at the 2002 Delhi workshop at which the findings were presented.

20 Marriage within the caste.

References

Agnes, F. 1992. 'Protecting women against violence? Review of a decade of legislation, 1980-1989'. *Economic and Political Weekly.* XXVII(17). pp. WS19-WS33.

Agnihotri, I. & Mazumdar, V. 1995. 'Changing terms of political discourse: Women's movement in India, 1970s–1990s'. *Economic and Political Weekly.* XXX (29). pp. 1869–78.

Agnihotri, I. & R. Palriwala. 2001. 'Tradition, the family and the state: Politics of the women's movement in the eighties' in *Gender and Nation.* New Delhi: Nehru Museum and Library.

AIDWA. 2003. *Expanding dimensions of dowry.* New Delhi: All India Democratic Women's Association.

Blanchet, T. 2008. 'Bangladeshi girls sold as wives in North India' in *Marriage, Migration and Gender.* eds. R. Palriwala & P. Uberoi. *Women and Migration in Asia.* vol. 5. New Delhi: Sage. pp. 152–79.

Calman, L.J. 1992. *Toward empowerment: Women and movement politics in India.* Boulder, CO: Westview Press.

Chowdhry, P. 1994. *The veiled women: Shifting gender equations in rural Haryana, 1880–1990.* New Delhi: Oxford University Press.

CSWI. 1975. *Towards Equality.* Report of the Committee on the Status of Women in India. New Delhi: Department of Social Welfare, Government of India.

Darling, M.L. 1947. *Punjab peasant in prosperity and debt.* London: Oxford University Press.

Gandhi, N. & N. Shah. 1992. *The issues at stake: Theory and practice in the contemporary women's movement in India.* New Delhi: Kali for Women.

Gupta, J. 1993. 'Land, labour, dowry in West Bengal'. *Social Scientist.* 21. pp. 74–90.

———. 2005. 'Women, land and law—Dispute resolution at the village level' in *Dowry and Inheritance.* ed. S. Basu. New Delhi: Women Unlimited. pp. 194–213.

Kapadia, K. 1995. *Siva and her sisters: Gender, caste, and class in rural India.* Oxford: Westview Press.

Kapur R. & B. Cossman. 1996. *Subversive sites: Feminist engagements with law in India.* New Delhi: Sage.

Karat, B. 2005. *Survival and emancipation: Notes from Indian women's struggles.* New Delhi: Three Essays Collective.

Kaur, Ravinder. 2004. 'Across-region marriages: Poverty, female migration and the sex ratio'. *Economic and Political Weekly.* 39(25). pp. 2595–2603.

Kishwar, M. 1988. 'Rethinking dowry boycott'. *Manushi.* 48. Sept.–Oct. pp. 10–13.

———. 1989. 'Towards more just norms for marriage: Continuing the dowry debate'. *Manushi.* 53. Jul.–Aug. pp. 2–9.

Kumar, R. 1993. *The history of doing: An illustrated account of movements for women's rights and feminism in India, 1800–1990.* New Delhi: Kali for Women.

Mazumdar, V. 2000. 'Political ideology of the women's movement's engagement with law'. Occasional Paper 34. New Delhi: Centre for Women Development Studies.

Menon, N. 1999. 'Introduction' in *Gender and politics in India.* ed. N. Menon. New Delhi: Oxford University Press. pp. 1–36.

Palriwala, R. 1985. 'Women are not for burning: The anti-dowry movement in Delhi'. Mimeo presented at Symposium No. 99 'Anthropological perspectives on women's collective actions: An assessment of the decade, 1975–1985'. Mijas, Spain: Wenner-Gren Foundation for Anthropological Research. (forthcoming in T.K. Oommen. ed. reader on social movements in India. New Delhi: Oxford University Press).

——. 1989. 'Reaffirming the anti-dowry struggle'. *Economic and Political Weekly.* 24(17). pp. 942–4. Reprinted in *Dowry and Inheritance.* ed. S. Basu. New Delhi: Women Unlimited. pp. 279–90.

——. 2003. 'Dowry in contemporary India: An overview' in *Expanding dimensions of dowry.* Delhi: AIDWA. pp. 11–27.

Sen, I. ed. 1990. *A space within the struggle.* New Delhi: Kali for Women.

Sheel, R. 1999. *The political economy of dowry.* New Delhi: Oxford University Press

Singh, K. 1987. 'The Dowry Prohibition Act'. *Women's Equality.* Inaugural Issue Oct.–Dec. pp. 19–20.

Srinivas, M.N. (1984). *Some reflections on dowry.* New Delhi: Oxford University Press.

Legacies of the
Dowry Prohibition Act in India
Marriage practices and feminist discourses

SRIMATI BASU

Introduction

In the last few years, I have regularly received enquiries connected to dissertation and grant proposals from postgraduate students in Europe or the US hoping to work on dowry. Meanwhile, since 2001, I have also observed the work of a range of Indian women's organisations that deal with marriage, violence and law (primarily in Kolkata, some in Mumbai), and strategise and organise around diverse economic and social issues such as maintenance, right to residence, or domestic violence, but they rarely focus their activist energies on anti-dowry measures per se. This paper addresses the disjuncture between these two moments: while dowry continues to be a hypervisible signifier in etic[1] analyses of Indian women, it has become relatively invisible as an organising focus in Indian women's associations. This latter scenario, I argue here, is not neglect, fatigue, despair, or the onset of sexier organising topics, and certainly not the disappearance of monetary exchanges at marriage, but a transformation of the economic and anti-violence goals of anti-dowry organising. Organisations now address more broad-based problems located in economic entitlements of marriage and the dailiness of violence rather than looking to the largely ineffective Dowry Prohibition Act (1984) and to piecemeal demonstrations around alleged 'dowry deaths' and their legislative trajectories; whether these changes in strategy follow primarily from the failure of legal provisions or from emergent successes in modes of organising is impossible to determine. Dowry concerns thus get folded into larger discussions of kinship, exchange and transaction.

South Asian feminists have come to dread the Orientalist and hegemonic feminist associations of the term 'dowry,' loaded with connotations of abject patriarchal oppression, of women as trafficked victims of their families and mute objects of exchange. Uma Narayan compellingly names this phenomenon 'death by culture,' arguing that Western Feminist (and especially Radical Feminist) analyses have looked to dowry to justify a homogeneous, universalised patriarchy, attributing the problem to irreducible problems of 'Indian culture' in broad terms rather than looking to complex interactions of gender, class, region or consumer culture. In the process, such analyses have often conflated systems of marriage payments such as dowry with possibly related domestic violence using arson, and further with the phenomenon of widow immolation which was quite limited in scope but has assumed gargantuan proportions in feminist imagination. Few parallels are drawn in these analyses with problems connected to dowry that affect western women systematically as well, such as gendered subordination built into heterosexual marriage as an institution, women's unequal access to financial resources, or widespread physical and structural violence against women. These conflations and assumptions of lack of agency, Narayan contends, makes for troubled relationships between western and Indian feminists, where 'the very constitution of cultural "similarities" and "differences" [in analysing "dowry"] is a politically complicated project' (1997: 86) because overdetermined cultural difference rather than structural similarity is emphasised in western feminist accounts of dowry. This paper, to the contrary, argues that problems with dowry are fundamentally related to the political economy of compulsory heterosexual marriage, and the associated trajectories of gendered property entitlement and permissible violence, in ways that are entirely consonant with cross-cultural feminist theorising of marriage. Rather than the exotic burning woman, the object of enquiry is the all-too-common impoverished divorcee.

In academic discourse, the phenomenon of dowry continues to provide a lively intellectual puzzle, particularly for economists and anthropologists. Recent research on dowry often reflects its iconic and fundamental status in India as a particular cultural problem. Anderson (2003) attributes the rise in dowries in India in contrast to their decline in Europe to the irreducibility of caste in the former case and to 'modernisation' in the latter. Shenk (2007) draws on functionalism and behavioural ecology of dowry to argue for dowry as purposive and strategic, in the best interests of parents and the daughter as an investment and a tool to increase her bargaining power. Dalmia and Lawrence (2005: 71) deem dowry to be a mechanism that 'equalises measurable differences' between households and individuals in marriage, i.e. signifies 'the price for a "good match".' Batabyal and Beladi (2007) use a game model to determine the parameters of an optimal dowry offer for bride and groom, and the information that a marriage broker/mediator needs to glean from the parties about these optimal offers in order to calculate his/her own best offer to accomplish the deal; brides and grooms are calculated as actors with equal agency in this formulation, and mediators as being genuinely impartial about parties and outcomes. In all the above analyses, dowry is a living experiment for speculating on theory, located in a world of rational economic actors where systemic patriarchal inequities can be balanced through compensatory economic mechanisms, where feminist interventions are quite irrelevant.

Other recent research reveals more dynamic conditions explaining particular factors for dowry, often locating its predominance and rise in consumption and labour practices. Biao (2005) studies the emergent scenario of Information Technology professionals migrating between Sydney and Andhra Pradesh, reading the migration as both driven by dowry demands and generating demands, in a vicious cycle. Srinivasan (2005) finds that the rise in female infanticide in Salem, Tamil Nadu, occurs in the context of increasing dowry expectations (dowries are higher for each successive daughter). With impoverishment from ever smaller plots of land, as it is sold to pay for dowries, devaluation of female labour and female disinheritance from land—driven by attempts to enhance and defy caste status through displays of wealth—dowry expectations impoverish families without enhancing daughters' power. Srinivasan and Lee's study in Bihar (2004) reports that dowry practices stayed resilient given intense materialism and the desire for daughters to make high-status marriages in that area; two-thirds of women in the study disapproved of dowry but still carried it on, while younger and wealthier women showed higher approval of dowry. With concrete economic and cultural practices foregrounded in these studies, there is a sense of the inexorability of dowry in the context of ever-growing consumerist and status-enhancing practices. Modernisation works to favour rising dowries, and no vectors of change seem evident or effective. Although sympathetic to the social inequities resulting from dowry systems, these analyses do not engage with legal or cultural strategies or the effectiveness of social movements.

My first memories of feminist organising as a young adult, on the other hand, come from graphic invocations of social transformation, such as the demonstrations and street plays of the 1980s. As the discussion of feminist arguments later in the paper testifies, these interventions were deeply influential in making us think about dowry as a lethal phenomenon, and drew connections with women's status within marriage and their access to property, drawing many of us into feminist movements. As resonant as these ideas were, the elaborate dowries of friends and families in the 1990s onward made me realise that vigorous passions around anti-dowry agitation had waned somewhat in public discourse: 'dowry deaths' had become marked as atypical and bestial, but prevalent discourses of class and consumption had normalised dowry itself as customary, a marker of affection, and a channel of cementing kin relations (Basu 1999). Whether these changes came about from new consumer identities in a post-1989 liberalised market economy, from a backlash against feminist challenges to marriage and its accompanying lure of presents, or from a realisation of the frailty of legal remedies against the depth and extent of the problem, is a matter of social movement analysis beyond the scope of this paper, if it can even be thus operationalised. In tracing later responses to dowry, this paper seeks to map the salience of anti-dowry agitations. Is their disappearance from the foreground of social movements timely and necessary? What stands in their place, and does it sufficiently address problems arising from dowry abuse?

Rising from the ashes of the Dowry Prohibition Act

It is difficult enough to conceptualise what we are trying to 'reform' or 'transform' when we talk of dowry, and far harder, perhaps, to agree on 'solutions' to a multifaceted and complex problem necessitating broad-based social change. The legal realm is often seen as the most concrete means to seek solutions to gender equity, whether with regard to family law, or labour, or violence. The hope is that instituting a law may signal recognition of a social problem, act as a deterrent, and in the ultimate instance, as a punitive instrument. In practice, however, cultural behaviours often adapt their way around legal loopholes (Agarwal 1994; Basu 1999; Kishwar 1999; Menon 1999).

Dowry laws are, par excellence, an example of such slippery legal terrain. The amended Dowry Prohibition Act (1984) makes the giving and taking of dowry 'as a condition of marriage' (excluding "voluntary gifts") punishable by law,' while suicides and murders attributed to dowry have a special apparatus of evidence and arrest.[2] However, the execution of these legal provisions does little to address the social mechanisms through which dowry flourishes. The ubiquity of exorbitant marriage expenses and the fact that both sides are held equally culpable, despite the very different pressures on them, means that there is no incentive to make a report except after death or as retaliation or in association with other lawsuits (Umar 1998; Gautam and Trivedi 1986).

In being unable to clearly distinguish coercion from custom and gift from demand, the Dowry Prohibition Act (1984) is functionally ineffective: it stands as a symbolic marker of the State's response to feminist organising that exemplifies the difficulties of transforming material-cultural practices into law. On the other hand, more specific and narrow legal provisions have allowed organisations and assistive counsellors to bypass the hypertrope of dowry per se and provide concrete solutions to problems proceeding from economic subservience, lack of residential options, and family domestic violence in marriage. In addition to the Indian Penal Code provisions given in Note 2 specifically against forms of violence, these also include Section 406 for criminal breach of trust if dowry goods are not returned, as well as civil remedies of divorce through the (theoretically) speedier Family Courts and the new Domestic Violence Act (2005). Criminal and civil venues, courts, police stations and mediation organisations are often simultaneously approached to address various aspects (e.g. divorce, alimony, violence, return of goods) of the same situation. As the cases discussed here illustrate, people seem well aware of legal guidelines and are constantly defining creative ways to get around them or manipulate them for 'off-label' uses.

Marshalling evidence for criminal trials under legal provisions has proved difficult: police have refused to use dying declarations as grounds to investigate deaths thoroughly; corroborative evidence from neighbours about violence or torture is often discounted; abetment to suicide seems impossibly difficult to prove; burning is a particularly efficient method of destroying evidence on the body; bribery is rife; and police are often reluctant to interfere in 'domestic disputes' (Umar 1998; Kumar 1994; Gautam and Trivedi 1986). On the other hand, Section 406 of the Indian Penal Code (criminal breach of trust applied to non-recovery of dowry goods) has come to be regarded as one of the most easily accessible legal grounds, and is promptly invoked (by threat or as an actual filing) to leverage a variety of issues related to divorce, maintenance and even physical violence. The recovery of *stridhan*[3] or wedding goods from affinal homes by women going through divorce was one of the most common tasks undertaken by the Family Court's counsellors (helpers/mediators) I observed (field work details in the next section), who were responsible for accompanying the wife, hunting through the man's (often extended family) household, and maintaining the integrity of the process. A Family Court judge complained to one of the counsellors about her previous day's foray from which the litigant had emerged unsatisfied: 'There should be a limit to this! How can she ask for her wedding saris back 15 years after the wedding, when the saris have been eaten up by termites?' While this statement was an overblown caricature of recovery efforts, such forays were often thorough and extensive, including furniture and items of daily kitchen use, seeming to be deeply symbolic moments of severance and recompense even if the goods had depreciated with little monetary recovery value. Recovering cash amounts may have been hard for women's families to pursue given the legal limitations, but these wedding goods were not in dispute as having been gifted. In terms of cultural practice, the response from organisations assisting with the process has been not to curb the giving of dowry but to see it as a space where legal strategies may be fruitfully applied after the fact, and where future economic leverage may be exerted in case of marriage breakdown.

Similarly, Section 498A relating to 'torture' (commonly used to characterise domestic violence) and the recently passed Domestic Violence Act (2005) provide alternate legal pathways to address physical harm that may or may not be related to dowry demands, thereby centring on the violence per se rather than emphasising dowry as the putative central cause of violence. Though Section 498A cases represent another nebulously worded law that is depicted as culturally inflammatory and has resulted in few convictions, it provides a space to articulate a range of economic and social grievances in juxtaposition with physical violence, and to leverage civil and criminal cases against each other with the expectation of obtaining some resources for sustenance (Basu 2007; Solanki 2001). Similarly, the new Domestic Violence Act (2005) seeks to transform married women's relationship to affinal property and household by positing their right to occupy that space, with the provision that they can claim right to residence in the marital household even if they allege violence (Rajan 2005). While no trajectory of its effectiveness or the means to get around it exist at the moment, it also, notably, does not single out dowry as the predominant form of violence, and hails a broader locus of material and physical control. The use of these legal provisions occurs partially in response to the ineffectiveness of the Dowry Prohibition Act (1984), but also from ongoing realisations by activists, scholars and front-line workers in organisations about the complexity that falls under the rubric of 'dowry,' in particular the need to notionally separate the issue of giving of gifts at marriage from the broader issues of violence, property and residence in marital dissolution.

Hiding in plain sight: deflected dowry

My current project of studying Family Law and Family Violence in courts, police stations and mediation organisations, is based on two periods of extended fieldwork in 2001 and 2004–5, as well as shorter visits since—mainly at the primary site of ethnographic data Kolkata, but also visits to Family Courts and mediation and legal advice organisations in Mumbai, Pune and Dhaka. This included daily observations in the Family Court, and at the Women's Grievance Cell and non-governmental mediation clinics in a regular rotation, travelling with Family Court counsellors on their tasks, and interviewing judges, court and police workers, and mediators. In my recent fieldwork, dowry matters inevitably emerged in the niches of conversations around family breakdown, in ways both furtive and overdetermined, settled and anxiety-ridden. It was clear from the well-choreographed responses of legal venues, mediation organisations and people who had brought marital disputes to these settings that dowry claims did not constitute strong legal grounds, but also that they were part of the existent quasi-legal apparatus that could be marshalled for negotiations. A couple of cases in point follow.

I accompanied some Family Court counsellors on a long train ride to Machlandapur from Kolkata in search of a young man who had been a no-show at his divorce hearings, and was in danger of being arrested for non-payment of court-mandated maintenance. Before the counsellors had a chance to explain, and to our initial confusion, he assumed we were there to investigate a dowry claim and that the court papers he had received were a notification of an FIR (first information report) filed with a police station in Kolkata. He was confident but belligerent and said, 'Her parents shouldn't have messed with me, I'm a nice guy but I can be tough. Let the police come to enforce the order; I can just show up in court and explain, they can't catch me.' It became evident that he was worried about the wife's family lodging a dowry case, but insisted that there was no way of tracing the dowry cash back to him and his immediate family (mother and brother). He believed he was in the clear because he had been advised to leave no direct trail; thus, his wife's family had paid his married sister (who was deemed to have no financial stake in wedding transactions) the agreed-upon amount, and it had come to him eventually through this roundabout route. It had not occurred to him that he might be in (civil and criminal) danger for not showing up at the divorce hearings in order to have his responsibility for maintenance determined.[4] The case demonstrates the difficulties of sending out legal notices in formal language for criminal charges, and the related difficulties of poorer sections of the population with less access to literacy, including legal literacy, and less resources to obtain legal advice. It also exemplifies how dowry is often seen as the primary criminal worry associated with a failing marriage. As opposed to the complicated civil apparatus of divorce (including the potentially criminal negligence of failing to pay alimony or maintenance that he was charged with), dowry becomes the identified problem in families' pre-emptive management of marriage.

The second scenario concerns a complicated negotiation at the offices of a well-known non-governmental organisation that undertakes family law counselling between the bride's and groom's families. The case revolved around definitions of fraud and informed consent. The husband and his family alleged that the wife had welts all over her body, could be deemed to be sexually repulsive, and was therefore liable for fraud since this had not been disclosed before marriage, which constituted grounds for divorce or annulment. The wife was not present, but her family contended that he was using some temporary boils as an excuse to get out of the marriage, that he was involved with a married woman and had married for the dowry money. Here too, the dowry payment had come to him through an indirect route to avoid legal liability, having been paid by the bride's aunt to the groom's sister's husband.

The mediation came to an eventual impasse, and having failed to persuade the husband and his family to take the wife back, the agency's representatives (now functioning as an informal substitute for lawyers) turned to negotiating conditions for maintenance (during litigation and after divorce). They focused on the return of wedding goods, exerting pressure on the man through the economic accountability of legal provisions. The financial terms of the dowry became evident only at this latter stage: the woman's family claimed to have given Rs 40,000 (about US$ 800 at that time) for dowry and the man's family said they had spent it already, on wedding-associated costs among other expenses. Her family was poorer by far than his and sought fiercely to recover the amount. His family had substantial agricultural and orchard land, though he himself claimed to be unemployed (a familiar stance for husbands during maintenance negotiations). While the mediation attempts by the organisation broke down at this point, it seemed that dowry amounts were being notionally compared against alimony payments, legal ways to 'recover money' being considered through a range of civil and criminal options.

These anecdotes exemplify the changing problems of dowry, and the socio-legal tactics that meet its transformation. The women's movement had a strong influence on delineating the word 'dowry' in legal parlance, but the Dowry Prohibition Act (1984) that emerged at the end of political negotiations was a weak legal tool because it failed to draw clear distinctions between coercion and customary exchange, and to demarcate criminal liability in gift-giving associated with marriage. Legal remedies did not take into account feminist critiques, such as the gendered differences in power of the parties to the marriage, and the problems of looking to dowry as women's optimal, if indirect, access to property resources. The more recent forms of leverage described here do not directly address questions of gender and power either, but seek to open up a better strategic space for targeting material issues, to diminish the economic impacts of marital dissolution. In the decades since the Act, the women's movement has continued to point to loopholes in the prosecution and proliferation of dowry, and has linked it to other forms of violence (infanticide, sex-selection, domestic violence), but the above examples show the flexibility of cultural practices despite these ongoing attempts at reform. Practices like deflected dowry arise as people respond to socio-cultural perceptions of the obstacles posed by the Dowry Prohibition Act and adapt to its loopholes, while mediation organisations seek to stay one step ahead of evolving practices. Both these negotiations occur ahead of legal change, transforming the scope and form of dowry that law seeks to contain.

Feminist theories: dowry as a problem of gender norms

Long before the anti-dowry social movements of the 1980s, however, problems of dowry had been framed in the comprehensive context of articulated gender hierarchies, the intersections of gender, class and caste oppressions, and particularly patrilocal marriage as a prime site of potential violence. The notion that dowry should be tackled through social pressures and incentives, rather than legal manoeuvres, was a recurrent theme in numerous venues, such as the Parliamentary debates on dowry and also various phases of the women's movement. The 1975 Report of the Committee on the Status of Women in India located the problem of 'dowry evil' as being 'against the goal of a socialistic society' and connected it to women's economic dependence, with the authors suggesting measures that 'though aiming at proximate ends, should take a determined step forward toward an egalitarian society' (1975: 76). Both problems and solutions identified in the document addressed fundamental difficulties of women's economic subservience and marriage as a site of subordination, rather than gifting per se; thus the goals were that 'social consciousness needs to be aroused particularly amongst women, to enable them to understand that by encouraging dowry they are perpetuating the inequality of the sexes. Reforms in marriage custom to simplify the ceremony, increasing opportunities for employment, condemnation of the ideal of a parasitic existence for women, a reassessment of the value of household work and homemaking as socially and economically productive, and the enforcement of the Anti-Dowry Act are some of the measures necessary' (1975: 76). The Committee also suggested setting a cash limit on the amount of gifts to the groom and his family as well as entertainment costs, prohibiting displays, and re-examining gifts to the bride if they are just an excuse for the transfer of wealth (1975: 115–6). It is notable here that specific anti-dowry measures (all of which were deemed too restrictive to be a part of the eventual law) are placed within a nexus of problems related to gender discrimination, underlining the connection between ideologies of gender, and class- and gender-based accumulation of resources.

This 1975 Report was an official government product, but it is an integral part of the feminist activist discourse on dowry that was especially visible and influential in the late 1970s and 1980s. It worked on several fronts: legal interventions, such as filing Public Interest lawsuits (Jethmalani 1995), mobilising to lobby politicians and publicly shame dowry murderers, and sustained campaigns to interrogate norms of gender. Stri Sangharsh, Mahila Dakshata Samiti and Nari Raksha Samiti organised demonstrations which gave a great deal of national visibility to the issue of domestic violence and murder connected to dowry, as well as marches which protested the commercialisation of weddings (Kumar 1994). Sometimes, demonstrations exerted pressure by taking place in the victim's workplace and home, as well as the victim's husband's workplace. Street plays such as *Om Swaha* in Delhi and *Meye Dilam Shajiye* in Kolkata became an important and popular means of interrogating the culpability of families in providing dowry, revelling in displays of status, staying silent on domestic violence, and making married dependence the ideal of women's lives.

As these interventions indicate, the anti-dowry movement addressed this question through a comprehensive and intersectional model of gender, incorporating the domains of economy, marriage, culture and violence against women. Indeed, most feminist organisations involved in the anti-dowry movement illumined the *connection* between these domains. They pointed to the ways in which conspicuous consumption and family dynamics contribute to the proliferation of dowry in its specific forms, but located the source of the problem in the political economy of patriarchy. Rajni Palriwala quotes the 1982 memorandum of the Dahej Virodhi Chetana Manch (the anti-dowry consciousness forum) which insisted that dowry not be viewed as an 'isolated phenomenon' but '[i]ts increasing incidence is symptomatic of the continuing erosion of women's status and devaluation of female life in independent fashion. It is equally related to the worsening socio-economic crisis within which structural inequalities have accentuated and black money power grown to fuel greater human oppression' (1989: 943). C.S. Lakshmi's essay 'On Kidneys and Dowry' focused on the nature of marriage itself: the problem, she contended, was the alienation of women from their natal families through marriage and the construction of their identity and status solely in terms of their affinal families, and the solution was to repudiate the compulsory nature of marriage. She provided an apt illustration of this principle: Sister Subbalakshmi's response to a question about what would happen 'if women can't get married because they refuse to give dowry?' was, 'Then women must have the dignity and courage to remain single' (1989: 189). A variety of activists, even while differing bitterly on the specifics of strategy, identified the nexus of patriarchal ideologies about women's alienation from the natal family and the devaluation of women's labour as being at the heart of the problem, and they all concurred that the solution lay with inheritance rights and less dependence on marriage for survival.

These comprehensive approaches to dowry focused not on

the details of gift-giving practices but on the systemic problem of marriage, arguing for simultaneous legal reform and social change on multiple fronts. Proposals to counter the impact of dowry by instituting property rights for women instead, for example, point to the need for multi-level changes: if women's structural subordination remains constant, strict legislative attempts to either ban dowry or enforce equal inheritance are likely to increase women's vulnerability and dowry-related violence against them. On the one hand, removing dowry entirely in the absence of guarantees of inheritance (wills, gifts, etc., being common strategies to bypass legal directives against equal inheritance) deprives women of the few natal resources they garner and value. On the other hand, emphasising inheritance for women without being able to stem the custom of wedding prestations leaves open possibilities for harassing women and their families for years over property, while dowry expenses are not curtailed in any way, and there is no return flow of resources from daughters in the form of eldercare or other financial help (Basu 1999: 225–6).

The current emphases on maintenance and anti-violence measures also illustrate the problems with challenging gendered norms through law or policy alone. The large number of women who regularly make rounds in court complaining of non-payment of legally granted maintenance, and the minimal convictions that finally result from domestic violence cases filed under Section 498A, as discussed earlier, reveal the difficulties of seeking legal solutions, and the empty promise of legal wins. They exemplify stark inequalities within marriage grounded in women's broader economic subordination, as well as cultural resistances to dealing with family violence. While these legal strategies provide better grounds for negotiation than the Dowry Prohibition Act, they are limited by the imbrications of law within patriarchal relations.

Contemporary interventions discussed earlier, both in feminist organisations and in Family Courts or mediation services,[5] seem to have stopped focusing conspicuously on dowry. However, their strategies, while markedly less radical, perhaps far more wary of formal legal interventions, may be seen to strike at modulating economic inequalities in marriage and bringing diverse forms of intra-family violence under scrutiny, which happen to be close to the broader goals of the original anti-dowry movement in ways that the Dowry Prohibition Act did not succeed in achieving. These are primarily pragmatic manoeuvres that work in the shadow of law rather than radical revisualisations of power relations, often embedded in affirming patriarchal privileges rather than challenging them. They are not necessarily an improvement on existent legal provisions but serve as adaptations to emergent problems.

Both comprehensive theoretical formulations coming out of the anti-dowry movement and these on-the-ground adaptations confront a problematic of enormous proportions: given the near-universality of wedding prestations, the task of eradicating or even transforming marriage customs such as gifts at weddings seems formidably difficult, but the more fundamental task of rendering (heterosexual, patrilineal) marriage more equal is at least as daunting. Powerful feminist analyses of the problem by individuals and organisations in the 1980s, as discussed earlier, point to the difficulties of translating theory into broad-ranging change in social practices, whether through law, policy or education. However, they also indicate the flexibility of cultural responses to legislation, and the importance of seeing the legal as a site of ongoing vigilance for feminist practice. If the violence and impoverishment related to dowry practice is to be substantively eradicated, then strategic configurations of gender, or power relations embedded in gender norms, need to be the first line of resistance, within which opposition to dowry might be one locus of negotiation.

Conclusion: dowry signifies a problem of marriage

'The practice of dowry itself is a crime, not just its excesses,' a recent AIDWA (All India Democratic Women's Association)[6] report declares in its title (2002). Launching a call for a renewed national campaign against dowry, it points out that feminist organising around dowry seemed to fade away in the 1990s (and, my own fieldwork confirms, in the new century). Mobilisation around dowry violence has perhaps died out in the women's movement as the practices of gift-giving and the forms of violence and legal strategies have been transformed; moreover, piecemeal legal reform has failed to address broader questions of gender subordination. Presently, the energies of women's non-governmental organisations dealing with marriage and family law have been taken up with finding precise and effective ways to deal with domestic violence, rather than dowry deaths as the proxy for forms of domestic violence. This includes interventions in the Family Courts to curb overreaching judicial bias, deliberating whether Section 498A of the Indian Penal Code against 'torture' is misused through police discretion, and campaigning for a focused Domestic Violence Act including the controversial provision to grant married women protected residence in affinal homes despite their allegations of domestic violence. Dowry may have become a shadow antagonist in the process.

In conclusion I return to the two legal cases about innovatively avoiding or 'deflecting' dowry, as a reminder that the analysis of dowry practices leads us to the crux of the problem at the intersection of compulsory heterosexual marriage as a mechanism of enforcing gender subordination, and the reproduction of economic/class relations through marriage practices. The perception of this coalescence, present in many analyses from the anti-dowry movement but minimised in legal reform efforts and organising strategies, can provide a comprehensive rubric, a transformative feminist mode of moving beyond piecemeal solutions such as dowry goods recovery and domestic violence. In the first case of the young man who did not appear on a maintenance hearing, his wife's family was so poor that they struggled daily for food and had been able to come up only with Rs 5000 (just over US$ 100 at the going rate) for their daughter's wedding. Their struggles were compounded by the fact that another daughter had died shortly after marriage and they had to raise her daughter. They had not even thought to enquire of the full name and address of the groom, or his vulnerable living situation and the lack of any income, happy to have found someone who would (temporarily, it turned out) 'take' a daughter for the small sum they had. In the second case, of the woman's physical scars being the apparent point of contention, the woman's family, also quite poor, had sold the only land they had for a dowry of Rs 40,000 (about US$ 800), because the groom's family had a lot of farm and orchard land. They chose not to enquire too closely about his lack of employment or his alleged sexual affairs, and in the negotiations, clearly wanted to persist with the marriage despite their accusations of his greed, cruelty and adultery.

Hypergamous marriage practices, the idea that daughters need to marry 'up' to be better off, coalesce in these cases with ideas of marriage as the prime form of property and sustenance for daughters, resulting in vicious cycles of impoverishment through sales of meagre property shares or other resources. While dowry (or marriage expenses generally) becomes the vehicle for passing the daughter on, the bride's economic and physical vulnerability make her the ideal locus for destitution and violence. The fundamental problems lie here with the symbolic status of dowry (or bride wealth) as transfers of wealth marking women's status as transacted objects, and importantly, the corresponding assumption that marriage itself will provide a woman with all the security she needs. Doing away with dowry in any substantive fashion thus requires confronting this fundamental formulation which is at the core of the patriarchal transmission of resources and structures of class. Strategies such as seeking comprehensive legal solutions for maintenance and against violence, boycotting dowry, avoiding extravagant weddings, extending full inheritance to daughters, or instituting marital property rather than making women dependent on affinal and personal resources, all function here as critical pieces of the comprehensive project of challenging gender subordination by transforming 'culture' at the level of intimate practices. The crucial task ahead is to link these strategies in developing tools that address fundamental structural problems with marriage and the concomitant control of property and sexuality, within and around the slippery terrain of law.

Notes

[1] 'Etic' here includes perspectives that are outside Indian women's movements, and does not refer to non-Indian perspectives.

[2] This includes: Section 498A of the Indian Penal Code relating to 'cruelty' which may drive a woman to suicide or 'harassment' related to 'unlawful demands for property'; Section 304B of the Indian Penal Code and Sections 113A and 113B of the Evidence Act relating to presumption of dowry deaths for unnatural deaths within seven years of marriage carrying a term of seven years to life; Section 174 of the Criminal Procedure Code relating to compulsory post-mortems for women dying within seven years of marriage; and Section 32(1) of the Evidence Act which accords importance to dying declarations in assessing guilt of the accused.

[3] Literally women's property, legally deemed to include gifts given to her at marriage which might include goods of common use.

[4] Divorce is a civil matter, but maintenance in case of financial hardship may be determined under Section 125 of the Indian Penal Code, in which case default on payment would be a criminal offence with fines and a potential jail sentence.

[5] There are a plethora of mediation organisations that deal with questions of Family Law, such as mediation services offered by the State through the Family Court or Women's Grievance Cell in the police station, mediation through local branches of the ruling political party, non-governmental organisations loosely connected to the party by the involvement of senior party members, alternate dispute resolution offered through village/community level boards and independent women's organisations that engage in avowedly 'feminist' politics to a greater or lesser extent. Most of these venues offer few critiques of gendered hierarchies as a significant problem, but the very fact of their prolific existence gestures in part to the mainstreaming of feminist emphases on the need for mediated interventions in Family Law.

[6] The women's wing of the Communist Party of India (Marxist), one of the most prominent political parties in India.

References

AIDWA (All India Democratic Women's Association). 2002. *The Practice of Dowry Itself is a Crime, Not Just its Excesses: A Report on the National Workshop on Expanding Dimensions of Dowry.* New Delhi: September 1–2.

Agarwal, Bina. 1994. *A Field of One's Own: Gender and Land Rights in South Asia.* Cambridge: Cambridge University Press.

Anderson, Siwan. 2003. 'Why Dowry Payments Declined with Modernization in

Europe but Are Rising in India'. *Journal of Political Economy.* 111.2.

Biao, Xiang. 2005. 'Gender, Dowry and the Migration System of Indian Information Technology Professionals'. *Indian Journal of Gender Studies.* 12.2–3. pp. 357–80.

Basu, Srimati. 1999. *She Comes to Take Her Rights: Indian Women, Property and Propriety.* Albany: SUNY P.

———. 2007. 'Playing Off Courts: The Negotiation of Divorce and Violence in Plural Legal Settings in Kolkata, India'. *Journal of Legal Pluralism and Unofficial Law.* 52. pp. 41–75.

Batabyal, Amitrajeet and Hamid Beladi. 2007. 'Mediator Learning and Dowry Determination in an Arranged Marriage Setting'. *Economics Bulletin.* 15.12. pp. 1–10.

Committee on the Status of Women in India. 1975. *Towards Equality: Report of the Committee on the Status of Women in India.* New Delhi: Ministry of Education and Social Welfare, Government of India.

Dalmia, Sonia and Pareena G. Lawrence. 2005. 'The Institution of Dowry in India: Why it Continues to Prevail'. *The Journal of Developing Areas.* 38.2. pp. 71–93.

Gautam, D.N. and B.V. Trivedi. 1986. *Unnatural Deaths of Married Women with Special Reference to Dowry Deaths: A Sample Study of Delhi.* New Delhi: Bureau of Police and Research and Development, Ministry of Home Affairs.

Jethmalani, Rani. ed. 1995. *Kali's Yug: Empowerment, Law, and Dowry Deaths.* New Delhi: Har-Anand Publications.

Kishwar, Madhu. 1999. *Off the Beaten Track: Rethinking Gender Justice for Indian Women.* New Delhi: Oxford University Press.

Kumar, Radha. 1994. 'The Campaign Against Dowry' in *The History of Doing: An Illustrated Account of Movements for Women's Rights and Feminism in India, 1800–1990.* New Delhi: Kali for Women.

Lakshmi, C.S. 1989. 'On Kidneys and Dowry.' *Economic and Political Weekly.* 24. 28 Jan. pp. 189–91.

Menon, Nivedita. 1999. 'Embodying the Self: Feminism, Sexual Violence and the Law' in *Community, Gender and Violence: Subaltern Studies No. 11.* eds. Partha Chatterjee and Pradeep Jeganathan. New York: Columbia University Press. pp. 66–105.

Narayan, Uma. 1997. ' Cross-Cultural Connections, Border Crossings & Death by Culture' in *Dislocating Cultures: Identities, Traditions and Third World Feminism.* New York: Routledge. pp. 81–117.

Palriwala, R. 1989. 'Reaffirming the Anti-Dowry Struggle'. *Economic and Political Weekly.* 29 Apr. pp. 942–4.

Rajan, Rajeswari S. 2005. 'Rethinking Law and Violence: The Domestic Violence (Prevention) Bill in India, 2002' in *Violence, Vulnerability and Embodiment: Gender and History.* eds. Shani D'Cruze and Anupama Rao. London: Wiley-Blackwell. pp. 276–300.

Shenk, Mary K. 2007. 'Dowry and Public Policy in Contemporary India: The Behavioral Ecology of a "Social Evil".' *Human Nature* 18. pp. 242–63.

Solanki, Gopika. 2001. 'Women's Experiences through the Police Lens: Analysis of Cases Registered under Section 498(A).' *Journal of Gender Studies* 10. pp. 83–6.

Srinivasan, Padma and Gary R. Lee. 2004. 'The Dowry System in Northern India: Women's Attitudes and Social Change'. *Journal of Marriage and Family.* 66. pp. 1108–17.

Srinivasan, Sharada. 2005. 'Daughters or Dowries? The Changing Nature of Dowry Practices in South India'. *World Development.* 33.4. pp. 593–615.

Umar, Mohammad. 1998. *Bride Burning in India: A Socio-Legal Study.* New Delhi: APH Publishing Corporation.

Dowry and Transnational Activism

MANGALA SUBRAMANIAM, KAREN REMEDIOS

and DEBARASHMI MITRA

Introduction

Challenging gender inequalities in education, employment, and reproductive rights has been a priority for women's groups all over the world. Predictably, attempts to address these issues have led to the questioning of accepted norms as well as protests against practices that have been reified in the name of 'culture'. As the movements have matured, local and national organisations have broadened their scope and formed local and international coalitions with other women's groups aiming to create and/or strengthen transnational ties (see Ferree and Tripp 2006; Moghadam 2005; Ferree and Mueller 2004; Ferree and Subramaniam 2001; Basu 2000 among others). The United Nations Women's Conferences since the mid-1970s provide fertile ground for networking and forming coalitions among women's movement groups, including NGOs, based in the global North and South. These conferences are also sites for lobbying by women's groups; the targets are more often than not specific national governments as well as international organisations. Over the past two decades, a multitude of issues across the North and South have been taken up at these conferences by women's groups; they range from reproductive rights, provision of basic needs, and gendered violence. We focus on one issue, the practice of dowry.

In this paper, we adopt a sociological social movement approach to analyse the framing of the practice of dowry at a national and local level within India and at a global level. The practice of dowry has been closely linked to violence and death often without attention to contextual factors, such as gender hierarchies in society and unequal marriage practices and expectations which feeds into what Narayan (1997: 87) refers to as the tendency to suggest that Third-World women suffer 'death by culture'. We argue that there has been a tendency in scholarly work (particularly that by western feminists) and the media to reduce the dowry issue to its violent outcomes and to also consider that dowry violence/death is a product of South Asian 'culture'. We suggest (see also Basu; Bradley; Palriwala in this volume) that while violence and death are outcomes of dowry practices and that South Asian culture can support unequal dowry customs, to reduce dowry to either is simplistic and works against the interests of initiatives to end abusive dowry practices.

This paper explores the argument that the tendency as noted above, however, can be explained by a focus on violence against women, particularly by transnational networks which emerged as early as 1974 (Tripp 2006). By the 1990s the issue of gender-based violence had gained prominence at the global level (Keck and Sikkink 1998) where it had a broad meaning including state violence against women, particularly in Latin America, trafficking of women, domestic violence and rape, violence caused by economic deprivation, structural adjustment, and war. However, particular experiences of violence, such as 'dowry deaths', are mentioned without reference to women's subordination as related to dowry and marriage, and nor is any information included about women being harassed and abused for dowry without being murdered. These details are not captured in the global frame. We suggest the reasons for this can be seen as deliberate or strategic but the global frame can also have a tendency to overlook the specific context of what is categorised as violence against women in particular locations.

Dowry deaths (also often termed as 'dowry murders') refer to the deaths, by burning, of young married women by their in-laws and emerged as a new phenomenon in the late 1970s in India. In the 1950s, dowry was viewed as a problem of expensive weddings and unreasonable demands that prevented many middle-class families from finding suitable grooms for their daughters. Over time, the requirements from the groom and the family have grown making it difficult for the bride's families to meet them. This was often followed up by periodic requests for additional items and cash. Not meeting the demands often led to the harassment and murder of the bride.

The violence perpetuated against women in marriages can comprise more than one 'frame', including domestic violence, harassment for dowry and murder as related to dowry. A frame (a noun and a product) can be seen as a 'story line' (Gamson and Wolfsfeld 1993: 117), while framing (a verb and a process) is the active process of creating the story line. A frame is an 'interpretive schemata that simplifies and condenses the world out there by selectively punctuating and encoding objects, situations, events, experiences, and sequences of actions within one's present or past environment' (Snow and Benford 1992: 137). Frames may be deployed by various actors (women's groups/movement organisations within nations and transnational networks, the state, and international organisations) and may be similar or may differ across the local/national and global levels. Framing refers here to the special category of cognitive understandings—collective action frames—relating to how social movements construct meaning (Snow and Benford 1992; Benford and Snow 2000). A global frame gains centrality and primacy for an individual such that it fundamentally reorders his or her world view. This frame takes on a dominant status because of its inclusiveness and scope (all encompassing) which allow it to be adopted by movements across borders and cultures and to interact with political structures and larger societal ideologies to achieve substantial change. Interestingly, there has been little analysis of such framing of the practice of dowry per se, a practice that in itself has reinforced women's subordination and in many instances perpetrated violence against women.

Modern dowries include large amounts of gold, cash, and consumer goods and transcend caste and class. Over the past few decades, the demands of the grooms and their families have grown in proportion and volume. The pervasive practice of dowry reinforces gender inequality by structuring power in marriage and within the family. Yet the practice of dowry and the violence associated with it have not gone unchallenged. While some of these challenges are captured in scholarship examining the dynamics of the women's movement, little attention has been directed at the ways in which dowry and/or related violence are framed. How are challenges to the practice of dowry framed locally and transnationally and why?[1] We address this question by focusing on local and national organised action against dowry and the ways in which the issue has been framed within India, particularly by the Indian women's movement, and international organisations (United Nations) at the global level.

While dowry has been challenged as a fundamental issue at the local and national level (within India) by referencing the practice and the violence frequently associated with it, at the global level the emphasis has been on violence against women per se. This is because of the increasing emphasis on the universal framing of human rights as a global frame of violence that encompasses various forms of violence (see also Basu in this volume). However, this circumvents the need to question gendered practices that are defended by some as cultural practices, thus failing to acquire a sufficient understanding of the context of the changing dowry system. Although there may be 'problematic explanations' of dowry murders as argued by Narayan (1997), there is also the possibility of using culture as a convenient reason for not intervening to address the gendered power dimension of practices such as dowry. We explore the activism against dowry as well as the local/national and global framing of dowry by drawing on data from multiple sources: primary textual data in the form of reports and conventions from the UN, and secondary sources that document protests and organised action against it. We also draw on our own experiences and research on women's movements in India. Using these data sources and theoretical framework that follows, we ask: 'How is the practice of dowry framed locally and globally and why?'

Activism and framing: local and global

Although widely used by feminist scholars, the term 'activism' is often less preferred than the concept of 'agency', because the idea of activism is perceived as lacking theoretical relevance within mainstream sociological scholarship. Broadly defined, it involves consciously taking action to effect some level of social or political change. Ferree and Subramaniam (2001: 1) posit that activism 'encompasses all collective efforts to change power relations at all levels'. However, activism often involves individual action (Bell 2001).

Explicating what constitutes activism is complex, as it may encompass a myriad tactics to confront sexism, classism, heterosexism, or racism, for instance (Springer 1999). The term comprises a variety of forms of action, focusing on daily practical needs at a local grass-roots level and policy advocacy at a national level. It could involve collective effort through public protests or simply individual action, such as signing petitions or writing, or transforming consciousness through teaching. Thompson (2001: xxvi) eloquently describes this variation through her interviews with activists, noting that 'a common stereotype of activists is that of placard-carrying protesters attending rallies and demonstrations. Although protests have often been used as markers for the telling of social movement history, activists' everyday lives tend to be much less dramatic, much more mundane, and much less collective than activist-as-demonstrator icon suggests'. Less dramatic daily resistances can be central to challenging power subtly, even if such subversion involves grass-roots organising (see Subramaniam 2006; Bell 2001; Bystydzienski and Sekhon 1999). Moreover, localised grass-roots organising is not isolated or separate from translocal struggles or movement initiatives.

Movements involve networks of individuals and organisations across the local and global (Subramaniam, Gupte and Mitra 2003;

Ferree and Mueller 2004; Moghadam 2005). This complex transnational networks of individuals and organisations, as well as international conventions and reports (such as country reports submitted to the UN), facilitate or constrain movement action locally. Local and global meanings attributed to issues of concern, such as gender-based violence and dowry in this paper, may differ for two reasons. First, local women's groups negotiate and strategically deploy frames that resonate with their immediate constituency, in that contextual information already available is used by local groups to provide meaning to an issue. Second, movement groups at a local versus national or global level may frame gender-based violence based on their targets for action; international institutions such as the UN at the global level, national governments such as the national parliament for the creation of legal instruments, courts for enforcement of law, and so on. Thus, movement groups may target different sets of actors locally and transnationally and thereby be strategic in choice of frames.

Local and global framing

Social movements and movement organisations are deeply involved in 'naming' grievances, connecting them to other grievances and constructing larger frames of meaning that will resonate with a population's cultural predispositions and communicate a uniform message to power holders and others (Gamson 1992). Frames can be seen as 'part of the world, passive and structured' (Gamson and Meyer 1996: 276), but, can also be perceived as active, as constructed by people, the state, religious institutions and the like. Opportunities shape or constrain movements depending on how events are imbued with meaning by groups or specific agencies, and the outcome of such an interaction (Gamson and Meyer 1996). For instance, framing by the state on any pertinent issue concerned with gender is influenced by organisations within the women's movement. Changing global conditions and the international mobilisation of women can also influence the framing of an issue.

Local movement actors often garner transnational support through the successful sharing of vision and information across borders. Movement organisations frame messages in a manner in which people are able to 'perceive, identify, and label' the social phenomena as something deserving of their attention and subsequent action (Snow, Rochford, Worden and Benford 1986: 464). This process of mutual information exchange possesses unique challenges as organisations must present issues that resonate with people living in various cultural contexts with a multitude of culturally significant frames (Ferree 2006). Exchanges of information occur within a political context of meanings. Specific frames resonate when they are able to capitalise on a dominant discourse. Such hegemonic discourse appears in formal political institutional texts as state legislation, but also in other (though no less political) forms as in the media and other cultural texts. Discourse, like material goods, diffuses across borders. Diffusion refers to the spread of an innovation, idea or practice that is being framed (Della Porta and Tarrow 2005; McAdam and Rucht 1993; Soule 2004) and is useful in explaining how ideas, beliefs, and practices move from one movement to another or one culture to another. But frames are likely to be modified or entirely altered in the diffusion process to ensure they resonate with the audience being addressed. Such modifications may depend upon the information that movement organisations, within and across nations, have and choose to use to compose meaning. Thus, frames deployed at the local and/or national level may differ from those drawn upon at the global level which occurs at a supra-national level, such as that by international women's groups based outside India in the case considered in this paper. Such a supra-national effort may not consider the local/national context and/or involve networks between local/national women's groups and international women's groups.

We argue that while movement networks and organisations may have similar beliefs and goals, framing strategies may vary across the local and global levels and have implications for ways in which practices, such as dowry, may be challenged, or otherwise be redefined and encompassed in a broader frame to seek the support and understanding of a wider constituency. Institutions at the local and global level are possibly being strategic in their framing effort particularly when it concerns gender and culture/ cultural practices. Global level organisations, such as the UN, are likely to draw on a frame that is meaningful to an international audience and avoid being drawn into a debate about cultural practices that may be perceived as being sensitive within a particular society.

Data and methods

We draw from several primary and secondary sources to trace movement challenges to dowry at the local, national and global level. A grounded theory approach was used to analyse the reports described below which facilitated identifying the varying emphasis and descriptions about dowry.

For analyses of the local and national level movement activity and framing we utilise a synthesis paper of 'violence against women' research published by the International Centre for Research on Women (ICRW) under its four-year grant programme, 'Promoting Women in Development' (PROWID). This report (Burton, Duvvury and Varia 2000: 12) is based on eight research studies in India which document the 'prevalence, trends, and responses to domestic violence' and analyse multiple forms of data. The studies include primary survey data from Gujarat, hospital records in Thane district (Maharashtra), a population-based survey of domestic violence in several major towns and cities of India, and court records in Bangalore district (Karnataka). While the findings do not explicitly consider dowry-related violence, the report calls for developing women's consciousness of their human rights and emphasises the need for discussion of the concepts of gender and human rights. We also draw on several valuable secondary sources and our research on the women's movement in India and internationally for the analyses (cf. Subramaniam 2004, 2006; Subramaniam, Gupte and Mitra 2003; Chacko 2001; Forbes

1996; Basu 1992; Calman 1992; Dietrich 1992; Desai and Patel 1985).

For the global level analyses, we rely on reports from two agencies of the United Nations: the Office of the Special Rapporteur of Violence against Women (Coomaraswamy 2000, 2002) and the Division for the Advancement of Women that handles details related to the Convention for the Elimination of All Forms of Discrimination against Women (CEDAW). The 1999 CEDAW report aims to integrate the human rights of women and the gender perspective by focusing on violence against women in the family across the various regions of the world, including India. In sharp contrast, the 2002 and 2003 reports of the UN Economic and Social Council (ECOSOC) focus specifically on cultural practices in the family that are violent towards women across the world. They are an analysis of cultural practices, such as female genital mutilation, incest, son preference and marriage. Dowry as a practice is covered in the discussion of marriage. Also included is one report from the Indian government as a response to the UN (2005). This refers to the 'principal areas of concern and recommendations' of CEDAW (2005) as outlined in the concluding comments on India's report (2005) and includes the information that was lacking in the Initial Report (1999). It also highlights the developments that have taken place during the years 1997 to 2005. Under violence against women, the Indian government outlines a four-pronged strategy to address violence: (a) legislative action; (b) training and awareness; (c) support services, through crisis intervention and rehabilitation centres, crimes against women cells, strict enforcement of poverty alleviation programmes, enhanced opportunities for education of girls and proactive measures by enforcement machinery with participation of NGOs; and (d) action at the social level, such as encouraging NGOs to generate public opinion on law enforcement agencies, to set up self-help groups of women and to organise gender awareness weeks. Dowry is specifically referred to only to explain the state initiatives such as the dowry prohibition legislation. The report notes that practices like dowry are 'detrimental to the development and empowerment of women' (p. 93) and therefore a national policy (National Policy for the Empowerment of Women) was being considered.

Activism against dowry

In this section we trace resistances and protests against dowry led by women's groups in local communities and state capitals in India, the framing of the issue of dowry and violence locally and nationally, and discuss the global framing of dowry.

Although the practice of dowry has its roots in the traditional upper caste marriage rituals of *kanyadan* and *varadakshina*, dowry-related issues are widely prevalent among all other castes of Hindus, Muslims (in the practice of *zehez*, which literally means dowry) and Christians (Caplan 1987; Kumari 1989). The pervasiveness of dowry-related violence against women in contemporary India is evident in the increasing number of cases. India's National Crime Records Bureau documents crimes committed under 'cruelty by husband and relatives' not amounting to death. Such harassment increased by about 51 per cent over a 10-year period; from 28,579 in 1995 to 58,319 in 2005. By some estimates, more than 15,000 women die in dowry related homicides each year (Banerjee 1997). A report by the UN's Special Rapporteur of Violence against Women notes that 'millions of women are missing in less developed countries' (Coomaraswamy 2000: 6) as a result of violence against them including domestic violence such as dowry deaths and sex selective abortions. This figure is likely to be underestimated because crimes against women by the spouse and in-laws are often misrepresented or under-reported because of social stigma.

An initial response of the state to the concerns about the effects of dowry was the creation of legislation, the Dowry Prohibition Act, passed in 1961, but it did little to reform marriage, and dowry as a practice continued. According to the law, both the families that gave dowry and those that took it were guilty; but not a single case was registered until the late 1970s. Women activists became disillusioned with the state's inability to enforce dowry laws and redefined the problem by drawing attention to these deaths that began to be increasingly reported in the media.

Women's groups describe dowry-related deaths as 'murders' and 'forced suicides.' Follow-up of such deaths by women's organisations led to the appointment of a Joint Committee of the two Houses of the Indian Parliament (Lok Sabha and Rajya Sabha), to re-examine the existing law. The ensuing legislation (Section 498A of the Indian Penal Code) raised the punishment for accepting dowry and decreed that in cases where a woman died an unnatural death, her property would devolve on her children or be returned to her parents. The new legislation was passed in 1986 but dowry deaths continue (Purkayastha et al. 2003). Anti-dowry activists have claimed that the law continues to evade demands for justice on the part of victims and point to police indifference, corruption, low rates of conviction, a backlog of cases, and legal technicalities as impediments to swift justice. More recently, activists have taken up public interest litigation to represent individual victims of dowry deaths and provide legal counsel and support for those who wish to use the court system (see Basu in this volume). But most importantly, women's organisations have continued to intensely protest the practice of dowry at the local level within towns and city suburbs as well as at the national level through major campaigns and rallies such as in the national capital of Delhi and the city of Mumbai (Kumar 1993).

Indian women's activism at local and national levels

Women's groups and activists at the local level have protested against dowry deaths, suicides related to dowry, and dowry harassment in various states in India. Their importance lies in the sharing of experiences in small consciousness-raising groups that is somewhat significant compared to the more visible campaigns of women's organisations in Delhi and other state capitals. Consciousness-raising efforts facilitate individual and collective challenges to gender-based subordination and oppression. One of the first protests against dowry was organised by the Progressive

Organisation of Women in Hyderabad in 1975 (Kumar 1993). In subsequent years, similar protests were carried out in other parts of the country with Delhi having a more sustained anti-dowry demonstration owing to the highest number of reported dowry-related murders and suicides in the city (ibid.). Activism in the form of protests were spearheaded by a number of women's organisations such as Mahila Dakshata Samiti, Janawadi Mahila Samiliti, Karmika, Nari Raksha Samiti and Stri Sangharsh, which included student activists from Indraprastha College Committee, and the Progressive Students' Organisation (ibid.).

In 1979, a landmark demonstration was organised by Stri Sangharsh to protest against the death of Tarvinder Kaur, which was registered as a case of suicide by the police. Nearly 1500 people of the neighbourhood joined this protest in their support for a social boycott of the family of Kaur's in-laws (Kishwar 2003). The impetus for this demonstration came from the Indraprastha College Women's Committee (Kumar 1993). College students were actively involved in such protests against dowry in Delhi. Another strategy used by woman's organisations was to stage street plays to sensitise the public about the negative effects of the dowry system. *Om Swaha,* a street play, by Stri Sangharsh in Delhi depicted dowry-related oppression and women's resistance to its practice. For the first time, many women had the opportunity to question their position within the larger cultural system of marriage and dowry. Later, new campaigns began in Delhi with a focus on dowry harassment, suicides related to it and dowry murders. Around the same time, the state's involvement in the dowry issue began, with the Prime Minister's declaration of measures to combat dowry in 1978 (Kumar 1993). Soon, campaigns against dowry began to emerge in other states including West Bengal, Karnataka, Maharashtra, Punjab, Gujarat, and Madhya Pradesh. A number of activists, for example, the members of Forum Against Oppression of Women (FAOW) in Mumbai exposed and resisted violence against women in general by seeking legal changes. FAOW, which originally began as an anti-rape campaign in 1979, raised awareness regarding dowry-related violence in later years. It specifically demanded new laws and effective implementation of existing laws to protect women's rights.

Running parallel to the efforts to challenge dowry in particular were attempts to foreground the issue of violence against women in general. More recently, Non-Governmental Organisations (NGOs) in Bangalore, such as Vimochana, have studied dowry and domestic violence as a violation of human rights issue. Another example is from Tehri, Uttarakhand, where women-initiated community level responses to domestic abuse have included attempts to recover the dowry as well as monetary compensation for injuries (Burton et al. 2002). Locally based organisations and self-help groups have allowed women to share their experiences with each other and garner support to resist the practice of dowry. As documented by ICRW researchers, under their programme PROWID, local NGOs in Mumbai, and women's collectives in other parts of the country, organise against domestic violence 'through the formation of community watches, encouragement of active intervention of neighbours during fights, protests against villagers known for harassing daughters-in-law and special community welcomes for young brides' (Burton et al. 2000: 16).

At the national level, dowry as a gender issue and as an act of violence against women gained momentum in the scholarly work of several activists (Kumar 1993; Kumari 1989; Kishwar 1988), as well as through the women's movement. The literature on violence against women and dowry often grew out of women sharing their experiences in small consciousness-raising groups. Following the campaigns and protests in 1970s and 1980s, violence against women became a central issue for women's movement groups and organisations (Kumar 1989). Over these years, women's groups in India have been successful in generating awareness in media and civil society and in criminalising violence against women (Banerjee 1999). In an attempt to address dowry-related harassment and deaths, they have also challenged both patriarchy and capitalism, and have been able to shift the focus of dowry from being a private problem to a public issue, needing the attention of state and legal institutions among others. Politicising the issue of dowry required mobilisation of political and social forces along with protests, as well as lobbying and petitioning against the patriarchal social structure of the family, state and economy. State support in terms of legal amendments and involvement of court and police were also crucial measures that strengthened their goal to curb violence against women. In fact, researchers from ICRW note in their report that reforms have occurred in the legislative and institutional arenas (Burton et al. 2000).

As a consequence of lobbying and campaigning against the practice of dowry by women's organisations, two important laws including the Indian Penal Code and Dowry Prohibition Act were amended in 1986. The Indian Penal Code states that a woman's death any time within the first seven years of marriage will be investigated, and the Dowry Prohibition Act now requires the government to maintain statistics on dowry deaths (Banerjee 1999). Another sign of their success at the national level is the establishment of anti-dowry cells, renamed as Crime against Women Cells in 1986 for handling crimes against women. This institutional mechanism was initiated by the government in various states as a preventative measure. The government is also developing other institutional machinery such as all-women police stations and programmes for gender sensitisation of law enforcement personnel.

While the protests of women's organisations and local women's groups against dowry-related violence have been successful in bringing together disparate groups of women, such as grass-roots activists and researchers, the movement also faces challenges in its efforts to combat the practice of dowry. First, the bureaucracy often delays a timely attention to the issue of crime against women as the traditional gender norms about women's role in private spheres shape the issues of dowry harassment more as a private affair than a public issue. Second, dowry cases are still under-reported, partly owing to the social taboo and partly because of the low rate of convictions of perpetrators of dowry. In the absence of substantial evidence of dowry-related violence, legal interventions by police and courts have remained inadequate. Finally, there are differences in language and framing of dowry as violence against women within feminist movements, which demand and seek change across various arenas: legislative, institutional, as well as in the practice of marriage (child marriage, early marriage, and the power for women to determine choice of partner) and dowry.

Prior to the 1980s, violence against women in India received little attention from women's organisations, political parties, or the media. While state-initiated actions put issues involving women's economic welfare on the agenda, it was women's groups outside of the government that placed body politics on the agenda (Katzenstein 1989, 1991–92). The framing of dowry-related deaths as private and as an issue internal to a family were challenged by women's groups who showed that many official 'suicides' were 'murders.' In fact, the UN Declaration on Violence against Women (1993) adds dowry-related violence to other forms of violence (such as domestic abuse, sexual harassment) as harmful to women. Activists in India, however, disagree on the framing of dowry deaths. For instance, Kishwar (1988) points out that the issue of dowry was not linked to women's rights to property but that instead dowry-related violence was connected to domestic violence. Others, such as Agnihotri and Mazumdar (1995), note that the campaign itself projected the 'women as victim' image to seek change. While there are differences in projections amongst activists and women's organisations, there is an overarching concern and recognition to challenge dowry.

The PROWID synthesis report emphasises the importance of acknowledging domestic violence as a development concern, thus enabling the shift from individual to social responsibility while foregrounding the social, cultural and economic factors that contribute to or hinder this process (Burton et al. 2000: 8–9). Research studies carried out in India suggest that legislation proscribing violence against women has been ineffective in curbing domestic abuse because the laws are not strictly enforced. Thus, despite the existence of a special clause (Section 498A of the Indian Penal Code) which prohibits cruelty to a woman within marriage and specifically addresses dowry-related abuse, dowry harassment continues largely unchecked (Burton et al. 2000: 16).

The 1999 CEDAW report's section on India also emphasises this drawback in the judicial system, which is especially ineffective in prosecuting violence that occurs within the family unit. Ironically, the family is the seedbed not only for so-called cherished Indian values such as respect for elders but also for discriminatory attitudes towards women. As examples of the kinds of violence perpetrated against women within families, the authors cite '[f]emale foeticide, infanticide, dowry violence and torture,' again clubbing together manifestations of gendered practices rather than highlighting the practices per se (UN Committee on the Elimination of Discrimination against Women 1999: 27). We have seen the vibrancy of movement action, specifically women's groups, within India to challenge dowry. This action combines local consciousness-raising efforts with national campaigns organised by women's groups across major towns and cities in India to protest dowry-related violence and deaths. In fact, women's groups have targeted the state and have had some measure of success in seeking legislation and institutional reform to prevent dowry harassment and death, to make the filing of police complaints by harassed women possible, and to strengthen enforcement of legislation. Within India, women's groups frame dowry in specific ways: as oppressive to women and as involving harassment, abuse and death. Such framing captures issue- and context-specific details that are overlooked in a global frame. The emphasis on violence, as we discuss below, is the highlight of the global frame. We therefore first turn to briefly discuss activism related to it at the global level.

Transnational women's activism

A significant impetus for transnational movement action by and for women was facilitated by specific activities initiated and supported by the United Nations. Women's involvement in the UN stems from its inception in 1945 and the United Nations Decade for Women (1975–1985) was a watershed both for placing women on the international intergovernmental agenda and for facilitating their cooperation. While women participated in the official delegations and gatherings of the General Assembly at the three meetings of the Decade, their participation in the NGO. Forums that accompanied each official meeting was equally, if not more, important.[2]

The global conferences in the 1980s and 1990s proved to be fertile ground for raising issues of violence against women and which included the active participation of NGOs.[3] Attention and discussion on issues such as acts of violence against women in international forums has prompted the UN to propose international covenants for ratification by nations. Such macrolevel changes affect microlevel structures and processes and as local challenges develop they influence macrolevel process, policy, and change. From its first use, the term 'violence against women' encompassed a range of practices in diverse locations, from household brutality to the violence of state security forces. But this 'involved a process through which the network helped "create" the issue, in part by naming, renaming, and working out definitions, whereby the concept of "violence against women" eventually unified many practices that in the early 1970s were not understood to be connected' (Keck and Sikkink 1998: 171). The new international attention to violence against women facilitated rethinking the boundaries between the public and the private.

The initial report of the first Special Rapporteur on Violence against Women, issued in 1995, provides a comprehensive analysis of this issue, its roots, and incidents that have occurred throughout the world. Like other recent studies, the report confirms that violence against women persists at all levels and in all parts of the world (Gierycz 1997). It also confirms that some forms of violence are particularly alarming due to their high incidence, their continual increase and their political or cultural nature.

In recent years, violence against women has been a central focus of transnational feminist activism and literature (Keck and Sikkink 1998; Tripp 2006). The United Nations Declaration on the Elimination of Violence against Women (1993) identified three major categories including violence in the family, the general community, and perpetrated or condoned by states with recognition that violent acts against women can take physical, sexual, and psychological forms. The recognition of violence against women through CEDAW and the UN conferences has expanded to the extent of not only becoming a global issue beyond the purview of women's programmes such as UNIFEM and the CEDAW Committee, but to invoke responses from other legal interventions such as Human Rights Watch (1995) and Amnesty International (2004).

While activist organisations from across the world (within nations and transnational networks) focused prominently on violence against women at global forums, activists from India forming transnational advocacy networks have attempted to politicise specific crimes, such as dowry deaths, as instances of such violence. To emphasise our point, it is only in the context of concerns about violence against women that dowry becomes framed at the global/transnational level. Although women's activism against dowry deaths and dowry harassment has not received exclusive attention at the global level, as Keck and Sikkink (1998) note, advocacy networks and human rights groups have brought together various activist campaigns on issues, such as domestic violence, dowry burning, and sexual slavery into international campaigns to end violence against women. For example, women activists from India have recommended strategies to combat violence against women in international meetings, conferences and forums. One such attempt was made by the women's delegation from India, who placed violence against women at the top of the agenda at the Fourth World Conference on Women held in Beijing in 1995. Such international level discourse also facilitated a process of framing where the emphasis was on dowry as violence against women rather than on dowry as being a gendered practice. As discussed below, at the global level the focus is on violence against women which is often a consequence of pressuring the bride's family for dowry. This emphasis does not directly challenge the practice of dowry which subordinates and devalues women within marriage and the family.

Global framing

A majority of the existing international laws and documents that focus on violence against women include rape, sexual slavery, forced prostitution, trafficking of women, forced pregnancy, or any other comparable acts of sexual violence. While we argue that to focus upon dowry as an issue of violence at the expense of other contextual factors is problematic, it is also true that dowry-related violence only receives a rare mention in international laws and amendments; violence against women or domestic violence more broadly remains the main focus of the international documents. Consequently, dowry-related issues have been marginalised at the global level and to some extent in mainstream academia outside of India. To partially correct this lack of attention at the global level, a broader definition and formulation of violence against women that is inclusive of otherwise residual categories of violence against women should be in place. One such effort for the Indian women's movement would be its inclusion in women's human rights. This has still not occurred because women's groups in India, for instance, fear a diversion of attention as well as resources from issues pertaining specifically to women's rights. Moreover, Indian women's groups perceive the concept of human rights as western that is coined in the United States and Europe (Subramaniam 2008).

While violence against women was an issue rarely mentioned in international forums at the beginning of this decade, women's groups from across the world have since actively campaigned for bringing it to the centre of discussions and policy making (Keck and Sikkink 1998). Attempts have also been made by transnational networks and local/national activism in India to link violence against women and human rights (Keck and Sikkink 1998; Coomaraswamy 1997; Forbes 1996). However, although the global recognition of domestic violence and dowry deaths has offered scope for framing of dowry-related violence as violation of women's (human) rights, women's rights issues are relatively weak in many countries, particularly with respect to traditional gender roles in the family (Coomaraswamy 1997). Further, the conceptualisations of domestic violence and human rights that emerge from scholars in countries in the global North (Europe and the US) are challenged by activists in countries such as India as well as some scholars who may be located in the global North but whose work extends across borders into India (Grewal 1999; Narayan 1997; Subramaniam 2008). At the same time, a number of initiatives at the global level such as the Global Campaign for Women's Human Rights are based on a framework of mainstreaming awareness about domestic violence (and women's issues) into the human rights framework. Instead of focusing on the geographical boundaries between the North and the South, the conceptualisation of violence against women in this Global Campaign is based on the political, social and cultural dimensions of human rights (Reilly 1996), which are incorporated into a single legal-cultural-political framework. Such a framework does not sufficiently address women's varied needs, struggle and resistance to gender-based violence that is embedded, defined, and analysed in diverse cultural settings as well as political arenas.

Echoing the same arguments, the report of UN's Special Rapporteur on Violence against Women emphasises an approach to integrate the human rights of women and the gender perspective by recommending that states, international organisations and donor agencies should not only implement the laws but play an active role in eradicating the 'torture-like cultural practices' (Coomaraswamy 2002: 33). The same report recommends that states should not 'invoke any custom, tradition or religious considerations to avoid their obligations to eradicate violence against women and the girl child in the family' (Coomaraswamy 2002: 33), whether these acts are perpetrated by the State or by private actors.

The 2000 UN report on violence against women, funded by the Economic and Social Council (ECOSOC) and presented at the 56th session of the Commission on Human Rights by Coomaraswamy, the UN Special Rapporteur of Violence against Women, touches on the general social and economic situation of women, the effects of globalisation on them, as well as reproductive issues and birth control policies. It states that '[f]emale infanticide, widow murder, neglect of girl children and dowry-deaths are related to the economic potential of women,' and that several million missing specifically in the developing world 'owing to female foeticide, female infanticide, purposeful malnourishment and starvation, neglected health problems and murders, some of which related to dowry—so-called dowry deaths' (Coomaraswamy 2000: 5). This framing effort combines several gender discriminatory issues including dowry deaths without raising concern about dowry as connected to marriage.

Thus, at the global level, the combining of various forms of discrimination against women with dowry deaths, overlooks possible harassment and abuse of brides as possible consequences of dowry and does not question the practice of dowry per se as it relates to marriage. The global frame undermines the complexity of specific issues of violence, such as state-sponsored violence, trafficking of women, domestic violence and rape as well as violence caused by economic deprivation, structural adjustment, and war, by lumping them together. In particular, recognition of particular experiences of violence such as 'dowry deaths' should be connected to the gendered dimension of the practice of dowry to capture the roots of such violence and ensure it does not go unnoticed and unchallenged. While the practice of dowry is described in the Special Rapporteur Coomaraswamy's report, the emphasis is on the outcome of a dowry system that was originally intended to ensure the bride's financial independence: 'If the woman's family fails to pay the full dowry or does not meet demands for further payments, dowry deaths are a frequent consequence' (Coomaraswamy 2000: 7). The 2000 UN report on violence against women deals with cultural practices in the family that violate women's rights, ideologies that perpetuate these practices and state responsibility in this regard. Dowry is briefly mentioned in the section titled 'Marriage,' and once again the focus is on dowry deaths (Coomaraswamy 2000: 20). As noted above, this report focuses on India among other countries of the world.

The advantages of using a global framework of women's rights as human rights (with a broader definition of violence against women) in the context of dowry-related violence are twofold. First, a broader framing of violence that is inclusive of otherwise residual categories of violence against women can have a wider appeal, across geographical borders and would not necessitate specific explanations. Second, in implementing the laws and monitoring dowry-related violence against women, a global framework of women's rights as human rights can be viewed as a process of both legal and cultural transformations, bringing about changes in the cultural practices that marginalise women in various societies.

Conclusion

This paper discussed organised action against dowry in India and challenges to the practice particularly around the issues of violence as a consequence of it, at the global level. Women's movement groups in India have actively sought to organise demonstrations and campaigns against dowry at the local community level as well as the national level. Activists and organisations have also constantly lobbied the state to seek legal action. The Indian state has responded legally and institutionally. Legal initiatives include the law of 1961 to prevent families from giving or receiving dowry and specifically the 1986 Act (Section 498A) that requires investigation of the death of a woman within seven years of marriage. Institutional mechanisms include a concerted effort to maintain statistics on dowry deaths, the establishment of anti-dowry cells within the police system, and all-women police stations to facilitate access for women facing dowry harassment. By referring to the practice of dowry as involving the subordination and control of women, women's groups in India specifically refer to the violence and deaths as related to dowry. There is little or no hesitation in framing dowry as problematic in that it is oppressive, even as the violence against women, specifically 'dowry deaths' are mentioned as a consequence of it. This is in sharp contrast to the frames drawn upon at the global level where the violence and specifically dowry deaths are emphasised without acknowledging the problems with the practice of dowry itself.

Discourse at the global level, and specifically the United Nations documents, refer to the issue of cultural relativism as the greatest challenge to women's rights and the elimination of discriminatory laws and harmful practices. This 'is the belief that no universal legal or moral standard exists against which human practices can be judged' (UN ECOSOC 2003: 16). It is argued by cultural relativists that the rights discourse is not universal but emerges from Europe and as such, is an imposition of European values on other parts of the globe. Therefore, the struggle to eradicate practices is often complicated by what is termed the 'arrogant gaze' of the outsider (UN ECOSOC 2003: 18). This explanation derives from the differential North-South (or developed-developing country) power dynamic which often translates into making the 'third world' appear as the primitive 'other.' Such complexity has possibly led to a strategic choice at the global level in framing dowry as an issue of violence rather than as a gendered cultural practice. This can expand the constituency supporting this cause because the issue of violence resonates amongst women's groups and activists from around the world. Most importantly, such a framing effort is a means to circumvent the cultural relativism debate and simultaneously demonstrate sensitivity to a cultural practice in a developing country. Therefore, it is relevant to point out that the emphasis on (gender) violence rather than the practice of dowry is the essence of the global frame.

However, it is important to note that invoking cultural relativism is often an excuse to allow continuance of discriminatory practices. By not explicitly denouncing practices like dowry (by maintaining it is cultural), global level organisations and activists *appear* to condone and overlook the consequences of the undervaluing of women through societal social practices. The differential framing between the local/national and the global levels could be explained as a transformation of a frame as it diffuses across borders. This transformation is occurring across levels without any attempts to create a transnational linkage involving dialogue and exchange between local/national level women's groups in India and those based outside to build a common platform and meaning. This global framing occurs at a supra-national level that may not account for meanings created by local/national women's groups. Such a lack of linkage between women's groups may constrain flow of information across levels and result in a variation in framing; the emphasis at the global level on violence without attention to the gendered basis of dowry in contrast to the local/national level framing of both the practice of dowry and related violence. It is this inconsistency in framing across levels that made us refer to the local and global level framing rather than transnational framing. Our reference to transnational activism is about linkages that women's groups/organisations have established across borders; within India and at a global level. These linkages do not directly imply that framing of challenges to dowry are the same across these borders. We refer to the framing of dowry primarily as violence in the UN documents as global level framing of the practice because they do not indicate or reflect transnational ties or connections in their documents.

Finally, we suggest two possible ways to bridge the local and global frames. First, global initiatives against dowry should consider taking direction from local (within India) efforts to challenge the practice and seek rights for women. Working with local women's organisations can also bring about meaningful partnerships and collaborations to pressure for change in gender and overall social relations, such as challenging dowry. Second, we call for a greater number of initiatives, such as this volume, to address and analyse the practice of dowry from a variety of angles and lenses. Moreover, by bringing scholars from across borders to discuss the various social, cultural, and legal dimensions of dowry, this volume attempts to bridge the local and global frames; thereby creating a transnational network to challenge the practice of dowry.

Notes

[1] Narayan (1997) discusses the complexities in the movement of information about dowry across borders, and how such distortions lead to references of dowry as what she calls 'death by culture.' We note the importance of this work but at the same time distinguish our research and analyses as important to the social movement scholarship on framing occurring within India and the global level.

[2] The Division for the Advancement of Women provides UN Secretariat support for the Economic and Social Council and its Commission on the Status of Women. The Economic and Social Council is listed as one of the main bodies of the UN. It may make or initiate studies and reports with respect to international economic, social, cultural, educational, health, and related matters and may make recommendations with respect to any such matters to the General Assembly, to the members of the UN, and to the specialised agencies concerned. The Office of the Special Rapporteur of Violence against Women is listed within the Human Rights Programme (in the list of sub-topics). See details at http://www.un.org/issues/m-women.html.

[3] The three meetings of the Decade were held at Mexico City in 1975, in Copenhagen in 1980, and in Nairobi in 1985.

References

Agnihotri, Indu and Vina Mazumdar. 1995. 'Changing Terms of Political Discourse: Women's Movement in India, 1970s-1990s'. *Economic and Political Weekly* 30. no. 29. July. pp. 1869–78.

Amnesty International. 2004. *It's in Our Hands—Stop Violence Against Women.* London: Amnesty International.

Banerjee, Kakoli. 1999. 'Gender Stratification and the Contemporary Marriage Market in India.' *Journal of Family Issues.* 20(5). pp. 648–76.

Banerjee, Partha. 1997. 'A matter of extreme cruelty: Bride burning and dowry deaths in India.' *Injustice Studies* 1.

Basu, Amrita. 1992. *Two Faces of Protest: Contrasting Modes of Women's Activism in India.* Berkeley, CA: University of California Press.

———. 2000. 'Globalization of the Local/Localization of the Global: Mapping Transnational Women's Movements.' *Meridians: Feminism, Race, Transnationalism* 1. no. 1. Autumn. pp. 68–84.

Bell, Beverly. 2001. *Walking on Fire. Haitian Women's Stories of Survival and Resistance.* Ithaca, NY: Cornell University Press.

Benford, R.D. and D. Snow. 2000. 'Framing processes and social movements: An overview and assessment.' *Annual Review of Sociology.* 26. pp. 611–39.

Burton, Barbara, Nata Duvvury and Nisha Varia. 2000. *Justice, Change, and Human Rights: International Research and Responses to Domestic Violence.* Synthesis Paper. A report of the International Centre for Research on Women and the Centre for Development and Population Activities.

Bystydzienski, Jill M. and Joti Sekhon. eds. 1999. *Democratization and Women's Grassroots Movement.* Bloomington, IN: Indiana University Press.

Calman, Leslie J. 1992. *Toward Empowerment: Women and Movement Politics in India.* Boulder, CO: Westview Press.

Caplan, Lionel. 1987. *Class and Culture in Urban India: Fundamentalism in a Christian Community.* New York: Oxford University Press

Chacko, Shubha. 2001. *Changing the Stream: Backgrounder on the Women's Movement in India.* Mumbai and Bangalore: Centre for Education and Documentation.

Coomaraswamy, R. 1997. 'Reinventing International Law: Women's Rights as Human Rights in the International Community'. Edward Smith lecture, Harvard University Law School. Available (http://www.law.harvard.edu/programs/hrp/Publications/radhika.html).

——. 2000. United Nations Economic and Social Council Report of the Special Rapporteur on Violence against Women, its Causes, and Consequences submitted in accordance with the Commission on Human Rights resolution 1997/44. Addendum—Economic and Social Policy and its Impact on Violence against Women. E/CN.4/2000/68/Add. 5. 24 February.

——. 2002. United Nations Economic and Social Council. Report of the Special Rapporteur on Violence against Women, its Causes, and Consequences submitted in accordance with the Commission on Human Rights resolution 2001/49. Cultural Practices in the Family that are Violent towards Women. E/CN.4/2002/68/83. 31 January.

Della Porta, Donatella and Sidney Tarrow. 2005. *Transnational Protest and Global Activism.* New York: Rowman and Littlefield.

Desai, Neera and Vibhuti Patel. 1985. *Indian Women: Change and Challenge in the International Decade 1975–85.* Bombay: Popular Prakashan.

Dietrich, Gabriele. 1992. *Reflections on the Women's Movement in India: Religion, Ecology, Development.* New Delhi: Horizon India Books.

Ferree Myra Marx. 2006. 'Globalization and Feminism: Opportunities and Obstacles for Activism in the Global Arena' in *Global Feminism: Transnational Women's Activism, Organizing, and Human Rights.* eds. Myra Marx Ferree and Aili Marie Tripp. New York: New York University Press. pp. 3–23.

—— and Carol Mueller. 2004. 'Feminism and the Women's Movement: A Global Perspective' in *The Blackwell Companion to Social Movements.* eds. David A. Snow, Sarah A. Soule and Hanspeter Kriesi. Oxford: Blackwell Publishing. pp. 576–607

—— and Mangala Subramaniam. 2001. 'Activism.' *International Encyclopedia of Women.* New York: Routledge.

222

—— and Aili Marie Tripp. eds. 2006. *Global Feminism: Transnational Women's Activism, Organizing, and Human Rights*. New York: New York University Press.

Forbes, Geraldine. 1996. *Women in Modern India*. Cambridge: Cambridge University Press.

Gamson, William. 1992. 'The Social Psychology of Collective Action' in *Frontiers in Social Movement Theory*. eds. A. Morris and C. Mueller. New Haven, CT: Yale University Press. pp. 53–76.

—— and David S. Meyer. 1996. 'Framing Political Opportunity' in *Comparative Perspectives on Social Movements*. eds. Doug McAdam, John D. McCarthy, and Mayer N. Zald. New York: Cambridge University Press. pp. 275–90.

—— and Gadi Wolfsfeld. 1993. 'Movements and Media as Interacting Systems.' *Annals of the American Academy of Political and Social Science*. (Citizens, Protest and Democracy). 528. pp. 114–25.

Gierycz, Dorota. 1997. 'Education on the Human Rights of Women as a Vehicle for Change' in *Human Rights Education for the Twenty-First Century*. eds. George J. Andreopoulos and Richard Pierre Claude. Philadelphia: University of Pennsylvania Press.

Grewal, Inderpal. 1999. ' "Women's Rights as Human Rights": Feminist Practices, Global Feminism, and Human Rights Regimes in Transnationality.' *Citizenship Studies*. 3(3). pp. 337–54.

Human Rights Watch. 1995. *The Human Rights Watch Global Report on Women's Human Rights*. New York: Human Rights Watch.

Katzenstein, Mary F. 1989. 'Organizing against Violence: Strategies of the Indian Women's Movement.' *Pacific Affairs*. 62. Spring. pp. 53–71.

——. 1991–92 'Getting Women's Issues onto the Public Agenda: Body Politics in India.' *Samya Shakti*. 6. pp. 3-4.

Keck, Margaret E. and Kathryn Sikkink. 1998. *Activists beyond Borders: Advocacy Networks in International Politics*. Ithaca, NY: Cornell University.

Kishwar, Madhu. 1988. 'Rethinking Dowry Boycott.' *Manushi*. 48. Sept.-Oct. pp. 10–13.

——. 2003. 'Laws Against Domestic Violence: Underused or Abused?' *NWSA Journal*. 15(2). pp. 11–122.

Kumar, Radha. 1989. 'Contemporary Indian Feminism'. *Feminist Review*. 33. pp. 20–71.

——. 1993. *The History of Doing. An Illustrated Account of Movements for Women's Rights and Feminism in India, 1800–1990*. New Delhi: Kali for Women.

Kumari, Ranjana. 1989. *Brides are not for Burning: Dowry Victims In India*. New Delhi: Radiant Publishers.

McAdam, D. and D. Rucht. 1993. 'The cross-national diffusion of movement ideas'. *The Annals of the American Academy*. 528. pp. 56–74.

Moghadam, Valentine M. 2005. *Globalizing Women. Transnational Feminist Networks*.

Baltimore, MD: The Johns Hopkins University Press.

Narayan, Uma. 1997. *Dislocating Cultures: Identities, Traditions, and Third World Feminisms.* New York: Routledge.

Purkayastha, Bandana, Mangala Subramaniam, Manisha Desai and Sunita Bose. 2003. 'The Study of Gender in India: A Partial Review.' *Gender & Society* 17. no. 4. Aug. pp. 503–24.

Reilly, Niamh. 1996. *Without Reservation: The Beijing Tribunal on Accountability for Women's Human Rights.* New Brunswick, NJ: Women Centre for Global Leadership.

Snow, David A. and Robert D. Benford. 1992. 'Master Frames and Cycles of Protest' in *Frontiers in Social Movement Theory.* eds. Aldon D. Morris and Carol M. Mueller. New Haven, CT: Yale University Press. pp. 133–55.

Snow, David A., E. Burke Rochford, Jr., Steven K. Worden and Robert D. Benford. 1986. 'Frame Alignment Processes, Micromobilization, and Movement Participation.' *American Sociological Review.* vol. 51. no. 4. pp. 464–81.

Soule, Sarah. 2004. 'Diffusion Processes Within and Across Movements' in *The Blackwell Companion to Social Movements.* eds. David Snow, Sarah Soule and Hanspeter Kriesi. Malden, MA: Blackwell Publishers.

Springer, Kimberly. 1999. 'Introduction: African American Women Redefining Activism for the Millennium' in *Lifting, Still Climbing: African-American Women's Contemporary Activism.* ed. Kimberly Springer. New York: New York University Press. pp. 1–13.

Subramaniam, Mangala. 2004. 'The Indian Women's Movement.' Introductory and Synthesizing Essay for Symposium in *Contemporary Sociology.* 33(6) Nov. pp. 635–39.

———. 2006. *The Power of Women's Organizing: Gender, Caste, and Class in India.* Lanham, MD: Lexington Books (imprint of Rowman and Littlefield).

———. 2008. 'Women and Religious Nationalism: Framing Women's Rights in the Religious Based Violence in Gujarat, India.' Paper presented at the Annual Meeting of the Global Studies Association. New York. June.

———, Manjusha Gupte and Debarashmi Mitra. 2003. 'Local to Global: Transnational Networks and Indian Women's Grassroots Organizing.' *Mobilization.* 8(2). pp. 253–70.

Thompson, Becky. 2001. *A Promise and a Way of Life: White Antiracist Activism.* Minneapolis, MN: University of Minnesota Press.

Tripp, Aili Marie. 2006. 'The Evolution of Transnational Feminisms: Consensus, Conflict, and New Dynamics' in *Global Feminism: Transnational Women's Activism, Organizing, and Human Rights.* eds. Myra Marx Ferree and Aili Marie Tripp. New York: New York University Press. pp. 51–75.

United Nations. 1993. *General Assembly Declaration on the Elimination of Violence against Women.* A/RES/48/104. 20 December.

———. 1999. Convention on the Elimination of Discrimination against Women

(CEDAW). Consideration of Reports Submitted by State Parties Under Article 18 of the Convention of the Elimination of all Forms of Discrimination against Women. Initial Reports of States Parties: India. CEDAW/C/IND/1. 10 March.

———. 2003. Economic and Social Council. Integration of the Human Rights of Women and the Gender Perspective: Violence against Women. Commission on Human Rights. 59th session. Item 12(a) of the provisional agenda. E/CN.4/2003/75. 6 January.

———. 2005. Committee on the Elimination of Discrimination against Women. Consideration of reports submitted by States parties under article 18 of the Convention on the Elimination of All Forms of Discrimination against Women. Combined second and third periodic reports of States parties—India. United Nations CEDAW/C/IND/2-3. 19 October.

Conclusion

EMMA TOMALIN

Introduction

Consolidating some of the key themes discussed here leads us to think about future directions of the Dowry Project. One of the main concerns of this volume has been to bridge the gap between academic theory and research, on the one hand, and practice to end dowry injustice, on the other. However, what should form the focus of dowry campaigns is by no means clear. As we have seen, both scholars and activists are divided about whether dowry itself should be banned or whether the target should be the abusive practices associated with dowry, particularly in the absence of solid inheritance rights for women. Basu, for instance, explains how dowry is fading as a central focus for feminist organisations in India. The limits of legislation to eliminate dowry have caused some scholars and activists to question if it is still realistic or desirable to achieve the complete eradication of dowry. Moreover, if structural inequality between women and men remains, legislation could serve to increase women's vulnerability. Removing dowry can mean taking away women's access to any resources and, in the absence of marriage gift-giving, they are likely to be harassed and unable to secure a respected position in their new family. For some, therefore, the reform of dowry represents a more attainable goal (Kishwar 1999; Leslie 1995). For others, however, accepting dowry as part of women's lives is contested. Palriwala (1989) is clear that dowry should be abolished, as it is symbolic of deep-rooted gender inequalities played out within women's lives.

While this debate continues to rage, many scholars and activists on both sides do agree that solutions to dowry injustice go beyond the legal remedies. This volume supports the view that ending dowry abuse is not primarily or solely a legal issue and that instead we need to also look at the role of gender inequality in this. The law can tackle gender inequality, but it also requires other strategies and interventions. As Basu states, the 'analysis of dowry practices leads us to the crux of the problem at the intersection of compulsory heterosexual marriage as a mechanism of enforcing gender subordination'. She argues that attention must be drawn to marriage as the patriarchal foundation upon which dowry rests. This requires a deeper gaze beyond legislation that looks more closely at the different ways that gender inequality creates the conditions for dowry abuse in order to find solutions that include legal remedies but much else besides.

Drawing upon the contributions to this volume, my aim is to bring out the suggestions made about the sorts of activity and action that are necessary to end dowry injustice and to highlight the particular role that academic research can play. To take our discussion beyond the legal dimensions of dowry and to be able to target appropriate interventions, it is necessary to ask 'who and what underpins the cycle of culpability and how can it be broken?'

Understanding and breaking the cycle of culpability

The various ripple effects of the harms linked to modern dowry practices in South Asia, are exactly the kind of issues that international conventions such as CEDAW (The Convention on the Elimination of All Forms of Discrimination against Women)[1] are designed to address, where discrimination against women is defined as:

> any distinction, exclusion or restriction made on the basis of sex which has the effect or purpose of impairing or nullifying the recognition,

enjoyment or exercise by women, irrespective of their marital status, on a basis of equality of men and women, of human rights and fundamental freedoms in the political, economic, social, cultural, civil or any other field.[2]

This convention seeks to establish an international mandate to end activities in any society that discriminate against women. Thus, both the international community, as well as national governments, are compelled to undertake action to protect women's rights. The above definition of discrimination could be applied to dowry per se, since, even putting its violent manifestations aside, dowry as a practice arguably discriminates against women in a variety of ways. It relies on and reinforces patriarchal marriage as the norm and commodifies women, and, even where it does not lead to death or injury, it can cause women much mental distress. However, as Subramaniam et al. demonstrate the focus at an international level tends to be on dowry violence rather than dowry itself. More recently, the 1995 Beijing Declaration and Platform for Action[3] specifically mentions dowry-related violence in its pledge to:

> Enact and enforce legislation against the perpetrators of practices and acts of violence against women, such as female genital mutilation, *prenatal sex selection, infanticide and dowry-related violence* and give vigorous support to the efforts of non-governmental and community organisations to eliminate such practices.[4] (emphasis is mine)

The focus of action here is not against dowry per se, but the violent acts associated with it. As such it is important to group prenatal sex selection, infanticide and dowry-related violence together since research has shown that dowry pressure has markedly increased pre-existing tendencies towards son preference within South Asian societies (Dreze and Sen 2002; Sunder Rajan 2003). In particular, the practice of female infanticide and the sex-selective abortion of female foetuses can be linked to the spread and intensification of dowry (Basu 1999a; Banerjee 2002). In India these practices have led to a declining female sex ratio (Sen 1990). As Sen argued in his famous article 'More Than 100 Million Women Are Missing':

Conclusion

It is often said that women make up a majority of the world's population. They do not. This mistaken belief is based on generalising from the contemporary situation in Europe and North America, where the ratio of women to men is typically around 1.05 or 1.06, or higher. In South Asia, West Asia, and China, the ratio of women to men can be as low as 0.94, or even lower, and it varies widely elsewhere in Asia, in Africa, and in Latin America. How can we understand and explain these differences, and react to them? (1990: 61)

While these differences can be at least partially explained in terms of the level of care that women receive within the particular societies (i.e. in terms of diet and access to health services) Sen also wrote in 2003 that: (see also Klassen and Wink 2003; Klassen 1994)

Another more important and radical change has occurred over the past decade. There have been two opposite movements: female disadvantage in mortality has typically been reduced substantially, but this has been counterbalanced by a new female disadvantage—that in natality—through sex specific abortions aimed against the female fetus (2003: 1297).

That this preference for sons is linked to the spread and inflation of dowry in South Asia, has been argued by Sen and others (Dreze and Sen 2002). Thus, dowry-related violence extends beyond that committed against wives and affects females even before birth. The existence of legislation against acts of violence against females, such as prenatal sex selection, infanticide and dowry-related violence, is crucial, but there is also a need to strategise in other directions. Changing attitudes about gender stereotypes and stemming the tide of dowry greed is not only a legal issue.

The problem of dowry can be defined and framed in different ways. Some of the contributions to this volume ask who is to blame for the abuse of the dowry system as well as the failure of various attempts at ending such abusive practices. Understanding the failure of the law and the state's role in this has received attention in the wider literature (Sirohi 2003; Butalia 2002) and in this volume (Basu). Indeed, despite the emphasis upon the legal anti-dowry interventions within the Dowry Project's earlier 1998 edited collection (as discussed in the Introduction) this volume expresses doubt about the efficacy of legislation alone. As Menski argues 'dowry is indeed a grave social issue and not primarily a legal problem' (1998: 105). He also emphasises that it is a moral issue (1998: 55) where 'dowry, more than any other legal topic, illustrates the limited role of legal intervention in people's lives and the tangential legal impact on individual morality' (1998: 59). In particular, the complicity of parents is of concern where they succumb to cultural and social pressure and/or material greed, showing a worrying lack of moral responsibility towards their daughters. For instance, Kishwar (1999) and Leslie (1995) call not for the eradication of dowry but for parents to be encouraged to avoid lavish dowry practices. Instead, each suggests that parents use money set aside for dowry to buy land or to put a deposit down on a property, both of which would be left in the daughter's name and would thus increase her economic leverage within her marital home. The potential of such initiatives needs to be further popularised across communities in South Asia, by women's organisations and/or religious institutions, with academic research playing a role here in documenting and making available case studies of successful interventions.

However, such practices are rarely so easy to condemn and what might seem like a fairly straightforward moral issue is cross-cut by more complex factors. For instance, Rozario and Jehan (in this volume) support the idea of the '"patriarchal bargain" by which they [women] receive security and projection in exchange for accepting their own subordination (Kandiyoti 1988: 282–3)' (Rozario). Thus, women collude in what seems to be their oppression when they can perceive some ultimate benefit for themselves in the continuation of certain practices. As Kishwar writes: 'instead of dismissing the refusal of young women to say "no" to dowry as a sign of their low consciousness or lack of awareness, we would do better to examine why they are not willing to give it up' (1999: 12). While women's support for dowry could be for reasons other than a 'patriarchal bargain', such as not having the knowledge or means to challenge such a culturally embedded institution, we cannot overlook the fact that not all women experience dowry as repressive and not all men benefit from it. Some women may suffer because of it at points in their life and then later benefit from it. The idea of the patriarchal bargain is useful in disrupting straightforward understandings of the mechanisms of gender oppression. As Basu writes elsewhere, although

> troubling moments of agency, such as women's allegiance to dowry as [a] marker of love and esteem ... pose the most difficult challenges for feminist politics about what should be the means and who should be the focus of reform ... there is no getting away from the fact that the contemporary phenomenon of dowry marks a profound space of gender-based dependence and hence, vulnerability to multiple forms of violence (Basu 2005: xxi).

Thus, women may at times show allegiance to dowry (and this needs to be captured in analyses of the phenomena), but there is no suggestion here that it is nonetheless problematic. Women's complicity highlights the complexity of the issue and further points to the need for gender analysis to feed into anti-dowry initiatives. Jehan argues strongly for this approach. On the issue of culpability, she draws attention to the importance of considering men's views of dowry in gender analyses of the practice. While dowry is depicted as patriarchal, and it is hence assumed that it is men who are its main sustainers, we rarely find in the literature an attempt to reveal their views as a means of better understanding the mechanisms that enable its continuation and perversion. As Jehan writes in this volume:

> Yet to exclude men from the debate entirely seems erroneous. Firstly, men are dowry givers as well as takers. Secondly, achieving justice for both genders requires a critical engagement with both women's and men's roles. A pragmatic approach to dowry that incorporates men's experiences is recommended ... as men are typically given less space in the dowry literature, the focus here is on men's perspectives.

In addition to asking 'who' is culpable for the continuation of dowry the contributors also ask 'what' underpins the contemporary dowry problem. Bradley considers the role that religion plays. While dowry itself is not a practice sanctioned in the Hindu texts, she discusses the depictions of women within Hindu texts and traditions which promote gender hierarchies that allow patriarchal systems such as dowry to flourish. Considering the contribution of academic research to activism, Bradley believes that scholars have a role to play through producing scholarship on religious texts and promoting interpretations of texts and practices that are empowering for women. Academic research can also uncover and document examples of women's activism that engage with religious teachings in order to deal with concerns over dowry.

For Dalmia and Lawrence, by contrast, the spread and inflation of dowry is a result of Sanskritisation, modernisation and economic growth. They emphasise the importance of academic research in the role that it can play in collecting and analysing data on dowry practices and distribution as a crucial factor in bridging the gap between theory and practice. If we do not have an accurate and detailed picture of the nature of the dowry phenomena across South Asia then anti-dowry initiatives do not clearly know what they are dealing with and are doomed to failure.

In advocating that initiatives to end dowry injustice must be multifaceted, this volume might be seen perhaps as not adding anything new to the debate, and as though it is sidestepping the need to make actual decisions about what needs to be done. However, if we consider dowry injustice to be primarily an issue of gender inequality then quick fix solutions are not always immediately obvious or possible to operationalise. We need a combination of immediate practical initiatives to protect women from dowry abuse such as legislation, counselling, women's refuges etc., combined with strategic long term, well-informed interventions to challenge and transform gender inequality. In particular, this volume aims to demonstrate the role that academic research can play in understanding the benefits and limits of different practical interventions and embedding these within broader agendas for social change around gender relations.

How to overcome dowry? Considering women's 'practical' and 'strategic' gender needs

As Dalmia and Lawrence demonstrate, dowry becomes a symbolic carrier of status elevation and also reflects people's desire to take advantage of new economic opportunities as they arise in India. It is difficult for the state or women's organisations to implement initiatives that encourage people not to seek status elevation or to want to increase their wealth. Indeed to do so could be seen as anti-development according to the prevailing model of neo-liberal economic development that India is now embracing. However, as men become more valuable because they can command higher dowry payments and women compete to attract men of higher social and economic status, the worth of girls and women declines and modern dowry practices become fundamentally damaging to women. Moreover, as we have seen, the ability of legislation to curb dowry in particular has proved ineffectual. A recurring theme of this volume is that without deeper structural changes within society that aim to sustainably transform gender relations, practical initiatives to resolve the dowry issue are little more than window dressing. For instance, as Basu writes in this volume:

> If women's structural subordination remains constant, strict legislative attempts to either ban dowry or enforce equal inheritance are likely to increase women's vulnerability and dowry-related violence against them. On the one hand, removing dowry entirely in the absence of guarantees of inheritance (wills, gifts, etc., being common strategies to bypass legal directives against equal inheritance) deprives women of the few natal resources they garner and value. On the other hand, emphasising inheritance for women without being able to stem the custom of wedding prestations leaves open possibilities for harassing women and their families for years over property, while dowry expenses are not curtailed in any way, and there is no return flow of resources from daughters in the form of eldercare or other financial help.

Law, or any other initiative, that exists within a system of patriarchal relations is liable to failure since it cannot ultimately achieve what it sets out to do: reform a practice that requires the transformation of gender relations. One useful framework for approaching this dilemma is borrowed from the gender and development literature: the distinction between 'practical' and 'strategic' gender needs. A consideration of dowry requires understanding women's 'strategic gender needs' (Moser 1993). Moser developed this framework to find reasons why certain development initiatives did not fundamentally improve women's lives. She suggested that while 'practical gender needs' are important (including, for instance, access to employment, specific training opportunities or health care), they do not in themselves fundamentally 'challenge the gender divisions of labour or women's subordinate position in society. Practical gender needs are a response to immediate perceived necessity' (1993: 40). By contrast, 'strategic gender needs are the needs women identify because of their subordinate position to men in their society ... They relate to gender divisions of labour, power and control and may include such issues as legal rights, domestic violence, equal wages and women's control over their bodies' (1993: 39).

The law can of course have an impact upon transforming women's subordinate position in society and as such is 'strategic' in purpose. Laws that grant women equal rights with men, for instance, do work to flatten gender difference. However, specifically with respect to anti-dowry legislation, the legal solutions have not been integrated with other strategies to deal with gender inequality. In this case it has acted more like an intervention to serve a practical gender need (i.e. the immediate avoidance of dowry) and this runs the risk of exacerbating women's situation in the absence, for instance, of solid inheritance rights. Thus, the failure of the legislative approach to dowry can at least partially be explained by the lack of accompanying strategies to improve women's strategic position within the gender hierarchy in society as a whole. Moreover, while laws can be produced that on paper set out to curb abusive dowry practices the will to implement them is limited by social attitudes. Thus, creating legislation to protect women's rights is often difficult to enact unless social attitudes about women promote the view that they are potentially equal beings. We need legislation to protect women, but, as Basu argues, without deeper structural change in society it is likely to be less effectual in the long term.

Therefore, how can both women's practical and strategic gender needs be approached in the context of the dowry problematic? Rozario for instance, outlines a number of suggestions for Bangladesh, including 'working with religious authorities such as local imams, to encourage them to raise awareness about the situation of women' and the 'use of media, education and role models to contest village stereotypes of women'. She aims to tackle women's strategic gender needs, specifically arguing that the dowry problem can only be solved in Bangladesh if there are associated attempts to deal with the broader issue of patriarchy and gender relations. Subramaniam et al. look at the role of transnational or international women's movements in approaching the dowry problem. They recognise that international bodies, such as the United Nations, potentially play an important role in tackling the problems associated with dowry, but are critical that the UN tends to lump all forms of violence against women together and therefore specific cultural causes of violence in particular contexts become obscured. In order to improve the strategic value of such global initiatives against dowry they argue that they should consider taking direction from local (within India) efforts to challenge the practice and seek rights for women. They write that:

> The global frame undermines the complexity of specific issues of violence, such as state-sponsored violence, trafficking of women, domestic violence and rape as well as violence caused by economic deprivation, structural adjustment, and war, by lumping them together.

While the macrolevel at which the UN works has meant that the specificities of dowry have been overlooked, including other ways that it is problematic for women apart from its violent outcomes, Subramaniam et al. do also emphasise benefits to the 'global frame', in that:

The advantages of using a global framework of women's rights as human rights (with a broader definition of violence against women) in the context of dowry-related violence are twofold. First, a broader framing of violence that is inclusive of otherwise residual categories of violence against women can have a wider appeal, across geographical borders and would not necessitate specific explanations. Second, in implementing the laws and monitoring dowry-related violence against women, a global framework of women's rights as human rights can be viewed as a process of both legal and cultural transformations, bringing about changes in the cultural practices that marginalise women in various societies.

They suggest that there is currently a delinking between the local/ national framing of dowry and the global framing of dowry and specifically advocate a closer working relationship between international actors and local women's organisations in India 'to bring about meaningful partnerships and collaborations to pressure for change in gender and overall social relations, such as challenging dowry'. It is only with the emergence of such partnerships that 'transnational' rather than distinct 'local' and 'global' approaches to the dowry problem could evolve.

Research and activism: feminist activist scholarship

I have drawn attention to the argument that anti-dowry initiatives have been limited, firstly, because they have tended to focus upon the violent aspects of the practice and, secondly, because they emphasise legal strategies to curb abusive dowry practices. These critiques should not be understood as implying that dowry is not a violent practice nor a phenomenon that should not concern the law, but without attention to women's strategic gender needs dowry abuse cannot be eradicated. For instance, as Palriwala writes in this volume:

> That did not mean that dowry-related violence should not have been attacked, but that the attack had to be taken further. It also had to be recognised that the women's movement, alert and dynamic though it was, could not transform structures of gendered inequality in which dowry was embedded without a much larger socio-political movement

Conclusion

which addressed a range of socio-economic inequalities and the very
raison-d'être of the state (Karat 2005).

The enormity of this task, therefore, and the necessary participation
of a range of actors (e.g. from women's groups and the state to
international NGOs), can thus help explain the tenacity of this
practice which feeds upon gender hierarchies that are so difficult
to fundamentally remove. However, the interdisciplinary character
of this book highlights the role that academic research can play in
describing and theorising the factors that underpin gender
difference. As Palriwala continues:

> This paper considers how the links between dowry and a range of anti-
> women social practices, including son preference, rituals and caste
> discrimination, are shifting or being reinforced. How are dowry and its
> repercussions to be addressed in the current struggle for gender equality
> and emancipation, drawing not just women but also men into the
> struggle? (AIDWA 2003; Karat 2005).

Jehan in particular, points out that men must be brought more
directly into the struggle if real strides are to be made in eradicating
dowry and that academic research has a role to play here in bringing
to the fore masculine responses to dowry. However, the problems
of actually bringing academic research to bear upon social change
are noted by Basu, who states that 'powerful feminist analyses of
the problem by individuals and organisations in the 1980s ...
point to the difficulties of translating theory into broad-ranging
change in social practices, whether through law, policy or
education'. Similarly, as the feminist activist scholar Naples writes:

> On the one hand, many activists could be critical of these apparently more
> 'academic' constructions of activism, especially since the need for specific
> knowledges to support activist agendas frequently goes unmet. The texts
> in which such analyses appear are rarely made widely available and further
> create a division between feminists located within the academy and
> community-based activists. On the other hand, many activist scholars
> have developed linkages with activists and policy arenas in such a way as to
> effectively bridge the so-called activist/scholar divide (2006: 10).

237

Palriwala in fact highlights that the AIDWA survey itself—in the design of its methodology—did attempt to bring together academic research and practice. She writes that:

> The AIDWA survey achieved even closer insight by using people who were recognised as insiders, rather than academics who merely make efforts to connect with their informants. At the same time, the activists were critical of the gender and social relations of their context which gave them an 'outsider's' view. Their activism had also given them the skills needed to conduct a survey sensitively on issues which could not be understood through numbers alone or even the immediate conversation through which data was usually collected in large surveys. *The idea of praxis—of theory and political practice clarifying and building on each other—was central to the idea of the survey.* Thus, it was hoped that there would be a synergic process of knowledge-creation, awareness-generation, mobilisation and refinement of the politics and actions of struggle (emphasis mine).

Despite the challenges within feminist studies to achieving feminist praxis, there is a strong sense of the necessity for 'feminist activist scholarship' under the current global socio-political climate. As Naples writes:

> We are living in challenging times for feminist activism and for activist scholarship. The conservative backlash against women's reproductive rights, affirmative action and immigrant rights, among other challenges to social and economic justice, is shaping the work of feminists both inside and outside the academy ... [but] ... whatever can a feminist do about such things? How can activist scholarship and feminism be brought to bear on these large-scale policies and social problems? (Naples 2006: 1–2).

This volume is based upon the conviction that dowry is precisely the sort of issue that counts as a focus for feminist activist scholarship. The papers indicate places where such linkages already exist and suggest the need and scope for further work in this area.

Conclusion: future directions of the Dowry Project

The aim of the Dowry Project is to contribute towards the transnational framing of the dowry issue in ways that recognise the value of transnational alliances and partnerships but also that these must be grounded in the microlevel everyday realities of South Asian women and men. The network remains committed to bringing together academics, practitioners and activists in future events to consolidate past research and to build new areas of scholarship with respect to the dowry problematic. This volume has highlighted gender as the primary consideration for dowry campaigns and in particular recognises that research around masculinities and dowry is an important area for future work. There is still a tendency in feminist research to focus upon the female side of the gender relationship and there continues to be much less reflection upon men's attitudes. In an era where dowry continues to escalate under the influence of globalisation, in terms of its spread to other regions, castes and religions, it is essential to understand men's attitudes towards dowry as much as the ways in which women are disadvantaged by it. This is an emerging area of research, as Jehan indicates, and is an important focus for the future Dowry Project. Jehan's research also points towards the need to better understand the impact of globalisation upon dowry and, by extension, therefore, manifestations of dowry outside South Asia.

Rozario, in her work on the spread of dowry amongst Muslims in Bangladesh, also suggests scope for further research that could look more closely at dowry and non-Hindu communities, as well as dowry practices in the diaspora. While this volume focused on South Asia, there are significant numbers of women affected by dowry in other regions (e.g. the USA and Europe) and their situation has not received attention here. Moreover, a comparison of dowry with other marital gift-giving practices, such as *mehr* (a form of bride price or bride wealth practised amongst Muslim communities), could also help our understanding of what is

EMMA TOMALIN

distinctive about dowry as well as the ways in which different sorts of marital-gift giving reinforce gender inequality.

In conclusion is a quotation from Julia Leslie's contribution to the earlier 1998 Dowry Project volume. Here she squarely locates the dowry issue as one that is linked to gender inequality, both before a girl marries as well as in her marital life.

> But let us imagine a different scenario. Girls and boys have the same opportunities to education and work training. They are brought up, both at home and at school, to treat each other as human beings. They are treated equally in their natal home. When they marry, they marry as adults (physically, socially and psychologically), whether they live with her family or his, or on their own. Wife and husband treat each other as equals with equal rights to decision-making. The wife loses none of her inheritance rights. She receives her full share of parental property at the same time as her brother receives his, and therefore not at her marriage. When she marries, she loses none of her rights to her natal family. She can visit her parents or even live nearby; she and her brother are equally responsible for their ageing parents.
>
> Imagine if this were the case. A bride would then no longer hanker after dowry for her own protection, and her male relatives would no longer have the incentive to pay her off. The question of dowry would fall away of itself (Leslie 1998: 35).

Notes

[1] The Convention on the Elimination of All Forms of Discrimination against Women (CEDAW), adopted in 1979 by the UN General Assembly, is often described as an international bill of rights for women.

[2] http://www.un.org/womenwatch/daw/cedaw/cedaw.htm

[3] These documents were an outcome of the 1995 United Nations International Women's Conference held in Beijing.

[4] http://www1.umn.edu/humanrts/instree/e5dplw.htm

References

Bannerjee, N. 2002. 'Between the Devil and the Deep Blue Sea: Shrinking Options for Women in Contemporary India' in *The Violence of Development: The*

Conclusion

Politics of Identity, Gender and Social Inequalities in India. ed. K. Kapadia. London: Zed Books. pp. 43–68.

Basu, A.M. 1999a. 'Fertility Decline and Increasing Gender Imbalance in India, Including a Possible South Indian Turnaround.' *Development and Change.* 30(2). pp. 237–63.

Basu, S. ed. 2005. *Dowry and Inheritance.* New Delhi: Women Unlimited.

Butalia, S. 2002. *The gift of a daughter: Encounters with victims of dowry.* New Delhi: Penguin Books India.

Dreze, J. and A. Sen. 2002. *India: Development and Participation.* Oxford: Oxford University Press.

Kishwar, Madhu. 1999. *Off the Beaten Track: Rethinking Gender Justice for Indian Women.* New Delhi: Oxford University Press.

Klasen, S. 1994. 'Missing women reconsidered'. *World Development.* 22(7). pp. 1061–71.

Klasen, S. and C. Wink. 2003. 'Missing women: revisiting the debate'. *Feminist Economics.* 9(2–3). pp. 263–300.

Leslie, Julia. 1995. 'Dowry, Dowry Deaths and Violence against Women'. Keynote paper delivered at the first international conference on dowry and bride burning in India. Harvard Law School. 30 Sept.-2nd Oct.

———. 1998. 'Dowry, dowry deaths and violence against women: a journey of discovery' in *South Asians and the Dowry Problem.* ed. W. Menski. London: Trentham Books. pp. 21–35.

Menski, W. 1998. 'New Concerns about Abuses of the South Asian Dowry System' in *South Asians and the Dowry Problem.* ed. W. Menski. London: Trentham Books. pp. 1–20.

Moser, C. 1993. *Gender Planning and Development: Theory, Practice and Training.* London: Routledge.

Naples, N. 2006. 'Feminist Activism and Activist Scholarship in the 21st Century'. *FemTAP: A Journal of Feminist Theory and Practice.* Summer. http://femtap.com/sitebuildercontent/sitebuilderfiles/naples.pdf

Palriwala, R. 1989. 'Reaffirming the Anti-Dowry Struggle'. *Economic and Political Weekly.* 29 April. pp. 942–44.

Sen, A. 1990. 'More Than 100 Million Women Are Missing'. *New York Review of Books.* 37(20). December 20. http://ucatlas.ucsc.edu/gender/gratio.html

———. 2003. 'Missing women—revisited'. editorial. *British Medical Journal.* 327. 6 December. pp. 1297–98.

Sirohi, S. 2003. *Stories of Dowry Victims.* New Delhi: HarperCollins.

Sunder Rajan, R. 2003. 'The Scandal of the State: Women, Law, and Citizenship' in *Postcolonial India.* Durham: Duke University Press.

Contributors

SRIMATI BASU is Associate Professor of Gender and Women's Studies at the University of Kentucky in Lexington, USA. She graduated from Kolkata and moved from literary studies to an interdisciplinary approach to gender and culture in her academic research and teaching. Her focus is on questions of law, violence, development, feminist theory and methodology. She is the author of *She Comes to Take Her Rights: Indian Women, Property and Propriety* (SUNY Press, 1999; Kali for Women, 2001); editor/ compiler of *Issues in Feminism: Dowry and Inheritance* (Women Unlimited and Zed Books, 2005); and is currently working on an ethnography of family courts and the mediation of family violence.

TAMSIN BRADLEY is Senior Lecturer and Course Leader for the Social Anthropology (BSc) in the Department of Applied Social Sciences, London Metropolitan University, UK. She received her PhD from the School of Oriental and African Studies, University of London. Her research takes an ethnographic approach examining the interfaces between gender, religion and development in Rajasthan, in North India. Key publications include: a monograph *Challenging the NGOs: Religion, Western Discourses and Indian Women.* (I.B. Tauris, 2006); and peer reviewed journal articles including, 'Physical Religious Spaces in the lives of Rajasthani Village Women: The ethnographic study and practice of religion in development' (*Journal of Human Development*, January 2009).

Contributors

SONIA DALMIA is Associate Professor of Economics at Grand Valley State University, USA. She received her PhD from the University of Iowa and her primary areas of interest include marriage transactions, gender bias and demographic behaviour. She has authored and co-authored articles in journals such as: *Journal of Developing Areas*, *Research in Economics*, and *International Advances in Economics Research*. Her ongoing research projects pertain to (a) the efficiency of marriage markets, (b) immigration laws, and (c) contemporary marriage practices in India.

KATE JEHAN is at the Centre for Development Studies, University of Leeds, UK, studying for her PhD looking at the relationship between gender, dowry and globalisation. She has interviewed women and men over three generations in the southern Indian state of Tamil Nadu. Her research explores the extent to which present attitudes are derived from contemporary variables, and how they are contextualised amongst shifting concepts of gender, class, caste and religious identity.

PAREENA G. LAWRENCE is Professor of Economics and Management and Chair of the Division of Social Sciences at the University of Minnesota, Morris. She received her doctorate from Purdue University, West Lafayette, Indiana, USA, and her research explores the intersections of gender, households and the political economy. She has authored and co-authored several book chapters and articles in journals such as: *Agricultural Economics, International Advances in Economics Research, Journal of Developing Areas, Problemas Del Desarrollo: Revista Latinoamericana De Economia, Revista de Economia Institucional,* and the *Journal of Business and Leadership.* Her current research focuses on the empowerment of women through reservation in political participation in India.

DEBARASHMI MITRA is Assistant Professor of Sociology and Community Development at Delta State University in Cleveland, Mississippi, USA. She received her PhD in Sociology from the University of Connecticut. Her research focuses on gender, globalisation and political economy, women's activism and community engagement, and women and work in the global economy.

RAJNI PALRIWALA is Professor at the Department of Sociology, University of Delhi, India. Her research falls within the broad area of gender relations, covering care, citizenship, and the state, women and work, kinship and gender, dowry, women's movements and feminist politics, and fieldwork methodology. Cross-cultural comparison is an underlying interest. Her books and edited collections include *Care, culture and citizenship: Revisiting the politics of welfare in the Netherlands* (with C. Risseeuw and K. Ganesh, Het Spinhuis, 2005); *Changing kinship, family, and gender relations in South Asia: Processes, trends and issues* (VENA, Leiden University, 1994); *Marriage, migration, and gender* (co-edited with P. Uberoi, Sage, 2008); *Shifting circles of support: Contextualising kinship and gender relations in South Asia and Sub-Saharan Africa* (co-edited with C. Risseeuw, Sage, 1996); and *Structures and strategies: Women, work and family in Asia* (co-edited with L. Dube, Sage, 1990).

KAREN REMEDIOS received her PhD in Theory and Cultural Studies from Purdue University, USA. She is currently Assistant Professor of Modern British and Postcolonial Literature, Southern Connecticut State University, USA. Her areas of specialisation are postcolonial literature, theory and film, and constructs of place and space in gender studies.

SANTI ROZARIO is Senior Research Fellow in the School of Religious and Theological Studies, Cardiff University. She is a social anthropologist who has conducted extensive research with rural women in Bangladesh and with British Bangladeshis in the UK. She is presently directing a project on Islam, young Bangladeshis, marriage and the family in Bangladesh and in the UK. Her publications include the books, *Purity and communal boundaries: Women and social change in a Bangladeshi village* (Dhaka University Press Limited, 2001); *Return migration in the Asia Pacific* (with

Contributors

Robyn Iredale and Fei Guo, Edward Elgar Publishing, 2003); *Daughters of Hariti: Childbirth and female healers in South and Southeast Asia* (with Geoffrey Samuel, Routledge, 2002); a special edition of *Women's Studies International Forum* on 'Islam, Gender and Human Rights' (with Anne Marie Hilsdon, vol. 29, no. 4); and numerous articles and book chapters.

MANGALA SUBRAMANIAM is Associate Professor of Sociology at Purdue University, USA. Educated at the universities of Delhi, Pennsylvania, and Connecticut, her primary areas are gender, social movements including transnational women's movements, and research methods. Among her many awards is an American Sociological Association/National Science Foundation Grant for Cutting Edge Research and Research Activities: The Fund for the Advancement of the Discipline award. She has authored and co-authored articles in journals such as: *Critical Sociology, Gender & Society, International Journal of Contemporary Sociology,* and *Mobilization.* Her monograph, *The Power of Women's Organizing: Gender, Caste, and Class in India* (Lexington Books, 2006) focuses on the women's movement in India with specific attention to dalit women's organising.

EMMA TOMALIN is Senior Lecturer in Religious Studies, in the Department of Theology and Religious Studies at the University of Leeds, UK. Her research focuses upon the links between religion and international development, and religion and environmentalism with a particular emphasis on gender issues. Her forthcoming book is titled *Bio-divinity and biodiversity: the limits of religious environmentalism* (Ashgate, 2009). She is currently working on two research projects: first, on 'Religions and Development' (see: www.rad.bham.ac.uk) with partner institutions in Tanzania, Nigeria, India and Pakistan; and, second, on female ordination within different Buddhist traditions transnationally and the implications of this for women's development and empowerment.

245